PRAISE FOR

IN EUROPE'S SHADOW

"Timely and powerful . . . Fresh out of his service in the Israeli army in 1981, Robert D. Kaplan chanced on a neglected classic—a history of Central Europe in the interwar era. He crossed the Iron Curtain on a whim to see what had changed since then (a lot, as it turned out). Thirty-five years later Mr. Kaplan is one of America's foremost writers on the region. *In Europe's Shadow* is about his greatest love: Romania. It is part autobiography, part travelogue, part literary history and part geopolitical analysis. . . . In a series of deep dives into the region's past—Byzantine, Ottoman, Habsburg and Soviet—he finds parallels and echoes that help us understand the present."

—*The Wall Street Journal*

"This book reveals the confident, poetical Kaplan, striving as ever in his writing for the proverbial, but also a reflective, political Kaplan, seeking at times to submerge his gift for romantic generalization in respectful attention to the ideas of others. That tension—between an aesthetic sense of wholeness and the intellectual acceptance of complexity—is the real subject of the book, both as autobiography and as geopolitics. . . . Unlike almost every other strategist one reads, Kaplan makes no bones about learning from his own mistakes and from the scholarship of others. . . . Kaplan correctly recognizes that understanding the nation involves two sensibilities, the sympathetic and the critical, and he now wishes to put his own aesthetic and romantic impulses into perspective."

—TIMOTHY SNYDER, *The Washington Post*

"[A] haunting yet ultimately optimistic examination of the human condition as found in Romania . . . The author delves into the ancient roots of Romania's culture and religion. . . . Kaplan's account of the centuries leading up to the most turbulent of all—the 20th—is both sweeping and replete with alluring detail. . . . The rich characters who wander through these pages . . . dispense wisdom from book-lined homes, cafes, or chapels old and new. . . . Kaplan's Romania offers lessons on the value of malleability, and what endures."

—ALISON SMALE, *The New York Times Book Review*

"A serious yet impassioned survey of Romania . . . [Kaplan's] method is that of a foreign correspondent, firing off dispatches from the South China Sea to North Yemen to the darkest corners of Eastern Europe when it was still Iron Curtain country, and his approach has a Thucydidean texture: a gimlet-eyed realism as gathered by evidence, and guided by an understanding that the knee-jerk of history is self-interest. . . . Kaplan is a regional geographer par excellence, undeniably—whatever you think of his conclusions—a big-picture man."

—*The Christian Science Monitor*

"Kaplan is infatuated with Romania and has been ever since his first serious encounter with the country, in the early 1980s. That infatuation drives this book's historical explorations and philosophical reflections, which Kaplan merges with travel accounts to form a panorama including Romania's origins and identity, its political idiosyncrasies, its people's sense of victimhood, and the striking insights of its intellectuals. . . . Kaplan moves seamlessly from sights, sounds, and conversations to the resonance of history: Roman, Byzantine, Ottoman, and Soviet. Along the way, he considers works that he treasures from the underappreciated canon of Romanian literature and music. In Kaplan's hands, Romania emerges as no mere footnote, but as a historical and political pivot."

—*Foreign Affairs*

"Superb . . . Kaplan has spent a lot of time in Romania, and he has a knack for seeking out local scholars, dissident intellectuals, relics of the corrupt old order, and all sorts of other interesting and sometimes rather rum characters making up the Balkan Salad of present-day Romania. He has also read widely and deeply on his subject, something that sets him honorably apart from the common run of journalists. . . . Kaplan's narrative gift and eye for the telling bit of color or dialogue fill in many details. . . . Kaplan's closing reflections are by no means Panglossian, but they are moving and offer some hope for the future."

—*The National Interest*

"As a stand-alone work of reporting and analysis it ought to be required reading for Westerners looking to opine about 'the ultimate marchland' and key terrain of southeastern Europe, Romania. . . . As is Kaplan's way such musings are often personal, and this book is as much memoir as reportage. . . . Who knows what the United States will do in the face of the threat to liberal democracy posed by Putin? However it falls out, our luck continues in having Kaplan as our correspondent."

—*The Washington Free Beacon*

"Kaplan's work exemplifies rare intellectual, moral and political engagement with the political order—and disorder—of our world. . . . Kaplan's writing is like the places he visits. It's a terrain, a concentrated expression of a particular part of the world as he sees it. . . . *In Europe's Shadow* amounts to a kind of historical anthropology plus geopolitics, a deep study of a particular country and people. . . . It shows how, at one and the same time, Romania is distinctive and a key to a broader and deeper understanding of contemporary Europe."

—*The Huffington Post*

"Part travelogue, part cultural history, part academic literature review, Kaplan's book captures the reality of Romania's past, while pushing back against determinism. . . . Kaplan elegantly dismisses the idea of

Romania as a victim of history, a narrative ingrained in the national psyche through schooling and culture, as well as state propaganda in the almost 100 years of the country's modern history. But he also highlights the brutal, devastating effects that 50 years of nationalistic communism had on a frontier people who have yet to develop a coherent identity. . . . Can one make history, or has history already determined one's fate? This clash is what Kaplan, a longtime fan of the country, attempts to highlight."

—Minneapolis *Star Tribune*

"Foreign correspondent and travel writer Robert Kaplan firmly believes Romania is a country to be studied, as it sits on the edge of two frontiers—where east meets west. With *In Europe's Shadow*, Kaplan provides an excellent primer on the history and politics of this fascinating country, and takes the reader into the possible future of the nation. . . . Kaplan takes an important and much deeper look at the current situation in Romania, and the possible outcomes of the ongoing political turmoil in the region."

—*Winnipeg Free Press*

"Robert D. Kaplan was a 21-year-old college graduate when he first traveled to Romania in 1973 at the height of the communist era. The country under dictator Nicolae Ceaușescu was dark, depressing, and dangerous. But the journey kindled a lifetime passion for a little-known country in the heart of central Europe. . . . [*In Europe's Shadow*] weaves together the story of this first journey with subsequent travels to the region, cross-stitched with fascinating excursions down the byways of central European history, literature, and culture."

—*Smithsonian Journeys Travel Quarterly*

"Kaplan's is travel writing at its contemporary finest, weaving in the sights and sounds of a faraway land alongside interviews with its philosophers and politicians. . . . [*In Europe's Shadow*] provides an incisive, tactile introduction to the politics and potential prospects of

Central and Southeastern Europe—a region that finds itself once again caught in the headwinds of history."

—*RealClearWorld*

"Neither a conventional history nor a travelogue, *In Europe's Shadow* tries to look at Romania's past, present and future through the prism of those who matter most: its people. Admirably, Kaplan is not the kind of author to sit in his hotel and pass judgement on a country he barely understands. . . . Kaplan also succeeds in writing perhaps the clearest and most succinct summary of the fascist Ion Antonescu regime we have ever read."

—*Bucharest Life*

"Kaplan presents a large sweep of the history of Central and Eastern Europe as he captures a 'perishable moment in time' in *In Europe's Shadow*. He looks back so we can look forward. Will Russia continue threatening its neighbors? Will the European Union survive? . . . Reading this book is like finding Kaplan's diary left behind in some train station in the Balkans. You sit and read his personal reflections, insights, anger and love, half-hoping Kaplan will walk in to reclaim his journal so you can ask him more about what he's seen between the seas of time. Kaplan's travel writing sometimes brings Mark Twain to mind. Both know how to convert monochrome to high-resolution color."

—*Navy Reads*

"Captivating . . . a journalistic tour de force that will convince readers that [Romania is] a fascinating place whose people, past, and current geopolitical dilemma deserve our attention."

—*Kirkus Reviews*

"In this insightful fusion of history, travelogue, memoir, and contemporary analysis, Kaplan, a journalist and foreign affairs writer, recounts his travels through Romania and other parts of Central and Eastern Europe. . . . Well written, intriguing, and informative."

—*Publishers Weekly*

"[Kaplan] has developed an analytical style so distinctive that he can fairly be said to have invented a genre all of his own. On the one hand, his writing is firmly grounded in the uber-realist tradition of geostrategic abstraction; on the other, it dives down to a deeply personal level, combining travelogues with interviews, cultural critiques, intellectual history and very personal memoirs. The result is attractive and addictive, helping us see not only why we should care about distant countries but also what the vast impersonal forces of geography and history mean for human beings."

—IAN MORRIS, professor of classics, Stanford University

"A masterly work of important history, analysis and prophecy about the ancient and modern rise of Romania as a roundabout between Russia and Europe . . . I learned something new on every page. Kaplan is a master."

—TOM BROKAW

"A tour de force of cultural and political travel writing, in which Romania's complex past and uncertain present become vivid and newly urgent."

—COLIN THUBRON, author of *Shadow of the Silk Road* and co-editor of Patrick Leigh Fermor's *The Broken Road*

"Robert D. Kaplan has the remarkable ability to see over the geopolitical horizon, and he now turns his attention to Europe's marchlands—the former 'Greater Romania' lying between the Balkans and a resurgent Russia. In a triple journey through books, landscapes, and histories, he tackles the meaning of geography, the influence of intellectuals, and the daffiness—and power—of nationalism . . . A timely, insightful, and deeply honest book."

—CHARLES KING, professor of international affairs, Georgetown University, and author of *Midnight at the Pera Palace: The Birth of Modern Istanbul*

"For an appreciation of contemporary Romanian attitudes, Robert Kaplan's book has no equal. As an outsider, yet within, the author offers an analysis of Romania that combines erudition and authority. His sparkling, suggestive reflections, drawing upon history and landscape, capture the DNA of the country and its inhabitants."

—DENNIS DELETANT, Ion Rațiu Visiting Professor of Romanian Studies, Georgetown University, and emeritus professor, University College London

"A moving book—an illuminating and compassionate guide through the labyrinth of Romania's immensely convoluted and often traumatic past . . . In spite of the many dark, distressing moments that no one should ignore, *In Europe's Shadow* conveys a sense of hope, promise, and continuous renewal."

—VLADIMIR TISMĂNEANU, professor of politics, University of Maryland, and author of *The Devil in History: Communism, Fascism, and Some Lessons of the Twentieth Century*

"Robert Kaplan illuminates the extraordinary journey of the people of Romania, as well as millions of other East Europeans, from the tragic Soviet despotism of the decades after the Second World War to their more hopeful and democratic future as members of NATO and the European Union in our own time. Kaplan's unique ability to weave together complex histories, religion, memory and political thought is nearly unmatched in our country today."

—NICHOLAS BURNS, professor, Harvard Kennedy School, and former undersecretary of state for political affairs

"A favorite of mine for years, Robert D. Kaplan is a thoughtful and insight-driven historian who writes clear and compelling prose, but what I like most about him is his political sophistication. *In Europe's Shadow* makes you look up and think about what's on the page— a true pleasure for the reader."

—ALAN FURST

BY ROBERT D. KAPLAN

IN EUROPE'S SHADOW

RANDOM HOUSE

NEW YORK

IN EUROPE'S SHADOW

—

ROBERT D. KAPLAN

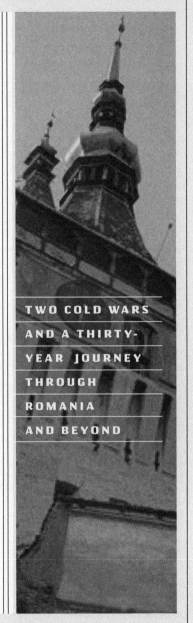

TWO COLD WARS
AND A THIRTY-
YEAR JOURNEY
THROUGH
ROMANIA
AND BEYOND

2016 Random House Trade Paperback Edition

Copyright © 2016 by Robert D. Kaplan
Maps copyright © 2016 by David Lindroth Inc.

All rights reserved.

Published in the United States by Random House,
an imprint and division of Penguin Random House LLC, New York.

RANDOM HOUSE and the HOUSE colophon are registered
trademarks of Penguin Random House LLC.

Originally published in hardcover in the United States by Random House,
an imprint and division of Penguin Random House LLC, in 2016.

Grateful acknowledgment is made to the following for
permission to reprint previously published material:
Persea Books, Inc.: Paul Celan, "Aspen Tree," from *Poems of Paul Celan*,
translated by Michael Hamburger. Copyright © 1972, 1980, 1988, 1995
by Michael Hamburger. Reprinted with the permission of
Persea Books, Inc. (New York), www.perseabooks.com.

LIBRARY OF CONGRESS CATALOGING-IN-PUBLICATION DATA
Kaplan, Robert D.
In Europe's shadow : two cold wars and a thirty-year journey through
Romania and beyond / Robert D. Kaplan.
pages   cm
Includes bibliographical references and index.
ISBN 978-0-8129-8662-4
Ebook ISBN 978-0-8129-9682-1
1. Romania—Description and travel. 2. Kaplan, Robert D.—Travel—
Romania. 3. Romania—History—1989– 4. Romania—
History—1944–1989. I. Title.
DR210.K37 2015
949.8—dc23
2015012726

Printed in the United States of America on acid-free paper

randomhousebooks.com

9 8 7 6 5 4 3 2 1

Title-page art and photo by iStock
Book design by Barbara M. Bachman

To
Joy de Menil

Who remembering,
Or foreseeing, ever smiled?

—FERNANDO PESSOA, 1926

True experience consists in reducing one's contact with
reality whilst at the same time intensifying one's analysis
of that contact.

—FERNANDO PESSOA, 1935

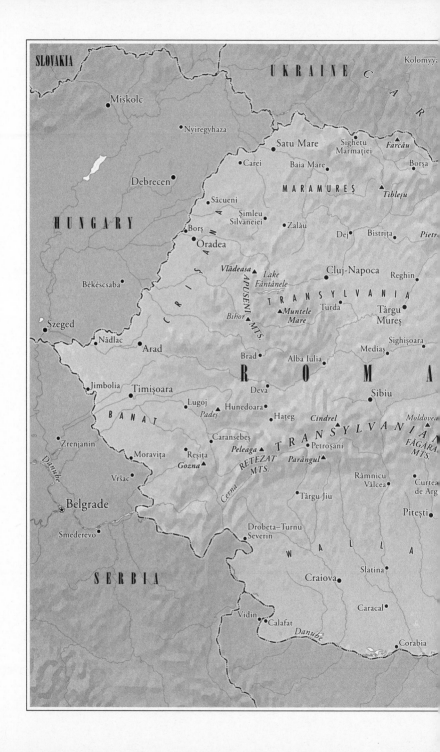

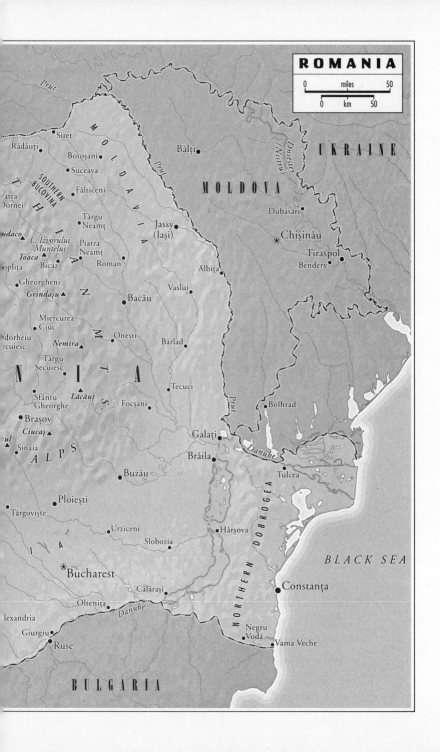

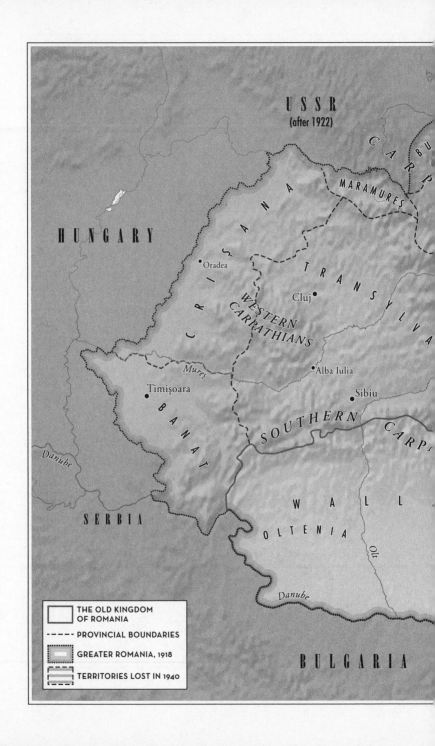

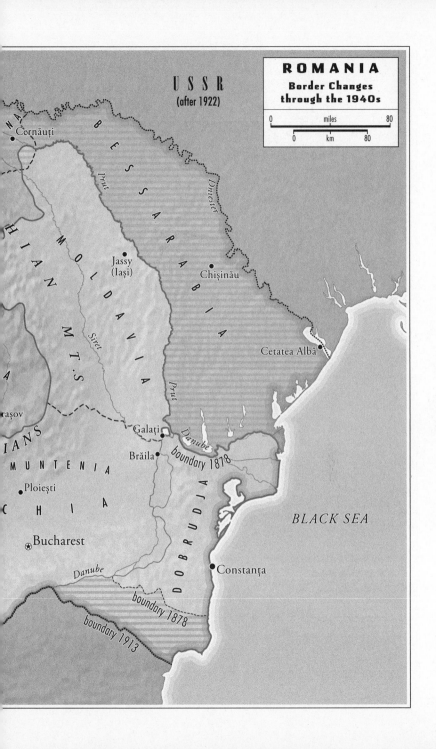

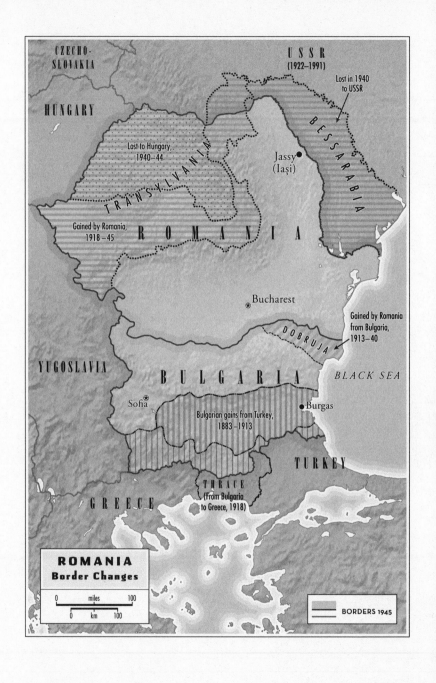

CZECHO-
SLOVAKIA

HUNGARY

USSR
(1922–1991)

Lost in 1940
to USSR

T R A N S Y L V A N I A

B E S S A R A B I A

Lost to Hungary,
1940–44

Jassy
(Iași)

Gained by Romania,
1918–45

R O M A N I A

Bucharest

YUGOSLAVIA

DOBRUJA

Gained by Romania
from Bulgaria,
1913–40

BLACK SEA

B U L G A R I A

Sofia

Burgas

Bulgarian gains from Turkey,
1883–1913

TURKEY

THRACE
(From Bulgaria
to Greece, 1918)

GREECE

ROMANIA
Border Changes

0   miles   100

0   km   100

BORDERS 1945

RUSSIA, AUSTRIA-HUNGARY, AND THE BALKANS

miles 0 — 200
km 0 — 200

RUSSIA

AUSTRIA-HUNGARY

Danube
Budapest

BESSARABIA

Pruth
Czernowitz

Dniester

TRANSYLVANIA

Jassy
(Iaşi)

Drava

Temesvar
(Timişoara)

Sibiu
(Hermannstadt)

Kronstadt
(Braşov)

Pruth

Sava

Brăila
Danube

Belgrade

ROMANIA

BOSNIA

Craiova
Bucharest

Silistra

Sarajevo

HERZEGOVINA

SERBIA

Danube

BLACK SEA

Mostar

Nish

Shumla

Varna

SANDJAK OF NOVIBAZAR

MONTE-NEGRO

Djakova

Sofia

BULGARIA

EASTERN RUMELIA

Burgas

ADRIATIC SEA

ALBANIA

Skopje

Philippopolis

Durazzo

Ohrid

Seres

THRACE

Constantinople

MACEDONIA

Salonica

Yanina

Larissa

AEGEAN SEA

GREECE

ASIA MINOR

OTTOMAN EMPIRE, 1815

OTTOMAN EMPIRE, 1908

CEDED TO ROMANIA, 1856;
RETROCEDED TO RUSSIA IN 1878

BOUNDARY DETERMINED BY
THE TREATY OF BERLIN (1878)

TERRITORY ALLOTTED TO BULGARIA BY
THE TREATY OF SAN STEFANO (1878)

TERRITORY ACQUIRED BY ROMANIA
FROM BULGARIA, 1913

BORDERS IN 1913

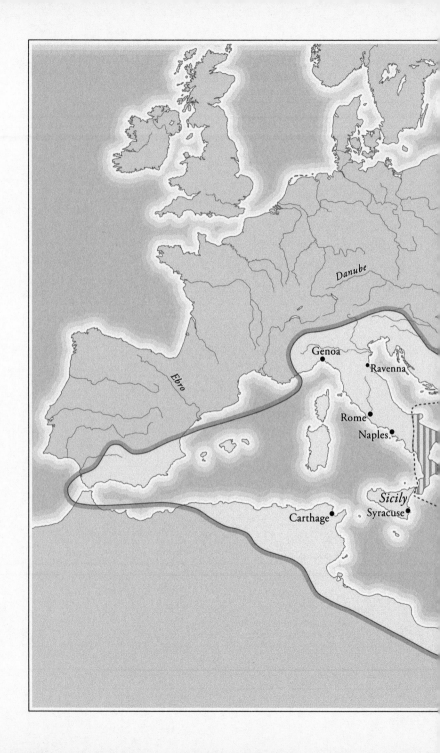

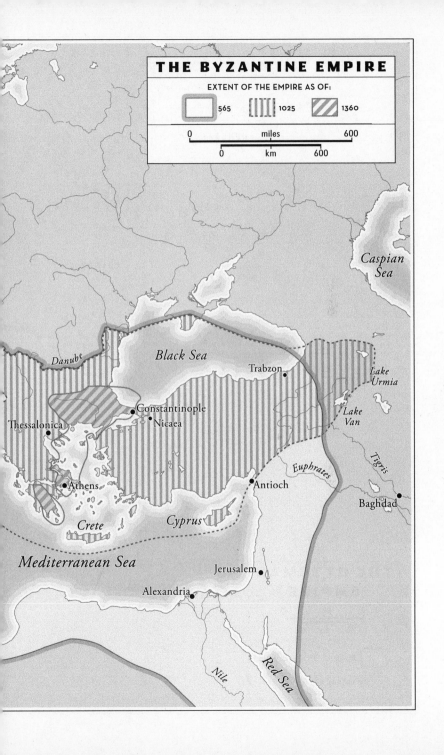

THE BYZANTINE EMPIRE

EXTENT OF THE EMPIRE AS OF:

565 | 1025 | 1360

0   miles   600

0   km   600

Caspian Sea

Danube

Black Sea

Trabzon

Lake Urmia

Lake Van

Thessalonica

Constantinople

Nicaea

Athens

Antioch

Euphrates

Tigris

Baghdad

Crete

Cyprus

Jerusalem

Mediterranean Sea

Alexandria

Nile

Red Sea

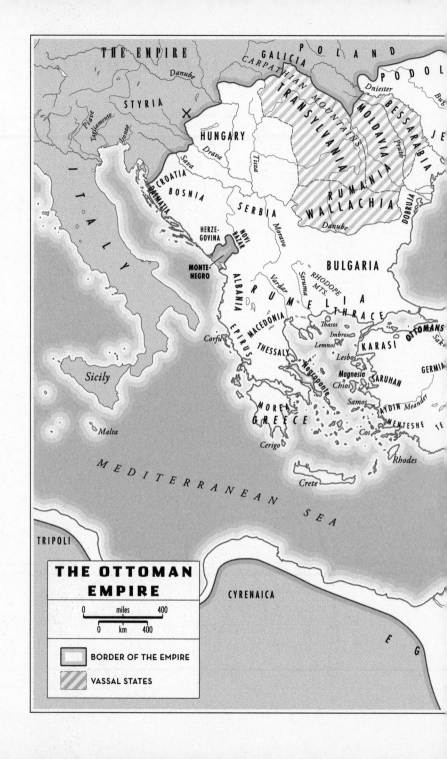

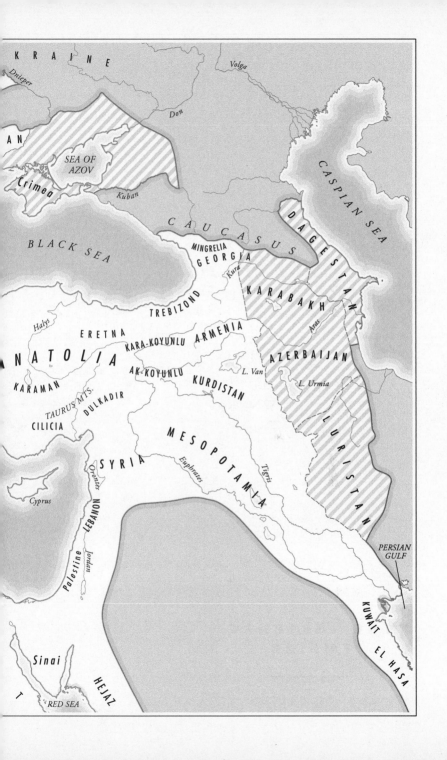

THE HABSBURG
EMPIRE

0 — miles — 100
0 — km — 100

AUSTRIA-HUNGARY
1867-1918

CONTENTS

NABOKOV'S ROOM

MY LIBRARY IS A BURDEN. IT CONSTITUTES THE NOTES THAT I am afraid to lose until I make use of them. So I need to write all this down. That way I can discard my library and continue to strip away my possessions—the foremost indignity of old age.

One book means freedom; too many books, though, act as a barrier to further discovery of the world. When you have a ready quote in your head for every new vista before your eyes, you can no longer see clearly.

Hardcovers are for sedentary life. I have relatively few of those, and even fewer first editions. No bibliophile would be impressed. My library mainly consists of battered paperbacks scrawled over with notes that I've made over the years. Nevertheless, each one is precious to me. A low budget makes you savor individual books, and makes you discerning as to which ones to buy. I did not have a full-time job until I was fifty-three, then I had several in succession, sometimes simultaneously. So in middle age I started to accumulate many more books which individually meant less and less to me. It is the books I acquired decades ago that really matter. Like old friends with whom you have lost touch, as flawed as they are, you can't shake your memory of them.

The problem is that like old memories, overtaken by more recent ones, the objects so dear to me have gotten pushed behind the stacks.

The icon given to me by a Romanian artist which once held such a prominent place is now squeezed sideways between a book on the Balkans and a Cambodian statue, behind which, in turn, is a print I bought at a museum in Lahore almost a lifetime ago. I must tear all this away. Beware the narcissism of collecting!

But it is hard. One worthy paperback beside the bed civilizes even the crassest hotel room. Sir Ronald Storrs, British governor of Cyprus, wrote after a mob burned down his library in 1931 that "even objects commonly called inanimate, over which one has mused often and long, may become almost like those beloved beings, that no seeming death can ever take. I can still shut my eyes and feel each book standing in its place. . . ." This from one of the handful of first editions I do own.[1]

The most sensuous inanimate object is a book. I hold in my hands a 1977 Hutchinson paperback of C. R. Boxer's *The Portuguese Seaborne Empire 1415–1825* (originally published in 1969): a holy text for those enamored by things Portuguese. I stare at its cover, the top half an elegant black and white typeface, the bottom half a painting of a caravel in a rich and turbulent turquoise sea, set against a map: this paperback has the texture of a medieval vase.

For decades, I began each new project with the purchase of a beautiful book on the subject: illustrated paperback editions of Alan Moorehead's *The White Nile* (1960) and *The Blue Nile* (1962) for a book on the Horn of Africa; the Oxford University Press/Karachi edition of Olaf Caroe's *The Pathans* (1958) for a book on Afghanistan; a first edition of John Reed's *The War in Eastern Europe* (1916), a rare splurge, for a book on the Balkans; the Charles E. Luriat Company edition of Basil Lubbock's *The Opium Clippers* (1933), another splurge, for a book on the Indian Ocean; and so on. Books that have been owned by someone for many years for a specific purpose carry not just memories (that is obvious); they also reveal their owner's true values. For the books we own may indicate something about us very different from what we think.

But don't wholly discount the value of memories that books confer.

A book can connote the place where it was read better than an old photograph can. For me, *Buddenbrooks* summons forth Prague in the early winter of 1981, when the Cold War granted a debilitating silence to the city, so that the squares were empty, making the statues and gargoyles all the more formidable. I remember returning from an interview with an official of the Communist government, being followed by a secret policeman to my hotel, and then reading in my hotel room about the little house on the Mecklenburg coast that smelled of coffee, where Antonie Buddenbrook develops an affection for a young medical student, a romance that dies with the summer because of family obligations. My copy of *Fathers and Sons*, which I read while I stayed alone in a lodge during two days of rainstorms in the summer of 1973, summons forth a Romanian forest of oak, fir, and beech. Because of Turgenev's dark, modern message embedded in a pastoral romance about nineteenth-century Russia, I experienced solitude rather than loneliness in Romania.

Young people are blessed by the ability to live in the present; those in middle age and beyond, undone by anxieties, are desperate to retrieve it. Books are an act of resistance, not just to the distractions of the electronic age, but to our problems, and to our pretensions. The goal is not *success*, but *presentness*, to recover those long moments — hours on end, actually — of absolute concentration in Turgenev's story. Turgenev took me inside the iciest of hearts as it is crushed by passion, so that I comprehended, for the first time, how ideology, with all its abstractions, founders on Shakespearean depths.

Like old records, old paperback books are quaint and delicious at first, but as the years roll on they threaten to assume the look of junk in an attic. Musty, yellowing pages will not do in a liquid crystal age. Get rid of books, I tell myself. Keep only the ones that matter most. Thin out my library. Reduce it to the essentials.

THERE IS A SHORT STORY by Vladimir Nabokov, "Cloud, Castle, Lake." The protagonist is desperate to escape from a noisy tour group—to escape from a world, really—that demands a horrific conformity. He happens upon an inn. "Upstairs was a room for travelers. 'You know, I shall take it for the rest of my life,'" he tells the innkeeper. It was a "most ordinary" room: "but from the window one could clearly see the lake with its cloud and its castle, in a motionless and perfect correlation of happiness." He realizes "in one radiant second . . . that here in this little room with that view, beautiful to the verge of tears, life would at last be what he had always wished it to be." He would require only a "few possessions" to fill that room, including a few books.[2]

What would be the books—two dozen at the most, enough for a shelf—that I would bring to such a room in order to live out the rest of my life? Each of these books would have to hold deep meaning for me; to have changed me; to have pivotally affected my life, and not altogether for the better, for life to be life requires complications and even unpleasantness.

Indeed, I have the books in mind that I would choose. Here is only the story of one.

I PULL A BATTERED VOLUME off one of my shelves, *The Governments of Communist East Europe*, by H. Gordon Skilling, the 1971 paperback edition; the book was originally published in 1966. I turn it over with affection. The title is dry, academic, and the cover is likewise: all gray with a brown heading, and no picture. There is nothing here of aesthetic or literary merit. This book, unlike the one about the Portuguese empire, is not beautiful. But this would be among the books I would take to Nabokov's imaginary room.

I was walking down King George Street in Jerusalem in the late summer of 1981. The sunlight was harsh, oppressive. I was tired and sweaty and had a mild headache, wandering aimlessly until I noticed a bookshop in an area roughly parallel by a few blocks to the King David Hotel. It was a little dusty warehouse with gray metal shelves and no place to sit, and little arrangement to the books. Like the walk I took, my life at that moment was directionless.

I would be released from the Israel Defense Forces (IDF) in a few weeks and was not sure what to do next. I was twenty-nine. I lacked a degree from the kind of college that helps in the world of journalism. I had worked as a freelance journalist in parts of the Arab world and Israel, and had read and traveled voraciously, but all to little published effect. In Israel for a few years, I had become fascinated not only with the country itself but with the "Holy Land" and its tapestry of different religions. I had acquired a passion not only for synagogues, but for Greek monasteries in the Judean desert and for medieval Muslim monuments. That had led me to write and ghostwrite a number of illustrated books on archaeology and Orthodox Christianity for Israeli publishers that had a negligible circulation. In short, I was basically unemployable. Moreover, I felt suffocated by my life in Jerusalem and just wanted to travel, once again.

The fact that I picked *The Governments of Communist East Europe* off a shelf the moment I saw it was not accidental, even if finding the book at that moment certainly was. The author, H. Gordon Skilling, was a Canadian expert on Cold War Eastern Europe of considerable note, who taught at the University of Toronto, from where he supported anti-Communist dissidents. He had a particular interest in what was then Czechoslovakia, about which he had essentially written its twentieth-century history.[3] But I knew nothing of this at the time. For me he was just a name on a drab, cheaply priced book. I decided to have a look at the book because it stirred a recollection:

In the summer of 1971, I had traveled by train for a few days through Yugoslavia. Inspired by that brief visit, upon graduation from college I made a three-month journey through Communist Europe in the summer of 1973, starting in East Germany and continuing through Poland and Czechoslovakia, and then southeast through Hungary, Romania, and Bulgaria. I stayed at youth hostels and in the homes of people I met along the way. This was during the height of the Cold

War, when all these countries were lumped together by the Western media into one gray mass as the "satellite states" of the Soviet Union. But as soon as I arrived in Warsaw from East Berlin, I began to notice vast differences between the various countries and how they were ruled. Whereas East Germany was a locked-down prison state, Poland had a much more liberalized atmosphere. And whereas Hungary, like Poland, was seething with convivial youth—with whom it was easy for me to make friends—Romania next door was far poorer and closed off to a Western visitor. I could strike up a friendship with no one there. Finally, there was Bulgaria, in whose countryside I felt I had left Europe altogether for what I then imagined to be the Middle East.

Nothing came of that 1973 trip. My attempts at publishing dispatches had failed because of my own inadequacy as a writer and insufficient interest, perhaps, in a region where there was so little news at the time. Returning to the United States, I found a job at a small newspaper and saved enough money to resume traveling, this time through the Arab world, ending up in Israel with no clear purpose. I was terrified of wasting my life.

Leaning against the metal shelves in the dusty bookstore, I began to read Skilling's narrative. On page five, I was roused by the realization that Great Britain's and France's policy of appeasement toward Hitler's Germany in the 1930s had damaged the reputation of the West in Eastern Europe even before World War II, an era when for significant periods it was mainly the Communists who were associated with standing up to the Nazis. Thus the loss of Eastern Europe to Stalin had its roots in Chamberlain's pact with Hitler at Munich in 1938. On page seven, I realized it was the disunity of the Eastern European states themselves that had facilitated the Soviet Union's conquest and continued hold over the region. Disunity between the satellite states had been my own impression of Eastern Europe eight years earlier. Too tired to continue reading in the store, I bought the book and took it back to my loft in Jerusalem's Musrara neighborhood, near the Old City.

Over the next few days, Skilling revealed to me a world of intense national conflict, internal political weakness, sharply defined geographical regions cutting one group off from the other, but all easy to penetrate by an outside power: be it Habsburg Austria in previous centuries or the Soviet Union in this one. "The Danube plain had been a route for migrating peoples and invading armies. . . . Over a dozen nationalities form an ethnic mosaic as varied as the geography. . . . Though the Slavs were mainly Asiatic, cultural kinship never transformed into political unity: inter-Slav and Slav-non-Slav conflict grew from different religious traditions and experiences of occupation." I am transcribing the shorthand notes I made in the back of what was at the time already a decade-old paperback. "Religion never caused unity because the Orthodox churches were autocephalous, besides there was the Catholic-Protestant rift." Of course, there was, too, the division between Catholics and Orthodox, harking back to that between Rome and Byzantium. On reading the word "Orthodox" in Skilling's book, my mind reeled at the connections with the Greek monasteries I often visited in the midst of the Judean Desert: glittering, musky enclosures, teeming with icons and egg-tempera frescoes, surrounded by a fiery, pie-crust landscape scorched the color of zinc.

Democracy, Skilling went on, had sunk meager roots in these countries between the two world wars, World War II had created ethnic winners and losers on a grand scale in Eastern Europe, and since 1945 history had virtually stopped. Meanwhile, the Romanians and the Albanians were still in significant measure peasants—thus did Skilling's explanation partly account for my shock of how Romania looked and felt in 1973 compared to Hungary. I stared for minutes on end at the ethnic map on page thirteen, so unlike the Cold War maps with which I was vaguely familiar.

Like the most valuable perceptions, the nub of a plan can formulate in your mind in the fraction of a second. Israel, though diplomatically isolated from the Warsaw Pact, did have formal relations with Communist Romania, and more crucially for my purposes it had a di-

rect air link to the capital of Bucharest. The very day after I was released from the military, I decided that I would fly to Romania and
begin a journey throughout Eastern Europe.

I had saved some money from ghostwriting. This time—I told myself—I would not waste the opportunity. This trip, with Skilling's book
as my guide, would be specifically about selling articles to newspapers
in order to establish the basis of a résumé. Eastern Europe, in 1981,
particularly the Balkans, was a journalistic backwater in the extreme.
Skilling's classification of "the rugged and mountainous Balkan Peninsula" forming one of three subregions within Communist Eastern Europe (the others being the North European and Danubian plains) gave
prominence to an area—and a word even—absent from the headlines
for decades on end. The "Balkans" at that moment represented the
opposite of Israel and the Middle East: rather than scores of journalists
chasing after the same story, as was the case in Jerusalem—and attend-
ing the same press conferences—here was a region within Europe itself with almost no one covering it, a region that was just as historically
and culturally interesting as where I lived at the moment. Skilling's
suggestion at the end of his book that all these states remained "distinctive" in their own right, despite their inclusion inside the Soviet
empire—with each practicing Communism in its own way, according
to its own culture and historical experience—would constitute a theme
of my reporting, I decided. It is the perceived differences between us,
as much as the similarities, that make us human.[4]

I BEGAN TO SCAN the press for anything about Eastern Europe and
especially the Balkans, and explored the newspaper microfilm archives
at the library of the United States Information Center in West Jerusalem. A pattern quickly emerged. A number of the major news organizations had correspondents in Warsaw or Vienna, who once a year or
so in the late 1970s and early 1980s would make a journey through the
southern tier of Communist Eastern Europe, writing a story about Yu-

goslavia, a story about Romania, and so on. I found a number of stories about how the Romanian currency was so worthless, people used Kent cigarettes as barter. While this was interesting, I got tired of reading the very same story from one correspondent after another. Surely more was going on in the country than that.

Finally, a wire service story at the bottom of an inside page of the *Jerusalem Post* caught my interest. The dateline was Belgrade, the Yugoslav capital. Apparently the Soviet Union was reducing the subsidy on fuel it provided the Eastern European states, resulting in periodic power blackouts throughout the region. I couldn't know it at the time, but this marked the beginning of a decade of economic decline that would eventually help ignite unrest within these societies themselves and against their leaders at the top. Also, in October 1981, I noticed another obscurely placed wire service story from Belgrade about disturbances among ethnic Albanians in the southern Yugoslav province of Kosovo. By the time I was ready to leave Israel, I had saved about a dozen clippings.

On my discharge date, after handing in my uniform and kit bag at BAKUM, the military processing center outside Tel Aviv, I made the ordinary request to travel abroad, now necessary as I would be eligible for reserve duty. The girl in uniform asked me where I planned to go. I told her Romania. She was a little surprised. Romania was a member of the Warsaw Pact, with close ties to the Palestine Liberation Organization and radical Arab countries. "Not many Israelis go there," she remarked. "Why?" she asked. "And at the beginning of winter?" I told her I wanted to visit Christian Orthodox monasteries, a subject I had written about in books. "Call the Foreign Ministry in Jerusalem for the address and phone number of the Israeli Embassy in Romania, in case you have any security-related problem when you're there," she said in an expressionless monotone, while issuing me the travel permit. She then added that the permit was for Romania only, and that I had no permission from the IDF to travel elsewhere in Eastern Europe, where Israel maintained no embassies. I accepted the conditions, knowing I had no intention of obeying them. However minor the infraction may have been, it was at that moment that I knew I might not be returning to Israel.

The next morning, as I boarded an El Al plane for Bucharest, I carefully placed my Israeli passport at the bottom of my carry-on bag. Upon arrival, I would discard my return ticket and produce my American passport, and use it to get visas to the other Communist countries at their embassies in the Romanian capital. Skilling's book had now given me a vocation, a direction: a fate. To read is to learn about the historical background in which one has grown up. By inserting me in Cold War Europe on and off for the next nine years, Skilling, more than anyone else, made me fully aware of the era into which I was born. That book made me a foreign correspondent, even though no one had hired me.

IN EUROPE'S SHADOW

Chapter I

BUCHAREST 1981

THE MOTION OF TRAVEL RELIEVES SADNESS. "THE NOVEL LOOK of streets in novel countries . . . The peace they seem to offer for our sorrows," remarks the early-twentieth-century Portuguese poet and existentialist writer Fernando Pessoa.[1] New surroundings prompt forgetfulness of old ones, and thus speed up the passage of time. The moment I left the plane at Bucharest's Otopeni airport, I exchanged a world of loud, intense colors in the sun-blinded Middle East for one of a black-and-white engraving in the shivery, November-hued Balkans. Only hours removed, Israel was, nevertheless, already part of a distant, earlier existence.

Otopeni was a marble and dirty glass blockhouse with passport officers in slummy cubicles. A red star and photo of the dictator hung from the otherwise lonely walls. I waited half an hour in the cold for a plywood seat in a bus to take me downtown. Bare wiry branches—beeches, poplars, and large-leaved lindens—crackled in the steppe wind breaching the bus windows, signaling winter in the dead afternoon light under an iron vault of clouds. The forest of deciduous trees—hardly known in the Eastern Mediterranean I had just left and here dominant—only sharpened the sense of distance I had traveled. So did the steep-roofed houses that emerged as we entered a grand boulevard of the city, with their northern baroque influence and expectations of snow.

For six years I had not traveled beyond North Africa and the Eastern Mediterranean. The times I had left Israel had only been for extended trips to Greece. The return to what—in comparison—was the north had a sudden and dramatic effect on me. "Nothing discourages thought so much as this perpetual blue sky," writes André Gide in *The Immoralist*. It is said that when we think seriously, we think abstractly: Gide suggests that a cold northern clime of leaden clouds encourages abstraction, and by inference, analysis and introspection.[2] For years I had held out the dream of living in a house on a Greek island in summer. My first hours in Bucharest began a psychological journey that would culminate decades later in the quest to live in Maine in darkest winter. With it would come a break in reading habits: exchanging the glittering Mediterranean sensuality of Lawrence Durrell for the cold, economical passion of Thomas Mann; leaving behind the occasional half-baked, Grecian ecstasies of Henry Miller and discovering anew the realist discipline of that most essential Greek, Thucydides, and by progression, his twentieth-century inheritors, Hans Morgenthau, Kenneth Waltz, and Samuel Huntington.

You don't grow up gradually. You grow up in short bursts at pivotal moments, by suddenly realizing how ignorant and immature you are. Bucharest, as I rode in from the airport and saw the ashen, moldy faces of the bus driver and other Romanians aboard, crushed in their overcoats and winter hats with earmuffs and their worries, made me instinctually aware of all the history I had been missing the last half decade. Here was a whole category of suffering foreign to the Levant.

The gargantuan *Scînteia* building, grand in a Stalinist sort of way—named after the Communist Party daily, "The Spark"—heralded the entrance to the city. The 1950s Stalinist architecture with the courtyard statue of Lenin on a high plinth spiritually defeated everything around it. Here, the next day, I would visit a Mr. Tuiu in an empty concrete office to the right of the entrance: this official of the

Communist wire agency AGERPRES advised me "to be careful about anyone you talk to except" whom he approved.

Eroilor Aerului ("To the Heroes of the Air") were the words emblazoned on the soaring monument on Piața Aviatorilor (Aviators' Plaza), dedicated in 1935 to World War I fliers and other aviation pioneers, which I caught a glimpse of as the bus rumbled by. I grasped immediately the word, making the connection with Beethoven's *Eroica* ("Heroic") or Third Symphony. From the travel guides I knew that Romanian was a Latin language. But the words on the monument made me abruptly, palpably aware of it: just as the altogether bleak, wintry surroundings and virtually empty streets and boulevards made me palpably aware that I was in a part of the world not ordinarily associated with Latinity. (True, an exotic geography provided Romanian with elements of Slavic, Hungarian, Turkish, Greek, and Roma, in addition to a Thracian substratum—and yet the Latin basis was dominant.[3])

Soon the bread and fuel lines began: beyond Piața Romană on Bulevardul General Gheorghe Magheru. The silence of the streets was devastating as I alighted from the bus with my backpack on Strada Academiei. The city had been reduced to a vast echo. There were few cars, and everyone was dressed in the same shapeless coats and furry hats that evoked internal exile somewhere on the eastern steppe. People clutched cheap jute bags in expectation of stale bread. I looked at their faces: nervous, shy, clumsy, calculating, heartrending, as if they were struggling to master the next catastrophe. Those clammy complexions seemed as if they had never seen the sunlight.

This was the beginning of a decade that would be among the worst in Romanian history, even if the political repression was actually more suffocating in the 1950s, when the Communists under Gheorghe Gheorghiu-Dej had to establish total thought control over an ideologically hostile population. A distinguished British historian would later write that in the 1980s Romanians had been "reduced . . . to an animal state, concerned only with the problems of day-to-day survival."[4]

The situation would deteriorate by stages: with food, fuel, water, and electricity shortages worse than during World War I. In late 1982, there was a widely circulating rumor that bread was deliberately held in the bakeries for twenty-four hours before selling, so it would become stale and the population would buy less. A local joke of the era: "If only the Russians invaded, then we would get to eat like the Czechs and get passports like the Hungarians." By the middle of the decade, the buses would no longer run on diesel, but on the much cheaper and more dangerous methane gas, with tanks attached to the roofs.

I had chosen the Hotel Muntenia on Strada Academiei from a budget guide: it was downtown and cheap enough, less than twenty-five dollars per night. All I can remember about the room was that it was brown with one bare lightbulb, with a common toilet and shower at the other end of a yawning and drafty hallway. I turned on the black-and-white television: speeches of the leader interspersed with folk dancing. The room had a phone with a corroded cord which required going through the hotel switchboard. In such mournful surroundings, I began to feel liberated from my previous life.

"Of course you can come in tomorrow for a briefing, and maybe we can get you in to see the ambassador," a friendly and welcoming second secretary or other at the U.S. Embassy told me over the phone, as if lightening all the brown in my room. I had suddenly gone from being a nobody in a crowded journalistic field in Jerusalem to a person with more status, simply by showing up in this Cold War backwater. "You're staying at the InterCon, aren't you?" she asked. My reply was nervous and noncommittal. The coming years would be about perfecting the technique of *so-to-speak* interviewing the prime minister while staying at the youth hostel.

The next morning I walked past the dirty cream-and-white, run-of-the-mill modernist hulk of the InterContinental Hotel, towering upward in a half arc, completed in 1970 and the epitome of luxury in late-Communist Bucharest. Behind the hotel lay Tudor Arghezi, the street named for the inexhaustible twentieth-century poet and writer, whose literary aesthetic and prodigious modernity had managed to survive Communist rule. Here the white and steep-roofed baroque mansion that housed the U.S. Embassy was located. Inside, the gleam of tooled dark wood; the neat, state-of-the-art file cabinets and photocopy machines of the era; and the strict Washington dress code of the occupants made for what in my eyes then was a pampered atmosphere of safety, elegance, and efficiency, an extraterritorial refuge from the prison-yard surroundings in nearby streets. I remember the mansion fondly because I was instantly embraced by a team of diplomats who entrusted me with not only their analyses but their frustrations. They treated me as a professional journalist, a small but crucial revelation, since in Israel I always felt that my professionalism was suspect because I was a freelancer and a member of the local armed forces, and therefore prone to be sympathetic to the right-wing nationalist government of the day.

On repeated visits to Bucharest in the 1980s, I would be reduced to relying on Western diplomats. The sheer terror that ordinary Romanians felt about confiding anything substantive to a foreign journalist, as well as the unwillingness of Communist officialdom to venture much beyond propaganda, left one with few alternatives. The Securitate, or secret police, were seemingly everywhere. The Romanian officials I did manage to interview would actually say such things as, "We never promised our people a rose garden," or, quoting President Nicolae Ceaușescu, "we are making the passage from the bourgeois-landlord society to the multilaterally developed Socialist society."[5]

While after 1989 the U.S. Embassy in Bucharest was an afterthought for a correspondent, before 1989 it was the central dispatch point for information and analysis on what was happening in this pulverized, half-forgotten country. Here, along with the American embassies in Sofia, Belgrade, Budapest, and so on, I received briefings remarkable for their insight, lucidity, and unsentimentality that, nevertheless, did not undermine an overarching idealism.

For in that white baroque mansion, I met an American diplomat and Balkan area specialist, Ernest H. Latham Jr., who had made it his passion to collect the memoirs and other writings of visitors to Romania prior to the onslaught of the Communist ice age. His point was that by preserving the memoir of a pre-Communist past, one would be able to conceive of a future beyond Communism. In the early and mid-1980s, when Ceauşescu's Romania bore the mood of Stalin's Russia, and the paramount assumption of the age was that the Cold War had no end, this was the best sort of prophecy.

The Cold War in the Balkans and Central Europe was a golden age for Western embassy reporting. In such settings I began to live history as it happened, at a time when none of these capitals were journalistically fashionable: for this was the decade of Beirut, Managua, San Salvador, and Peshawar, with the media preoccupied with wars in Lebanon and Central America, and to a lesser extent in Afghanistan.

I then began acquiring the habit of separating myself from the journalistic horde, looking for news in obscure locations, that is. For example, on a later trip to Bucharest in 1984, Latham casually told me that Ceauşescu was blasting a vast area of the capital into oblivion, with security forces plundering and then blowing up whole neighborhoods of historic Orthodox churches, monasteries, Jewish synagogues, and nineteenth-century houses: ten thousand structures in all, many with their own sylvan courtyards.[6] Residents were given hours to clear out with their life possessions before explosive charges were set. The blast site, where an austere Stalinist-style civic center and apartment blocks were to be built, was being called "Ceaushima" by Romanians brave enough to talk to foreign diplomats. Latham, who had seen the plans for the new Party complexes and ceremonial avenues, compared it to something "Albert Speer might have designed for Adolf Hitler, had the 1,000-year Reich become reality." When I revealed what was happening in a magazine article a few months later, I was made persona non grata in Romania for five years, until Ceauşescu fell.[7]

In neighboring Bulgaria in the mid-1980s, another American diplomat told me that, *by the way*, the Communist regime was forcing all 900,000 ethnic Turks, 10 percent of the Bulgarian population, to change their names—to Slavic equivalents, even as mosques were being closed and the Turkish language forbidden. In 1984, yet another

American diplomat, Dan Fried, this time in Belgrade, strongly recommended that I henceforth concentrate my energies on Yugoslavia, where, as he put it, ethnic, political, and economic divisions were worsening and therefore "this country has a great future in the news."

The 1980s, which professionally began for me that first morning at the U.S. Embassy on Tudor Arghezi, would constitute an onrush of current events, primarily in the Balkans, that I had more or less to myself—save, of course, for the relatively small number of dedicated foreign correspondents based in capitals like Vienna and Warsaw, themselves struggling to get their own stories prominently placed and appreciated, in the face of more cinematic events in the Middle East and Central America. In all of Eastern Europe, only Poland—because of Solidarity, martial law, and a Polish pope—figured prominently in the headlines.

Passion was usually lacking in my freelance dispatches: sent by airmail with self-addressed return envelopes, using post offices and occasionally diplomatic pouches. The facts alone were sufficient to communicate the extent of the nightmare, to which an air of unreality frequently hung.

On one occasion I even saw the tyrant close-up at a Communist Party congress. He had stridden up to the podium, and the four thousand Party members in attendance rose to their feet, chanting loudly "Cea-u-şes-cu, Cea-u-şes-cu . . ." The tyrant, his chin jutting forth, watched impassively for a full three minutes with his wife, Elena, beside him. Then he slightly raised his arm in a gesture vaguely reminiscent of a Hitler salute, the sight of which immediately silenced the great hall. Standing directly below a giant picture of himself, he began a speech interrupted five times: each time by several minutes of handclapping and chants of "Cea-u-şes-cu, Cea-u-şes-cu . . ." until he silenced them. He spoke for a full ninety minutes about socialist economics. After a break, he would speak for a further ninety minutes on socialist theory and ideology. The faces in the audience looked terrified throughout. Nobody dared stop clapping and chanting until he raised his arm.

——

I LEARNED HOW TO BE a journalist in Bucharest. Not all at once, not always intentionally, and, again, not altogether consciously, for Bucharest in 1981 was not only powerful at first sight, but powerful in retrospect as the years went on. I would ponder Bucharest often as a reaction to the books I later read. Learning to be a journalist happened as much in reflection as it did in real time.

By learning to be a journalist, I do not mean learning the commonplace but crucial mechanics of accurate note-taking, newswriting, or developing sources, which I had been taught in elementary form earlier in college and at a small newspaper. Instead, I refer to understanding the true character of objectivity. For what is taught in journalism schools is an invaluable craft, whereas properly observing the world is a matter of deliberation and serious reading over decades in the fields of history, philosophy, and political science. Journalism actually is not necessarily, whatever the experts of the profession may claim, a traditional subject in its own right. Rather, it is a means to explore and better communicate subjects that are, in fact, traditional areas of study: history and philosophy as I've said, but also government, politics, literature, architecture, art, and so on. I've never altogether trusted what journalists say about themselves. As Robert Musil, the great early-twentieth-century Austrian novelist, observes: "high-mindedness is the mark of every professional ideology." That's why "the image of a profession in the minds of its practitioners is not too reliable."[8] (Thus journalism schools have the particular responsibility of looking at their profession from the vantage point of outsiders.)

Reading history and political philosophy more and more as I got older, in the course of reporting from all over the world, taught me that a journalist simply cannot be expected to predict the distant future, or even the exact details of the near future. That is impossible, for so much depends not only on impersonal forces like geography and technology, but on the actions of individuals—themselves motivated often by the disfiguring whirlwinds of passion. However, a journalist, through his or her own observations, might be expected to make the reader measurably less surprised by the events to come in a given place within the space of a few years: the middle-term future. And the journalist's ability to do that, however imperfectly, is only made possible by being cruel-hearted.

"Truth is the successful effort to think impersonally and inhumanly," writes Musil in *The Man without Qualities*. "Truth arises when the blood is cold." He suggests that a banker is more dependable than an angel, because the desire for money preserves objectivity more than love.[9] Thomas Mann concurs, writing in "Tonio Kröger," "It is all up" with the writer "as soon as he becomes a man and begins to feel."[10]

I learned the value of such advice, in part, because of my raw reactions to Bucharest in 1981. Bucharest taught me that while a journalist perpetually seeks out people for information and insights, he must also embrace solitude in long walks in distant cities. I would deeply empathize with all categories of people over the decades—with Romanians especially throughout the Cold War—even openly sympathize when I was purposefully intent on showing readers the world from their point of view. But I also knew that while empathy helps, sympathy can distort. A journalist should be less concerned with outcomes—tragic or not—than with getting the analysis right. A journalist can never shade his observations for the sake of some imagined result. Outcomes are the responsibility of the policymaker, not the journalist. For however moral and uplifting the policy, it must be based on a realistic assessment of the facts on the ground. Thus a journalist must be a polite person who asks rude questions, leading sometimes to unsettling observations about both groups and individuals—the very questions and observations that may make one unwelcome at the dinner table and at some fancy conferences.

The real difficulty with journalists, and here I refer specifically to foreign correspondents, is that they are the ultimate empiricists. They are children of the moment, with experiences so intense that in their minds the entire universe depends on the fate of those about whom they write, to such an extent that what they don't experience firsthand—even such history that might put their own adventures into perspective—is relegated to the back of their minds, to the lower paragraphs as it were, especially if the local history implies something enduringly heartrending. As for the rest of the world, where equally serious dilemmas exist—and where action is also morally and otherwise demanded—it concerns them not, unless they have been there as firsthand witnesses.

So how does one get morally involved while also retaining a heart of ice? How does one describe suffering with the requisite sensitivity while not caring at the same time? Of everything I later read that caused me to reflect back on my ten days in Bucharest in 1981, nothing solved the conundrum between empathy and objectivity as much as the writing of Joseph Conrad, particularly in his two monumental works, *Lord Jim* (1900) and *Nostromo* (1904).

Conrad's rationalism never gives way to his adventures. His specific achievement is to re-create the overwhelming compactedness of what journalists experience when they are alone in far-off places, in trying circumstances. Yet, because he knows that the record of human experience indicates just how many problems in this world simply have no solutions, his fictional correspondences evince a majestic, godlike objectivity in which humankind is at once loved and deeply pitied. Love is fine, it turns out, as long as one sees it for what it is: an emotion necessary for full-bodied observation, even as that observation will ultimately renounce it. Indeed, Conrad makes you feel that the destiny of the universe depends upon one poor man, or one sick child, while also letting you know the seeming hopelessness of their situation. This is why Conrad could be history's greatest foreign correspondent, greater than Herodotus even. Because the future lies inside the silences—inside what people are afraid to discuss openly among themselves, or at the dinner table—it is in the guise of fiction that a writer can more easily and relentlessly tell the truth.[11] Such is what I got out of Conrad, partly by way of Bucharest.

Romanians and other East Europeans would ultimately have to liberate themselves. That, in the spirit of Conrad, was the hopelessness of their situation, even as the fact that they would ultimately do so years later vindicated the idealism of the American diplomats I knew.

DESPITE MR. TUIU'S WARNING, I visited several foreign embassies for briefings. The Israeli Embassy was off Strada Plantelor, southeast of the city center. It was in a villa that resembled a small and grim castle, on a section of street that for obvious security reasons was uninhabited. A block away was a set of barricades patrolled by Romanian militiamen armed with assault rifles. After a body search, the Romanians allowed me to proceed to the embassy compound, where I passed through a series of locking doors before arriving in a waiting room with two one-way mirrors and insipid posters about holidays in Israel. A voice through a microphone told me to stand up facing the mirror, then slip my passport through a steel slot. I was now on Israeli territory and as someone holding Israeli nationality it should have been my Israeli passport that I presented. When I pushed my American passport through the slot I knew I was crossing another, small psychological divide.

The passport came back through the slot, another locked door opened, and I proceeded through an undersea-like labyrinth of corridors coated with white tiles, through a curtain, on the other side of which I met the Israeli diplomat who would give me my briefing. His office was lined with undressed stone, like a bunker.

The diplomat was about my age, perhaps a bit older, with premature gray hair. He gushed with friendliness. He seemed honored that an American reporter had asked him for a briefing on a subject other than Romanian Jews. I flashed back to where I had been, what I had been wearing, and what language I had been speaking the week before. Israel was already deep in my past—at least it seemed at that moment. In Israel I had been someone passing through, in the military merely for an adventure, not integrated into the society in a profound enough way, and not intending to be. But here in Communist Romania, I felt that I was finally beginning to do what I always was meant to.

The briefing was the least informative I received from any foreign diplomat in Romania. Unlike the Americans, French, British, and West Germans, he was unwilling at any juncture to criticize the Ceauşescu regime. The reason was obvious. The Israelis were in Romania—their only outpost in Eastern Europe—on the whim of a tyrant, who was using his official ties with Israel to wheedle trade concessions out of the West, while being guilty of the worst human rights violations in the Warsaw Pact. The embassy's security arrangement and the tightfistedness of the diplomat's briefing were proof of this. The Israelis could be thrown out at any moment and the diplomat was not going to risk it for the sake of being honest with a young reporter.

"But people have to line up before dawn just to buy stale bread," I pleaded with him.

"Yes, but in this part of the world, you know, people are used to waiting in lines. It's in their culture."

In grandiose moral terms, his reply was pathetic. In terms of Israel's self-interest and difficult geopolitical position, his reply was merely awkward. For a price, Ceauşescu was permitting Romanian Jews to leave the country. Protecting that process constituted a morality in and of itself. Having removed myself from Israel to this bleak and emotionally neutral terrain where I barely knew anybody, I was better able to fathom Israeli logic.

IT WAS BOTH A REVELATION and an inspiration to feel so intellectually alive simply because I was alone, with no emotional attachments to this place, with no personal stake in its destiny. Lucian in the second century indicated that a true observer has to be in his writings "a foreigner, without a country, living under his own law only."[12] In Israel, I often listened to my Jewish friends attack some of the foreign correspondents in Jerusalem for being tacitly pro-Palestinian, mainly because the correspondents were outsiders, who had no investment in Israel's present or future, and therefore could not profoundly comprehend Israel's degree of endangerment. In Romania I instinctively grasped how those foreign correspondents in Jerusalem, whom my friends had criticized, were merely trying to strike a balance between two warring peoples: how they benefited emotionally and intellectually precisely by not having a stake in the outcome.

Romania might have been a news backwater and Israel a place where news was constantly happening. But that's not how I experienced it. Romania *was* the Cold War, the signal conflict of the age, whereas the Arab-Israeli crisis was but a critical sideshow of it. My mind reeled back to those long lines for bread and fuel, with the colors of people's faces and clothes and the surrounding sky and buildings all reduced to the two shades of gray in a photo negative. Sometimes I saw people sitting on the sidewalk in the cold, waiting in front of shops whose shelves were empty: following rumors of a forthcoming delivery of meat, eggs, or cheese. People waited in shifts, sometimes all night. They shivered, and it was only early November. At least my hotel room, for all its dinginess, was heated: not so in the case of many apartment blocks. In terms of human suffering, Romania was the ideological front line between Communism and capitalism. This was *the* history with which my time on Earth corresponded. As Mann writes in *The Magic Mountain:* "A man lives not only his personal life, as an individual, but also consciously or unconsciously the life of his epoch. . . ."[13]

Three years before, in 1978, I had been on the peninsula of Mount Athos in Greece, where I heard that the Soviet Union and its empire would collapse and do so in my lifetime. Two young Russian-American seminary students I had met at the Bulgarian monastery of Zographou, whom I accompanied on a hike to the Russian monastery of St. Panteleimon, spoke to me of the greatness of the czars and of the Russian Orthodox Church, and how the Church and the Romanov dynasty were more legitimate than Leonid Brezhnev's Communist regime of the day. Because it was godless, the Soviet regime had no moral purpose, and therefore Russia would have to be restored to its true self before long. They had said all this matter-of-factly. Because the Cold War had been in progress since before I was born, I unconsciously assumed its permanence, and so impulsively rejected their argument.[14] But now, observing the daily bread lines for one day and yet another and another, their argument hit me with full force. *This could not last, not inside Europe*, I suddenly realized at one point; even as, in calmer moments, I still strongly disbelieved the prospect of a categorical ending to the Cold War.

I recalled journalist Theodore H. White's visceral reaction to the Honan famine of 1943, and how the sight of masses of starving Chinese peasants effectively convinced him that the Nationalist government of Chiang Kai-shek was illegitimate and thus could not endure.[15] I had read White's memoir only the previous year in Jerusalem, and some of his pages affected me still in Bucharest.

Communism in Romania in 1981 appeared like something out of a grainy, nightmarish past, an industrial form of feudalism. And yet the Soviet empire was immeasurably tangible in the eerie submarine silence of these streets, even as it was morally illegitimate. Obviously, Ceaușescu's Stalinism was an affront to the Soviet leadership itself, which had moved beyond Stalinism more than a quarter century earlier and had long tired of Ceaușescu. But totalitarianism in Romania— with the photos of the dictator and his wife on nearly every wall, with a bust of him in every schoolroom—represented, nevertheless, a tolerated variant within Moscow's imperial system. As I would write later in 1984: "Far from being a bold maverick, Ceaușescu—who reigns over a Marxist banana republic of his own making—is a bird singing loudly in a cage."[16]

My third morning in Bucharest, fifty thousand people marched down the boulevards General Magheru and Nicolae Bălcescu— named for the radical luminaries of the 1848 revolutions—shouting, "Ceaușescu, Pace, Ceaușescu, Pace" ("Ceaușescu, Peace, Ceaușescu, Peace"). The tyrant was hailed as the mythic leader of all world peace and disarmament movements. Massive photos of him and his wife, adorned with ribbons, and festooned with blue, yellow, and red Romanian flags, were noisily carried aloft. Near dawn I had watched as the busloads and truckloads of peasants—hauled in by convoy from the

poverty-racked Wallachian countryside (underdeveloped even by Romanian standards)—alighted near Piața Universității, close to my
hotel, where gangsterish men in black fedoras and long trench coats
directed them with bullhorns into their parade formations. It was Har-
vest Day, a festival blatantly manipulated by the regime for its own
purposes. Occasionally an order was barked and people ran faster into
place. Terror filled the faces of these peasants, many in sleeveless
sheepskins, who looked far more wretched than even those at the
morning bread lines. *Ceaușescu, Pace, Ceaușescu, Pace.* And yet the
thunderous roar only seemed to intensify the silence I felt everywhere.
Silence was the regnant sound of repression.

It was Bucharest that led me to Elias Canetti's masterwork, *Crowds
and Power* (1960), about the manipulation of crowds in both their concrete and virtual forms. Canetti defines the *crowd* as a mass of people
who, knowingly or not, abandon their individuality in favor of an intoxicating collective symbol—ultimately, so as to escape loneliness.
Always have the same opinions as everyone else. For even if those
opinions are proven wrong, the crowd will still protect you, while once
outside the crowd, your opinions become suddenly vulnerable. The
trick is always to survive the moment—no matter the moral compro-
mises necessary—and worry about the next only when it comes.

Standing on the sidewalk of Bulevardul Bălcescu, I detected a contest between two crowds: the one marching, composed of a rural peasantry (among the last remaining in Europe), and the one of city
dwellers quietly observing. The crowd of city dwellers evidently could
not be trusted; or else why bus in people from outside the city? But the
peasants, too, were suspect according to the regime, if less so. I would
later confirm with foreign diplomats that the peasants had been both
bribed and bullied to attend the rally.

In their personal, family, and group histories those peasants surely
had suffered far worse than merely having to submerge their individual thoughts periodically into the enforced collectivity of a crowd formation. Their relative docility—compared, that is, to the more sullen
and untrustworthy city dwellers—was a natural survival mechanism,

one born, for example, of the Long European War, begun in 1914, and still inching forward as a tailpiece in Romania in 1981, even if the war had ended in Western Europe in 1945. Truly, Ceauşescu's national Stalinism was a Kremlin-approved substitute for Soviet military occupation, which, in turn, had been the direct product of Stalin defeating Hitler in Central and Eastern Europe.[17] The process of great power conflict, with all its epic hardships and sacrifices, had not ended here yet. In Romania as late as the 1980s, I could perceptibly close the distance with World War II.

East Europeans could adapt to anything, writes Czesław Miłosz. For "man is so plastic a being that one can even conceive of the day when a thoroughly self-respecting citizen will crawl about on all fours, sporting a tail of brightly colored feathers as a sign of conformity to the order he lives in."[18] After all, East Europeans—Romanians in particular—had known territorial dismemberment, occupation, monarchy, military dictatorship, fascism, and Communism all in one century, with two decades still left to run in it. And by the end of the century they would also know revolution and democracy. No wonder Romanians had a deep and tragic historical imagination, unlike Americans, who had never known violent upheaval on their soil since 1865. What the historian Modris Eksteins said about life in the trenches of World War I was also true to a significant degree of East Europeans and especially of Romanians: "honor, glory, heroism, valor" all "lose their meaning" as "the external world consists only of brutality, hypocrisy, illusion. Even the intimate bonds to family have been sundered. Man," Eksteins goes on, "remains alone, without a foothold in the real world."[19] Such was not an exaggerated description of life in Romania in 1981.

Dissidents there might be in Warsaw, psychologically buttressed by a Roman Catholic Church that was both universal in its values and nationalistic in its opposition to Soviet domination. But here in Bucharest, I would meet only one such dissident, a lonely and demoralized man, with no church or labor union to support him. In 1981 he told me, "Westerners expect Romania to be the next Poland, but it will never happen. There are no martyrs here. One half of the country is informing on the other half." Whereas in countries like Poland and Hungary there were such things as "liberal" and "reform" Communists to serve as an unofficial opposition, people like that existed only by the handful in Romania, and made certain to keep their heads bowed, their eyes closed. They barely surfaced except in the final years of the decade. All privately owned typewriters were required to be registered, along with the owner's fingerprints according to some reports, in order to cut off sources of antiregime literature.

Romanians had simply known no respite, political or economic, since the 1930s. World War II witnessed a Nazi-allied regime, the to-ing and fro-ing of armies across Romanian territory, and bleak choices about whether to back Stalin or Hitler following Chamberlain's pact with Hitler. ("*You* were nowhere," Silviu Brucan, the grand old man of Romanian Communism, would later tell me, referring to how the United States was altogether missing from Central Europe until 1944.[20]) And since World War II, three and a half decades of Communism-as-Oriental-despotism had made conditions, by some accounts, worse than in the 1940s. And they would certainly be far worse by the late 1980s.

"Throughout Rumania's history the country had survived because of clever pliancy rather than of the heroism of its people. . . . The Rumanians possess to the highest degree the capacity of receiving the blows of destiny while relaxed," writes the Countess R. G. Waldeck in a memoir of early 1940s Bucharest.[21] The Romanians, in Waldeck's intimation, were not so much fatalists as wise in the ways of history: in which, because there was no end to the process of permutation, there was always the possibility for adaptation and for finding new angles in order to survive. Just as con men had a better chance of surviving the Holocaust than those who played by the rules, Romanians endured the Ceauşescu years by corrupting the entire system. Thus, the country that both baffled and fascinated me for ten days in 1981 was nothing less than a very Latin-style tyranny, a blend of Joseph Stalin and Juan Perón, stuck in the underbelly of Eastern Europe. Even partially understanding it would require years of study and reading, reading that would take me beyond Romania itself—with its utterly chilling and riveting twentieth-century experience, particularly in the 1930s and 1940s—to the histories of the Habsburg, Byzantine, Hungarian, Russian, and Ottoman empires in the Balkans.

FOR THE REAL ADVENTURE of travel is mental. It is about total immersion in a place, because nobody from any other place can contact you. *You are alone.* Thus your life is narrowed to what is immediately before your eyes, making the experience of it that much more vivid and life-transforming. And it wasn't just the cityscape of Bucharest and the other capitals in Eastern and Central Europe I would visit in 1981 that was overpowering, but the conversations with the diplomats and everyone else, too. Real conversations require utter concentration, not texting on the side when you are in a café with someone. That is because travel is linear—it is about one place or singular perception or book at a time, each one etched deep into memory, so as to change your life forever.

Eastern Europe in 1981 would impact me as much as that first trip throughout the region in 1973: both occurred before postmodern communications technology destroyed all but the most extreme forms of travel. For not only could nobody from home contact me, but also there was little real news about the world in the English-language newspapers where I was (the *International Herald Tribune* was banned in many places or arrived days late). My interactions with the young East Germans, Poles, Hungarians, Romanians, and Bulgarians I met along the way in both 1973 and 1981 were concentrated in the utmost. Indeed, those were rich personal lives I often encountered, precisely because the political and public spaces were so barren. I will never forget those faces, and some of those conversations. For example, 1973 was a summer dominated by news of Watergate, about which, traveling alone in Eastern Europe, I could not have cared less.

Like serious reading itself, real travel has now become an act of resistance against the distractions of the electronic age, and against all the worries that weigh us down, thanks to that age. A good book deserves to be finished, just as a haunting landscape tempts further experience of it, and further research into it. Travel and serious reading, because they demand sustained focus, stand athwart the nonexistent attention spans that deface our current time on Earth.[22]

THE PRESENT MOMENT WAS then sacred. It allowed for the depth of awareness required to truly appreciate history and landscape. The two are inseparable. Landscape requires total and unyielding concentration. How else to tease history out of it? Take the architectural legacy of Bucharest: Byzantine, Brâncoveanu, Ottoman, Renaissance, Venetian Classical, French Baroque, Austrian Secession, Art Deco, and Modernist, all writhing and struggling to break free of a dirty gray sea of pillbox Stalinism, like Michelangelo's Unfinished Slaves struggling to break free of their marble blocks. The cloud cover and cold weather intensified my cognizance of all the Stalinist monstrosities. Perhaps had that November brought sunlight instead of clouds, I would have been more focused on the earlier architectural periods. But later visits in the 1980s and 1990s would make the cityscape whole to me.

Authentic, undistracted travel also introduced me to the challenges of area specialization: spending a professional lifetime in the study of a single geographic, cultural, and linguistic region; blending the appreciation of a particular aesthetic with the requirement for cold-blooded analysis of it. Slavists, Arabists, Sinologists, and so on were people who would become of urgent interest to me thanks to Bucharest.

Realism emerges from the tension between moral philosophy and area expertise. The weight of history and landscape limit what can be accomplished in any particular terrain, even as the possibilities for improvement must always exist. The area expert says, *This is the way things are in this part of the world, this is the material at hand with which one has to work*; the moralist replies, *Don't be a fatalist, such op-*

pression and poverty must not be permitted to stand. These are not over-whelming forces about which good men can do nothing.

Romania infused me with the wisdom of both positions. Romania's fate in the 1980s was without question a product of its geography, that is, of its closeness to the Soviet Union, even as Romania's distinctive brand of Latinity within Eastern Europe (another product of history and geography) allowed for its psychological isolation—and from that a peculiar, almost North Korean form of Communism could take root. This was the irreducible, deterministic material at hand with which one had to work, and which area specialists relished. The West was not going to topple such a regime and others nearby by military action, though such fantasies had been entertained by some Americans at the very beginning of the Cold War. The West could only remain militar-ily and politically vigilant, pressuring the Soviet Union wherever and whenever it could, and hope for the day when internal stresses, in turn arising out of Communism's unworkability and moral illegitimacy, would topple the East Bloc from within. Thus was containment—with its aggressive Reaganite component in the final phase—the proper compromise between realism and idealism. Thus were both area experts and moralists vindicated. The American diplomatic corps in Bucharest and other Eastern European capitals during the 1980s represented an exquisite synthesis of both these traditions and tenden-cies.

But I had a long way to go in order to become as wise and mature as they were. For this balance between realism and idealism is some-thing I only have become aware of in retrospect, over the years and decades. It is a balance that I still have not gotten right, and probably never will.

My impressions of Bucharest in the early 1980s became a faithful reference point for my thinking—and not always toward a good result. For example, my reporting trips to Iraq later in the 1980s convinced me that Saddam Hussein's regime was unlike any other I had experi-enced in the Arab world, and yet in its machinal, totalitarian intensity it bore a striking resemblance to Ceauşescu's in Romania. Thus, when the opportunity arose almost two decades later to topple Saddam, I supported the effort—for my obsession with Saddam was derivative of my obsession with Ceauşescu. But when that effort turned into an anarchic nightmare worse than the Iraqi regime itself, much like Prince Nekhlyudov in Tolstoy's *Resurrection*, I suffered for years a "moral nausea which turned into a physical sickness."[23] In my depression I saw the world, including Romania, as I hadn't before. And of the many things I saw more clearly, one was how Reagan was a great president precisely because he had surrounded himself with such realist and pragmatic luminaries as George Shultz, Caspar Weinberger, and James Baker III, men who understood that as awful as such regimes as Ceauşescu's and Saddam's were throughout the world, in the end their subjects would have to liberate themselves. The United States could not do it for them. As inspirational and unyielding as Reagan's rhetoric was—morally arming the United States against Communist oppression in Central and Eastern Europe as never before—Reagan and the men around him never would have countenanced the kind of military action chosen in Iraq.

The Foreign Service officers I met in Eastern Europe during the last decade of the Cold War had internalized that very balance, something else I only fully realized following the debacle in Iraq. Romania's terror in the 1980s had never diminished in my mind. But after Iraq, I understood better that Ceauşescu probably could not have fallen any sooner than he did. Reagan could help set history in motion in Eastern Europe, but the specific act of removing a tyrant could only rarely be the work of foreigners.

MY LAST EVENING IN BUCHAREST in November 1981, I walked with my backpack from the Hotel Muntenia three blocks to Piaţa Universităţii, where I took a bus to the North Station. Crossing by train into Bulgaria around midnight, I severed another of many small bureaucratic and psychological links with Israel. In the next few weeks, until 1981 turned to 1982, I traveled through Bulgaria, Macedonia,

Kosovo, Serbia, Croatia, Hungary, and Czechoslovakia. By the middle of the decade I was reporting from Iraq, Syria, Algeria, North Yemen, and other states in the Arab world, swallowing my fears about being an Israeli citizen traveling alone in the most radical parts of the Muslim world in order to earn a living. The wars in Afghanistan and the Horn of Africa were also part of my beat.

But it was Romania and the rest of the Balkans that principally held my interest throughout the 1980s, places I would return to again and again, usually in the cold weather. I interviewed hundreds in the course of that decade—nuns in Orthodox monasteries, sweaty politicians in cafés, roughnecks drinking plum brandy in train compartments, farmers at collectivized settlements, secondary school students in their classrooms, local historians and intellectuals in the poignant intimacy of their homes and libraries: all in addition to Western diplomats in the magisterial detachment of their embassies. In the July 1989 issue of *The Atlantic Monthly*, more than four months before the Berlin Wall fell, I wrote: "In the 1970s and 1980s the world witnessed the limits of superpower influence in places like Vietnam and Afghanistan. In the 1990s those limits may well become visible in a Third World region within Europe itself. The Balkans could shape the end of the century, just as they did the beginning." On November 30, 1989, less than three weeks after the Wall fell, I wrote in *The Wall Street Journal*: "Two historic concepts are emerging out of the ruins of communist Europe. One, 'Central Europe,' the media is now beating to death. The other, 'the Balkans,' the media has yet to discover. . . ." I went on in the article to consider the ethnic fissuring of Yugoslavia. War broke out there eighteen months later.[24] By then I had already completed the writing of a book, *Balkan Ghosts*, which though its early chapters dealt with Yugoslavia, devoted its largest section to Romania.

My fixation with the region—and its distinctive *otherness* compared to the rest of Europe—was a function of what I had first experienced as a journalist in Romania. The Balkans may not have had, at least theoretically, an especial predisposition to war and conflict, but the region's very poverty and underdevelopment, relative to the rest of the

Continent—and especially relative to the rest of the Warsaw Pact—
further inflamed its historical disputes. My reporting depressed an
American president on the possibilities of stopping a war in the former
Yugoslavia. I saw it differently. From the beginning, I supported armed
intervention there.[25] Nor did that contradict what I had written in *Balkan Ghosts*. After all, it is only the darkest human landscapes where
humanitarian action is ever required in the first place. And before one
intervenes anywhere, the worst about a place should be known in advance and discussed by officials directing the invading force. The invasion of Iraq ultimately failed because the depth of the suspicion
between Sunnis and Shiites was not adequately admitted and planned
for.[26]

Still, whatever I intended, the book's reported effect in policy terms
was, to say the least, tragic. Thus, if it is not guilt that I feel, it is profound sorrow. A writer, as I've said, must honestly describe what he
sees and hears during a moment in time regardless of the consequences, but sometimes the consequences can be difficult to bear.

ROMANIA WAS MY MASTER KEY for the Balkans. Here was the Poland
of southeastern Europe in terms of size, demography, and geopolitical
location vis-à-vis the Soviet Union: the ultimate marchland, a vast territory hacked to pieces by invading armies, and constituting the frontier extremities of the Byzantine, Ottoman, Habsburg, and Russian
empires, even as the language itself signaled a longing for the Latin
West. At the beginning of the modern era, Ottoman, Habsburg, and
Russian forces all converged where Romania now lies. The Carpathians, which snake through the heart of the country, separated Europe
from the Near East—or more specifically, Central Europe from Eastern Europe—as much as any single geographical gradation could.[27]
Though Ceauşescu happened to be the Russian-tolerated *voivode* at
the time of my early visits, Romania carried the seeds of other, manifold hopes and legacies, even if finding them back then was a matter of
groping in the darkness.

Chapter II

BUCHAREST 2013

A THIRD OF A CENTURY LATER, I RETURNED TO THE ROMANIAN capital. It was Holy Week, the marrow of Orthodoxy. There is no greater union of the sensual and the spiritual than the swinging censer-blackened icons and frescoes of the interior of an Eastern church, floating in frankincense, with inscriptions in Cyrillic and hymns on Good Friday sung in Greek. Near Saturday midnight, the Biserica Albă ("White Church") in Bucharest was entrenched in darkness, as people filtered in quietly from the Calea Victoriei, young couples with children and grandparents, ravishing women and destitute crones, each clutching an unlit candle, an otherworldly awe and humility erasing the differences between them.

The hymns evoked a melodious and somber deliverance; an irresistible undertow. Finally, two priests arrived from behind the iconostasis with flaming candelabras. People surged forward to have their candles lit. Then each person lit another's with his own, until a forest of light swept from the front of the church to the back and into the courtyard, annihilating the darkness. It was Easter. *Hristos a înviat* (Christ has risen). *Adevărat ca a înviat* (In truth, he has risen). Spring had been initiated in this most pagan ritual of monotheism. History is never so real as in the candlelit faces of Romanians at Easter. You can read every tragedy, every miracle, and every restoration in their eyes.

The Doric neoclassical church dated only to the early nineteenth century. But the fact that I connected it to one of Gregor von Rezzori's stories of late-1920s Bucharest in *Memoirs of an Anti-Semite* made it old. The early nineteenth century, like the Middle Ages, is an abstraction to someone born in the mid-twentieth. It is far too removed to bond with any living memory. But my father was born five years before Rezzori, and was almost twenty years old during the period Rezzori describes. My father would now be well over a hundred, if alive. My father at twenty: now that's old. Between the setting of Rezzori's story and the present, the Jews that Rezzori describes—not always politely, not always sympathetically—might well have been killed in the Holocaust; and if not, would have had to survive a Nazi-allied regime and decades of Communist-inflicted terror and poverty in Romania, unless they had been lucky enough to emigrate. Here was history unimaginably compressed, for the 1930s and 1940s constitute an unfathomable chasm between one epoch and another. And for Romania, to a greater extent than elsewhere in Eastern Europe, it was a chasm that lasted until 1989. Rezzori's story lay on one side of the chasm, my life lay on the other.

Such were my thoughts at Easter Midnight: the whirling mystery of time and what it meant; the Biserica Albă in the late 1920s, my visit to Bucharest in 1981, and my return now in early 2013. Nineteen eighty-one now seemed remote; the 1920s less so. I could almost touch the Bucharest of Rezzori's story, though it had existed before I was born, though it seemed so further removed in time than the 1820s.

Rezzori recalls a summer of "lavender-blue skies and unfulfilled longings" in Bucharest, listening in a "tiny apartment" to a chorus from a garden restaurant behind the Biserica Albă.[1] Soon his youthful protagonist would move into a rooming house run by a Jewish family, and the theme of these stories would present itself: that of anti-Semitism as background noise, as a minor personal tic exhibited by all the Romanian characters, the more shocking because it comes across as normal and understated, the horror noticed only because of Rezzori's gentle, occasional reminders that this is the 1920s and 1930s he is talking about. The inference of what would come afterward is left to the reader.

This interwar period in Central and Eastern Europe was one of "a light . . . extinguished,"[2] the light of the Austro-Hungarian Empire, a vivid world of Biedermeier furniture interposed with folkloric peasant weavings, of a withering Habsburg gentility overlaid on a turbulent, political carpet of ethnic minorities, a world in dangerously exposed disarray. Though this world lay on the far side of my own lifetime, when my father was still very young, Rezzori, an Austrian from the Bukovina, brought it close by.

For the more recent in actual time, the more distant it may seem. One's own life, with all of its intervening events of such supreme personal importance, can make relatively recent history—the history concurrent with one's childhood—appear far, far away. One's own life distorts historical time, in other words. I was born *only* seven years after World War II ended, I suddenly realized one day in middle age, when seven years no longer seemed like a long time, given that I had accumulated memories going back five decades. And so the interwar and fascist periods in Romania arose real and substantial, even as the Communist 1950s and 1960s, when I was still a child and teenager, became dim and unimaginably ancient. Only the candlelit faces I saw at Easter conquered those distances, making them all cohere.

EASTER 2013 IN BUCHAREST also illuminated the work of Patrick Leigh Fermor, that craftsman of irreducible godlike essences whose every sentence belongs in a time capsule—to call him a mere travel writer is to diminish him. I first read Fermor's rich descriptions of Romania in 1986 immediately upon the publication of *Between the Woods and the Water*, when the glacis of Communism still constituted an almost impenetrable barrier for traveling back in time to the 1930s, rendering his words antique almost. But late in 2013, when the next volume of his series finally appeared posthumously in Great Britain, his descriptions of 1930s Bucharest were altogether immediate and touchable: "the shop fronts with dashing modernistic lettering . . . one of them ultra-chic, containing a single gleaming scent flagon poised on a softly lit pyramid of dove-coloured velvet against a back-drape of ruched, lemon-yellow silk—the ferro-concrete facades, the rainbow tangle of electric signs, the blazing kiosks with their polyglot flutter of periodicals . . . interiors of unimaginable splendour . . ." Bucharest for Fermor was a "fascinating nightmare" and an "over-upholstered Babylon."[3] Decades of Communism would pulverize it all, and in 2013 Bucharest was now still in the process of rebirth.

ROMANIA IS TRULY A wondrous geographical and cultural confection. Its effect on me has always been both corporeal and abstract, leading in ways direct and indirect to a fixation with Orthodox icons, with the Cold War, time travel, and much else. *Rumania* it was, until some indeterminate point in the Cold War. (The change might have been the partial result of *Romînia* in the Romanian language becoming *România* in the 1960s.) But I always preferred the earlier English spelling and pronunciation, more suggestive as it was of the Balkans somehow, and thus seemingly more real.[4]

Romania, as I am forced to refer to it, constitutes one of those indigestible ethnic nations, like Georgia and Armenia, that have miraculously survived the millennia despite being oppressed, overrun, and vanquished. Yet Romanians have survived thus on a grander demographic scale than the peoples of the Transcaucasus, and have done so on the very edge of Central Europe. There was so much I had to be reacquainted with; to adjust to.

The decades between late 1981 and early 2013 had seen several evolutions in Romanian manners, which I had experienced firsthand in the course of two short visits, in 1990 and 1998. Returning barely four months after the 1989 Christmas Revolution, I saw how Bucharest, denied religion for decades, had been transformed into an open-air church, with roses, tulips, and beeswax candles at sacrificial pavement offerings in honor of the revolutionaries who had died fighting Ceaușescu.[5] By the late 1990s, downtown Bucharest would boast casinos, topless clubs, and Italian fashions in boutique windows that in one instance featured live models. As in New York and Paris at the time, black apparel was chic. A former Romanian diplomat, Ioana Ieronim, told me in 1998, "This is how we were in the interwar period, in the 1930s. We are resourceful, adaptable, exaggerated, pseudocosmopolitan émigrés in a new, global world. We are one-dimensional Latin-Oriental clones of the West." A local philosopher and essayist, Horia-Roman Patapievici, added: "When we buy computers, compact disks, and clothes, we borrow the material consequences of the West without grasping the fundamental values that created such technologies in the first place." Patapievici, in his book-lined apartment during the late 1990s, with the hallways plagued by stray dogs, and wearing jeans and a smoking jacket, condensed for me all that was intoxicating to me about Romania, a country resembling a sensual, macabre, perpetually fascinating, and occasionally brilliant film noir.[6]

But to scratch the surface was not enough. The more I had opportunities to write at length about other parts of the world—parts I had not yet seen even—the more I merely wanted to return to Romania and complete the picture I had been forming from earlier visits. I wanted to reacquaint myself with the country not as a trained historian with an advanced degree, which I wasn't; not as a memoirist whose linguistic gifts were matched by an equally fantastic family background like Rezzori, which I was not either; nor was I a literary travel writer like Fermor, armed with social gifts and the perfect metaphor always at the ready. I was a journalist with an obsession about one place—and about what lessons that place could teach us, and teach me, about Europe and the period of history through which I was fated to live. Simply because Rezzori and Fermor were in terms of their skills of observation unapproachable did not mean that Romania had to be retired as a subject of concern. It was too important for that, located, as it was, close to Ukraine, Russia, Central Europe, the Black Sea, and the Mediterranean.

I began not with people but with art and architecture, the material elements of a civilization that the Communists had tried for decades to undermine. I wanted to experience Romania's material heritage after color had poured back into the landscape, without the burden of the crushing gray immensity of oppression—the memory of the cityscape of 1981 that still haunted me.

AT THE THREE-HUNDRED-YEAR-OLD PALACE of Mogoșoaia outside Bucharest, the church steeples resemble Turkish minarets. The wafer-thin brick half domes and brick archways—the later held up by marble half columns—recall the early-medieval Byzantine world emerging out of late Roman antiquity, even as the steep leaden roofs yearn toward the baroque. I lost myself in the beauty of Muntenian carpets and Oltenian and Moldavian kilims, all colored in rich vegetal dyes, heavily influenced by the patterns of Turkey and Persia. For Muntenia and Oltenia are both subregions of the broad plain of Wallachia where Bucharest sits, less than forty miles north of the Danube, subject from late antiquity to the early modern age to the hoofbeats of Byzantine and Ottoman armies. (Before becoming the capital of Romania, Bucharest was the capital of Wallachia, adjacent to Ottoman-occupied Bulgaria, from where the Turks could launch raids and invasions.) The tragic Wallachian prince Constantin Brâncoveanu, who built this palace between 1698 and 1702, and whose name is associated with Romania's haunting architectural design system of Western and Oriental styles, was himself taken to Constantinople with his four sons and a son-in-law and beheaded there by the Turks in 1714, his sons dying first before his eyes. Brâncoveanu had been forced by circumstance to play the forces of Russian czardom off against those of the Ottoman sultanate, and he ultimately, understandably failed. The

Russians and Turks were a constant presence in Bucharest right up through the mid-nineteenth century. As late as 1866, Romanian coins displayed an Ottoman emblem.[7]

Silent amid the smoky Byzantine icons, lush carpets, and brick melon domes of Mogoşoaia, time once again vanished for me. Youthful memories of visits I had made decades before to the medieval Byzantine monuments of Athens, Sofia, and Istanbul, as well as to those of Mystra, Mount Athos, and Old Serbia, became suddenly vivid. A historical period, because of the artistic sensibilities it wrought, connected me with an earlier life.

Like the Brâncoveanu roofs at Mogoşoaia, the Athenaeum off the main square of Bucharest aspires to the Western tradition, yet also confirmed for me the Eastern one. Built by subscription in 1888, the Athenaeum had been refurbished in the wake of the Communist ice age. However, even back then I found it a visual—and thus an emotional— relief from the relentless brutality of Bucharest's Stalinist pillbox architecture: the Party and government buildings, as well as vast, grim apartment complexes, with their heavy accent of cheap and veiny-white stones from the Apuseni Carpathians, that sought to suffocate the capital's Byzantine, Renaissance, Venetian Classical, Vienna Secession, Art Nouveau, and Art Deco structural beauties. It had been Nikita Khrushchev in 1954, a year after Stalin's death, who promoted the "industrialization of architecture," with its emphasis on prefabrication and reinforced concrete that in later years would so deface Bucharest and which I would so come to hate.[8]

The Athenaeum and the age it represents constitutes a rebuke to the twentieth century and its ideologies, and to the Long European War, which started in 1914 and did not conclude in Romania until 1989. The Athenaeum is technically neoclassical. Thus it demands to be considered European and Renaissance. But with its abundance of ormolus, yellows, and fleshy pinks, with its curvatures and absence of hard angles, with its baroque spirit of exaggeration and ostentation, it is also Byzantine and thus captures the breath of the Orient—the very definition of Romania. I looked at Greek and Roman pillars and pilasters, but I almost felt as though I were in an antechamber of Hagia Sophia (the Church of the "Holy Wisdom") in Constantinople.

The Athenaeum never could have been conceived at any point after the outbreak of World War I. It was then that art and architecture, because of the human catastrophe of ten million battlefield deaths, lost their innocence altogether, and consequently retreated further into tortured abstractions and aggressive minimalism. The Athenaeum is unashamedly romantic art. I sat in the circular concert hall surrounded by Costin Petrescu's 1937 mural of Romanian history, which celebrates such personages as King Carol I, King Ferdinand, and Queen Marie, the foundational personalities of modern Romania— German and English royals who in the late nineteenth and early twentieth centuries tried to anchor Romania firmly in the West, and whom the Communists tried to purge from memory by knocking down their statues and all other evidence of them. But now this last architectural gasp of the Old World rules triumphant once more. Classical concerts and recitals fill the hall on many an evening, graced by a mural that was partly covered for decades until 1989. The ultimate purpose of existence is to sanctify beauty: the Athenaeum is a place of worship.

BECAUSE ROMANIA WAS SO VIOLATED in the course of the twentieth century, there was now the ever-present artistic and spiritual need to restore earlier, more normal epochs, to recognize the past and show a way to the future.

I spent two hours over an espresso in the former villa of Nicu Ceauşescu, the depraved son of the Communist dictator, who died of cirrhosis of the liver seven years after his father and mother had been executed in the final anti-Communist revolution of 1989. Within these walls it is said the younger Ceauşescu serially violated women in the course of his alcoholic excesses. Now the villa is a café evoking the iron penmanship of the Belle Époque, with chairs whose backs are carved into elegant swirls and daguerreotypes of fin de siècle beauties with sun umbrellas hung carefree over their shoulders. I thought of

Vaslav Nijinsky's choreography of Igor Stravinsky's *The Rite of Spring*, performed in Paris in May 1913 near the end of the Belle Époque, a work of music and dance that would define the dissonance and decomposition of the twentieth century, whose horrors lurked little more than a year away.

Elegance punctuated the Bucharest of 2013, a city where in the early 1980s I used to walk hundreds of yards in the pitch dark looking for a lit storefront and a decent place to eat. Even my poor and rugged tastes of that era were violated by the greasy canteen and mess hall atmosphere: waiters at the restaurant in the Union Hotel coughing up phlegm and flicking their cigarette ends into the ice buckets adjoining each table. Caru' cu Bere ("The Beer Cart"), a sausage house founded in the nineteenth century by a Romanian from Brașov, was back in those bad old Cold War days terrorized by fat, begrizzled waiters who ignored you for half an hour until they slammed a plate of sausages (*mititei*, or "meech") on your table with mustard and watery beer. Little else was on the menu. The dark and sumptuous wooden interior with its stained glass windows was a tub of cigarette fumes and body odor. Women were rare. Now a lavish menu boasted literally dozens of meat and vegetable dishes served by officious and lithe waiters and waitresses, with a clientele of young couples with children, all looking wholesome and middle class. There was a separate menu for wines, and Transylvanian *palinka* was offered along with the harsher and less convincing *țuică* from Wallachia and Moldavia. The once unspeakable restrooms had been renovated. Smoking was, of course, no longer permitted. It is almost as if the Ceaușescus had to be executed so Caru' cu Bere—and everything awful about Romanian Communism that it represented—could be domesticated and civilized.

There were just so many cafés now—bearing conceited names such as Charme, Rembrandt, La Muse—with their chairs and tables made of wicker, zinc, velvet, blond wood, and black metal, each establishment desperately trying to evoke Paris, Berlin, Vienna, Stockholm, or New York. Even the ashtrays bore edgy designer patterns evocative of Art Deco and the Belle Époque. And yet it has to be said that these new cafés of Bucharest lack the enfolding and layered elegance—and especially the intimacy—of cafés in Central Europe. I was still south of the Carpathians, in the former Byzantine and Turkish world. There was simply no *Gemütlichkeit* here: almost none of this organically emerged from a real past. Bucharest in 2013 was mainly a city of stagy contraptions. Rezzori's observations of interwar Bucharest were still applicable: a "garbagey modernity," a "futuristic element joined . . . with the ornamentation of carved shepherds' crooks" that is distinctly "Balkanese," a city that "for all its Art Nouveau villas and . . . glass-and-concrete buildings . . . was as Oriental as Smyrna."[9]

And yet on the other hand, a city with so many cafés, flower shops, and bookstores was by any measure civilized. For what could be better symbols of urban civilization, however nascent?

Bucharest in 1981 had a theme, a pattern: that of Communism—somber, formidable, and suffocating in the silence it inflicted upon the streets and boulevards. Bucharest in 2013 had no theme, no great urban plan of the kind that had prepared monumental cityscapes such as late-nineteenth-century Paris and Ringstrasse Vienna. The Civic Center of the Ceaușescus had not been a plan, but a mutilation. Rather than a plan, what defined the early-twenty-first-century Romanian capital were crass strata and deposits of change, no one element configuring with the other, each one driven by private risk. There was nothing to provoke a memory that I might harbor in the future in the way that the Bucharest of the 1980s had for a journalist with no personal stake in the suffering exacted on the inhabitants.

Downtown, in between the stylish cafés and restaurants, was a desert of broken sidewalks, chipped concrete, garbage, and abandoned buildings. It was taking the better part of a decade of legal wrangling to restore property to the rightful, pre-Communist owners. Just as the Kent cigarette barter economy had been a journalistic cliché of the Ceaușescu years, the gangs of stray dogs were of the early post–Cold War ones. But amid the dogs and general abandonment, one must insert the tinted Plexiglas and polymers of tall, cubistic, Lego-like edifices built in recent years, and the renovated, sandblasted exteriors of the old hotels in the vicinity of the Calea Victoriei. The Majestic, where I once stayed in 1982 for twenty-nine dollars, was now a small Ramada. The Muntenia, my address in 1981, was gone, the marquee completely coated in rust, the façade boarded up by sheet metal defaced, in turn, by graffiti repeating the word "fuckcrack," and partially covered in posters advertising both punk bands and classical concerts. A sign indicated that a hair salon would soon open on the premises: metamorphosis in a sideways direction, like so much of history.

I saw women in space-shoe heels, and others in bathroom slippers; some wore leotards, and others pajamas, with the pale ocher symmetry of the neoclassical former royal palace hovering in the background. Despite the haphazard gentrification, I felt as close to the dust-blown urban bleakness of Anatolia as I did to Central Europe. Scrape away the lipstick and there was still the mournful, mealy face. And yet on Magheru, amid stone walls gangrened with graffiti and layers of peeling posters, there were the most daring and plush boutiques. Postmodernism is about incongruous juxtapositions, and Bucharest combined the architectural legacies of Stalinism with capitalist decadence.

Cişmigiu Garden, a well-tended backdrop in Olivia Manning's World War II–era *Balkan Trilogy*, was in a derelict state: stray dogs, tall weeds, graffiti on the benches that were also missing planks, and people who, while not exactly homeless, looked like they had nowhere else to go. Silviu Brucan famously said in 1990 that it would take Romania a generation to move beyond what Ceauşescu had done to the country. At the time, people were shocked by such dark pessimism. But he was right.

Traffic clogged the streets, and was noisy and savage in the way of Middle Eastern and other third-world cities. The Communist metropolis of silence had become the city of drivers permanently pressing down on their horns. Every pedestrian below middle age was busy working a smartphone, even as the young bemoaned to me the absence of progress and claimed disillusionment. Many of them had no useful memory of the Cold War, so it could not constitute a point of reference, or of comparison. As the Arab proverb says, "People resemble their times more than they resemble their fathers."[10] Though it is an empowering thought, one that argues against essentialism and cultural determinism, the danger of such reinvention is loss of the past, with all of its useful lessons.

I wanted the city to be symbolic of something—symbolic of some consequential historical epoch. I wanted it to have a powerful effect on me, commensurate with the city of 1981. And of course, I was disappointed. True, I was younger then, a time when new experiences burned more deeply in one's memory. But more to the point, Bucharest was now a mishmash. That was its salvation and its humanity. It had not yet been overrun again by another utopian ideology or grand scheme. The city merely existed from day to day, adding dissimilar elements, while the politics of the capital were emblemized by petty, low-level intrigue and chaos. There was nothing archetypal about it anymore, thankfully.

"ALL POST-COMMUNIST SOCIETIES ARE uprooted ones because Communism uprooted traditions, so nothing fits with anything else," explained the philosopher Patapievici. Fifteen years earlier, when I had last met him, he had cautioned:

"The task for Romania is to acquire a public style based on impersonal rules, otherwise business and politics will be full of intrigue, and I am afraid that our Eastern Orthodox tradition is not helpful in this regard. Romania, Bulgaria, Serbia, Macedonia, Russia, Greece—all the Orthodox nations of Europe—are characterized by weak institutions. That is because Orthodoxy is flexible and contemplative, based more on the oral traditions of peasants than on texts. So there is this pattern of rumor, lack of information, and conspiracy. . . ."[11]

Thus, in 1998, did Patapievici define Romanian politics as they were still being practiced a decade and a half later. Though in 2013, he added: "No one speaks of guilt over the past. The Church has made no progress despite the enormous chance of being separated from the state for almost a quarter century. The identification of religious faith with an ethnic-national group, I find, is a moral heresy."

Dressed now in generic business casual and wearing fashionable glasses, Patapievici appeared as a figure wholly of the West—more accurately of the global elite—someone you might meet at a fancy conference like Davos or Bilderberg, even as he rose above the fads to which those events are prone. He remained, nevertheless, singular: an example of how, while individual genius might be partly rooted in a culture and family history, it owed its existence less to a specific historical landscape than to something as sublime as Spinoza's God. Patapievici's beautiful, complex mind was in and of itself a lovely manifestation of the mystery of universal existence.

"I believe in defending the Western Canon. I have a duty to remember my father, my civilization. For who else will? I am a liberal in the nineteenth-century sense—the liberalism of Tocqueville, Lord Acton, John Stuart Mill. From that follows my belief and admiration in twentieth-century liberal philosophers such as Karl Popper, Friedrich Hayek, Ludwig von Mises. These are the founders in my view. And, of course," Patapievici went on, "there is Isaiah Berlin and Michael Oakeshott, who upheld the liberal tradition against fixed ideologies. I am a liberal in terms of the individual and his rights. I am slightly conservative in terms of culture and the need to preserve it. And I am very conservative in terms of the preservation of fundamental values."

Complexity of thought is a defining element of great intellects, but such minds suffer in the public arena, where their ideas are crudely simplified. Consider the fate of the Romanian Cultural Institute, which Patapievici directed from 2005 to 2012. It was an organization and a concept he had tried to put his personal, humanist stamp on in the intervening years since I had last seen him. He had interpreted his mission as promoting artists and writers who, while in some cases Jewish and avant-garde, were Romanian provided that they expressed themselves in Romanian. This, after all, as he explained to me, "was the essence of cosmopolitanism." But a minor scandal ensued: he was

accused of not promoting true Romanian culture. Patapievici was defi-
ant: "There are no workable values outside cosmopolitanism, and
that's why our frame of reference [despite our geography] must be the
Western Canon."

Though disillusioned, he was not pessimistic about the overall national condition. "There has been tremendous progress since we saw
each other in 1998. There is no epidemic of mob crimes like in Bulgaria, no murders of journalists like in Russia." Neither had Romania's
economy collapsed like Greece's; nor had there been bouts of occasional anarchy like in Bulgaria and Albania since the Berlin Wall fell.
Romanians and ethnic Hungarians had avoided civil war. As for the
absence of any real philosophical values among Romania's leading
politicians, Patapievici saw this, perhaps, less as a Romanian failing
than as a development that transcended Romania. He explained:

"You will see, philosophical values will fade away in your country,
too. To advance themselves, politicians will increasingly claim beliefs
that they don't actually possess. Values are a reflection of the soul. And
as souls fade, people no longer need values. Souls fade gradually because of the substitution of the inner imagination by technology:
smartphones, intelligent toys, the array of electronics at malls, all make
soulful intelligence less necessary. [Martin] Heidegger was right, progress has been in key respects deprived of purpose. Homer endowed the
world with a rich soul. Now technology leads to an impoverished soul
for the public and politicians alike. In some respects," he went on, "the
soul is being replaced with the cult of the body. Have you seen the
advertisements in the fashion magazines lately? The young in particular don't need souls anymore, they need sensuality. Already, technology constructs images for us. In the future, more functions of the brain
will be replaced by technology. The mental muscles will atrophy.
Politics will further deteriorate."

He spoke calmly, like a psychiatrist pointing out a painful reality to
a patient. He believed the future was providing rich terrain for new
and extreme ideologies. He had lived through Ceaușescu, and had a
living memory of Gheorghiu-Dej, so he knew of what he spoke. He

combined a firsthand knowledge of the horrors of the twentieth century with vast reading and ample exposure to Western elites. He saw
how technology and primitivism could flow together. For me, he was
part of the rich tapestry of Bucharest, even as I knew his insights be-
longed to no national category.

IN THE LOBBY OF the Athénée Palace hotel, one of the country's leading analysts exposed the ground truth regarding Patapievici's more abstract, philosophical assessment of Romanian politics.

Romania's president in 2013 was Traian Băsescu, formerly head of
the Liberal Democratic Party. The prime minister was Victor Ponta,
head of the Social Democratic Party. They were at each other's throats
with vicious charges of corruption, plagiarism, and so forth. Romanian
politics were immobilized for a time by this rivalry, even as one suspected that years hence, few might even recall the names of those two
politicians, neither of whom enjoyed all that much presence or gravi-
tas (especially in Ponta's case). Băsescu officially represented a conservative tendency and Ponta a liberal one. But as this young analyst told
me in the hotel lobby, there was at root no philosophical struggle between them. They merely represented two clientelistic networks, competing for spoils. "Băsescu has personal interests and a good radar, but
no belief system, only formally is he a conservative. Ponta is similar.
His party is hungry for financial rewards after being out of power.
There is little important that they really debate. They both have
learned from the legacy of Communism how to siphon off state assets
and run networks. It is all angles and striking poses: the mix of post-
Communism and Latinity."

The young analyst quoted a local proverb:

"*Mămăliga nu explodează.*" Translation: Romanians are like polenta. Polenta doesn't explode. It is amorphous, without guts, always
adopting to whatever form is required.

Even if one rejects such essentialism, it was undeniable that the
transition from Ceaușescu's Communism was not over. The more en-

compassing the tyranny, the more decades required to overcome it. The judicial system was broken. The rule of law was only partially established. The property regime, as I saw from the vacant lots and abandoned buildings, was insufficiently clear. Too many Romanian politicians in the second decade of the twenty-first century had risen to power in a police state system, or one proximately derivative of it. Nor did they have the advantages possessed by a former Warsaw Pact ally like Poland, which, for example, had had a civil opposition, a liberal Communist wing, and the activism of a universalist Church long before 1989. This was not to mention Poland's helpfully tangible memory of a pre–World War II bourgeois, as well as the advantage that Poland had gained from massive German investment following the Cold War. The sheer variety within Communist (and post-Communist) Eastern Europe was still a defining factor of the region, as Gordon Skilling had noted nearly a half century before.

Yet, as Patapievici said—and as this young analyst admitted—the worst had so far been avoided. The Greater Romania Party of Corneliu Vadim Tudor, to which nostalgic former Communists and some far-right fanatics—themselves nostalgic for the Nazi-era Iron Guard— were attracted, was much less fashionable than it had been in the 1990s. "Vadim Tudor is a bit nuts, anti-Semitic, though a good rhetorician. A typical Romanian story. In any case, he is yesterday's man," said the analyst. Corneliu Zelea Codreanu, the charismatic Iron Guard leader of the 1930s, revered almost as a peasant-god in the fascist heyday—uniting, as he did, anti-Semitism, blood-and-soil Dacian myth, and a distorted version of Orthodox Christianity—simply never enjoyed a revival in post-Communist Romania. As for Marshal Ion Antonescu, the Nazi-era military ruler with a complex legacy (his alliance with Hitler was based more on necessity than on philosophical conviction, even as he fitfully began the process of switching sides in the midst of World War II, after the Nazis had been defeated at Stalingrad), "nostalgia for him never really emerged in full force" after 1989, even as a dispassionate, albeit obscure, scholarly debate about his wartime record continues. Yes, statues of him have been erected in the odd place here and there, and that is certainly a scandal given his complicity in the murder of hundreds of thousands of Jews in the eastern territories of Bessarabia and Transdniestria. But in 2013 he was not part of the conversation in Bucharest in the way he threatened to be for a time in the 1990s.

Then there was Ion Iliescu, the post-1989 symbol of corrosive stability—the ultimate compromise figure and bellwether between the Communist past and an anxious future—who served as president for a total of ten years following Ceauşescu's execution. A leading Communist, Iliescu postponed desperately needed reforms, but he may have saved the country from interethnic war and chaos in the early 1990s. In 2003, while serving a third term as president, he publicly admitted guilt for the murder of Jews in Romanian-occupied Bessarabia and Transdniestria during the World War II–era Antonescu regime (even if he would backtrack a bit).

The point is, things were inching forward, in spite of the political stasis. The economy had grown an average of 6.5 percent annually between 1999 and 2008, on the eve of the European crisis, after which it continued to grow at a reduced pace. Three million Romanians out of a population of over 21 million were working in Western Europe, even as the elite was still in the process of orienting itself westward, following more than four decades in the East Bloc. Meanwhile, there was this floundering, intrigue-ridden, seemingly purposeless interregnum, which nearly everyone with whom I spoke both bemoaned and compared to the 1930s, when King Carol II's regime governed in a style that was at once replete with plots and purposeless maneuvers, with corruption the great leaven, all the while leading to Romania's dismemberment by the Soviet Union and Nazi Germany (a circumstance that Carol probably never could have prevented no matter his actions or his personality; such was the nightmare of Romania's geography between Nazi Germany and Stalin's Soviet Union). In 2013, I heard the word "interbellum" repeated often in Bucharest. Of course, what keen observers like Patapievici also realized was that while German and Russian power were greater in the early twenty-first century than in the 1990s, the sinister shadows of Hitler and Stalin were, nevertheless, absent, and thus the forces of fascism and Communism were not exactly mobilizing on Romania's borders as in Carol's day.

This was all still a year before a new geopolitical age would dawn in Central and Eastern Europe with the crisis in Ukraine, which was still barely imaginable in the Bucharest of spring 2013. But in 2013, I felt Romanian politics lived on as an echo compared to the more dramatic and cataclysmic 1930s. Looking out over Piaţa Revoluţiei from the café of the Athénée Palace, fixing my eyes on the French Baroque University Library—now beautifully restored after having suffered damage during the 1989 revolution—and listening to the young analyst talk with light jazz playing in the background, I realized that, for the time being, this was normality: something the country had not known since 1914.

And that was no small circumstance. Just consider: World War I had seen a welter of foreign armies sprawl over and occupy the country. The Austro-Hungarians had marched deeper into Transylvania unto the Carpathian ridges, while the Germans occupied Bucharest in Wallachia in the south, and the Romanian royal family and political elite took refuge in Jassy in Moldavia in the northeast.[12] Disease, hunger, chaos. Only the eventual victory of the Western Allies and the collapse of the Russian front following the Bolshevik Revolution restored to Romania all its historic territories by 1920. Then in 1939, the Molotov-Ribbentrop Pact between Hitler and Stalin set the stage for Soviet Russia taking back Bessarabia and entering northern Bukovina, and Nazi Germany awarding northern Transylvania to Hungary. Romanian troops in their many hundreds of thousands then fought alongside Nazi Germany against the Soviet Union—unto Odessa and Stalingrad—in the first part of World War II, and later they switched sides and fought against Nazi Germany in order to recapture northern Transylvania. Then following World War II came the living death of Communism, when the Soviet Union treated Romania, because of its alliance with Hitler right up through and after Stalingrad, as a defeated country, suitable for predation.

In particular, it had been World War I that delegitimized armed conflict in a way that no other war had or could—the emblematic and meaningless sum total of all the wars that Europe had fought in its thoroughly violent and therefore discredited past. The record of armed conflict on this western extremity of Eurasia plainly boggles the mind. For example, I thought for a moment. There had been the Nine Years War, the Thirty Years War, the Eighty Years War, the Hundred Years War, the Italian Wars of the sixteenth century, the Northern Wars of the seventeenth century, the War of the Spanish Succession of the eighteenth century, and on and on. As for the fifteenth century, it was maybe the bloodiest since the fall of the Roman Empire, with "unemployed mercenaries ravaging France and Italy" and England torn by civil war. Then there had been the sacks of Brescia, Siena, Sancerre, Antwerp, Magdeburg, Augsburg, and again, on and on—wars in which the "ordinary business" of armies was to torment civilians.[13] As to the wars that Romanian *voivodes* themselves—far to the east in their shaky frontier principalities—had to fight against the Turks alone, they constituted a veritable nonstop torture and bleeding of the civilian population that went on for centuries. Following the Long European War of 1914–89 in Romania, the only thing that now seemed to matter was the individual and his well-being. The rest was madness. Even the idea of the ethnic *nation*, if not dead, was in momentary remission, for it led in one way or another to organized violence.

I would come to meditate on all of this during a visit a few months later to the World War I memorial at Mărășești in Moldavia. Here in a month-long battle from August to September 1917, the Romanian army fought the German army and some Austrian units to a standstill. The result of this stalemate was 27,000 Romanian dead, and 47,000 German and Austrian fatalities. The memorial itself holds the graves of 5,073 Romanians. The dreary gray walls of the well-socketed and cavernous mausoleum evince a slamming-shut-on-the-tomb finality, which seems to declare the futility of war in the grip of remembrance. Mărășești is a place of august horror, just one particular example of why Romanians require, as they say and wish for, *an escape from history.*

THE ATHÉNÉE PALACE ITSELF was symbolic of history as anticlimax. Opened in 1914 at the beginning of World War I, and perhaps the only place in early 1940s Europe—aside from the hotels of Lisbon—where Nazi officers, American newspapermen, and diplomats and spies from the West, the Axis powers, and the Soviet Union could sit at the same bar and restaurant tables and take each other's measure, this grand hotel of Bucharest constituted nothing less than a museum of twentieth-century Romanian intrigue. When I had last stayed here in 1990, the ghosts of Communism lived on in the gloomy serpentine staircase and purple wall-to-wall carpeting. Ceaușescu had turned the place into a veritable intelligence-gathering factory, with the lobby patrolled by prostitutes working for the Securitate.[14] Now it was a sterile, assembly-line Hilton, like many in middle America, lacking the cutting-edge elegance that makes luxury hotels in Asia so vaguely futuristic. There was an insipid English pub. The nearby café flaunted photos of international actors, rock stars, athletes, and cosmonauts who had stayed here in recent years, signing testimonials that betrayed no knowledge whatsoever of the significance of the place where they had slept. The old hotel lived on only in a row of fleshy Corinthian columns with faded gold capitals, and flirtatious, dark-haired waitresses who served red Moldavian wine with a nice metallic aftertaste.

Across the street from the hotel and by the Athenaeum had been Cina, the restaurant where in the 1930s and early 1940s Gypsy songs rose from under the trees, lamenting "oppression" and "foreign masters." One night in 1940, as the Countess R. G. Waldeck had remembered, "a woman in a silver fox jacket [hearing the music] began quietly to sob, mascara running into the paprika chicken on her plate. . . ."[15] Now the successor to Cina served a cuisine that was generically global Italian. Quite a few of the diners wore designer

T-shirts and baseball hats. There was no music. People kept their smartphones on the tables next to the food.

Beyond Cina and the Athenaeum stretched Piața Revoluției, the vast square holding the former royal palace and Communist Party headquarters, where tanks had rolled and the streets had run with blood during the uprising against Ceaușescu in December 1989, the singular event which terminated the Cold War in Europe. Here Ceaușescu had given his last speech before the crowd turned on him. The square, too, was a mishmash, the unfinished project of a high school shop class. The equestrian statue of King Carol I, unveiled in 2008, looked like a cut-rate copy of the one executed by the great Croatian sculptor Ivan Meštrović in 1930, which the Communists had destroyed in 1948. Meštrović had been deeply influenced by Rodin, and had Rodin's ability to convey an entire concept through a gesture, with the result being monumentality. This Carol looked like a mass-produced lawn sculpture.

Carol I must not be confused with his nephew's son, Carol II. Whereas the latter was undisciplined and sensual, the former was an anal-retentive German of the family of Hohenzollern-Sigmaringen, who, in the course of a forty-eight-year rule (1866–1914), essentially built modern Romania, complete with nascent institutions, from an assemblage of regions and two weak principalities. Following 1989, he had become the default symbol of legitimacy for the Romanian state.

Whereas Carol I signified realism and stability, the liberal National Peasant Party leader Iuliu Maniu, a Greek Catholic by upbringing, stood for universal values. As a mid-twentieth-century local politician in extraordinarily horrifying circumstances, Maniu had agitated against the assault on the Jews and in favor of getting Antonescu to switch sides against the Nazis; soon after, during the earliest days of the Cold War, he agitated against the Soviets and their local puppets. Nazi foreign minister Joachim von Ribbentrop once demanded Maniu's execution. As it turned out, the Communist Gheorghiu-Dej regime later convicted Maniu in a show trial in 1947. Defying his accusers, he spoke up in court for free elections, political liberties, and fundamental human rights.[16] He died in prison in 1953 and his body was dumped in a common grave. Maniu's emaciated treelike statue with quotations from the Psalms is, by itself, supremely moving. But there is a complete lack of harmony between it and the massive, adjacent spear pointing to the sky, honoring the victims of the 1989 revolution. The memorial slabs beside the spear are already chipped and cracked. Piața Revoluției in 1981 was dark, empty, and fear-inducing. Now it was cluttered with memorials, oppressed by traffic, and in general looked like an amateurish work in progress. But though it lacked any signal drama, which is the gift of inspired urban design, the personalities and ideas it commemorated spoke to the moral progress of the Romanian state.

YET AS A CLOSE FRIEND told me over my two-hour espresso at Nicu Ceaușescu's former villa, "our geography is still a nightmare."

Indeed, when Romania had joined the North Atlantic Treaty Organization (NATO) in 2004 and the European Union (EU) in 2007, Romanians thought that they would be absorbed into the West in a straightforward and mechanical fashion. They would therefore replace their historical tragedy with some version of utopia—that history itself would lie wholly in the past, and would not any longer be a drumroll of violent catastrophes that happened to them. But a military alliance is only as strong as its member states' defense budgets, and with some exceptions those had been steadily declining in Europe, throwing NATO's future into question. And no sooner had Romania joined the European Union than the European Union itself fell into the greatest crisis of its existence: a mountain of debt spiraling out of control that put the future of the welfare state—the political and moral response to centuries of war and suffering on the Continent—in doubt. Instead of one Europe into whose bosom Romania could escape history, several Europes began to emerge: those states inside the Eurozone and the Schengen border agreement; those outside; and those outside the EU altogether. More troubling, there was geographic logic to Europe's fracturing: those states constituting the medieval Carolingian core and the early modern Prussian Empire were in general the most prosperous, or moving in the direction of prosperity; those of former Habsburg Central Europe were somewhat less prosperous; and those in Catholic Southern Europe or in the former Byzantine-Ottoman Balkans were the worst off. Thus Romania found itself once more exposed and well inside its own vivid history, just at the time when Russia, under Vladimir Putin's authoritarianism (reminiscent of the bad czars rather than of the progressive ones), was once again a threatening geopolitical factor to Romania's northeast. Russia had evolved from Boris Yeltsin's weak and chaotic rule of the 1990s, something that had been actually very convenient to Romania.

Making all this worse was Romania's dependence on Russian natural gas for 25 percent of its energy needs. Russia was now trying to incorporate the Balkans in Pharaonic-style energy pipeline networks. Nor would Russia ever willingly cede influence in the strategic Ponto-Baltic Isthmus, meaning Moscow would keep the national conflict in Moldova simmering on Romania's northeastern border. Meanwhile, the United States was half a world away and distracted by events in the Middle East and the Pacific Basin. The United States did have two military bases in Romania, with troops rotating through them. But Romanians were increasingly worried that this was insufficient as a trip wire. The Bucharest University political scientist Radu Dudău told me that "all serious foreign policy discussions in Romania begin and end with geography." Again, by 2014 because of the Ukraine crisis, all my earlier discussions in this regard would seem that much more meaningful.

I thought of R. W. Seton-Watson's *History of the Roumanians,* from 1934. The very first words: "Roumanian territory was originally inhabited by Scythians, Cimmerians, and Getae," peoples all from the very outer margins of Europe, the area often associated with Ukraine. Then, a few pages on, we are told that the Roman emperor Aurelian decided in A.D. 271 to evacuate the territory of present-day Romania, because it "formed too exposed a salient amid the waves of advancing barbarism."[17] Romanians know from far back in their history (to say nothing of invasions in more recent centuries) that they have always been geographically marginal to Europe, and thus forever run the risk of being trampled upon, or of falling into some political abyss.

Mircea Geoană, a former foreign minister, counseled me in 2013 that Romania had to stop seeing itself as a victim of geography and history, condemned to a repetition of fate about which it could do little. Romanians needed to take their fate into their own hands. In that regard, the best defense against outside geopolitical forces was good governance at home, governance that would strengthen the state and make it a nodal point of global interactions rather than a marchland of empires. (Here he was in line with both Machiavelli and Frederick the Great, both of whom believed that strength abroad was usually built around a strong domestic edifice.[18]) Singapore had been a mere microstate against the vast and hostile forces of Indonesia and Malaya when it began its climb toward global economic and strategic prominence. Look, said Geoană, at how well Poland was doing despite its geography—mainly because of internal reforms. Russia would likely never again invade Romania but would try to subvert it—unless, that is, Romania built strong institutions. Romania's real enemy, Geoană suggested, might be less geography than "a lack of transparency: a nation of survivors and adapters without sufficient standards" of public and private behavior. Thus did Geoană agree with Patapievici.

So it was a matter of continuing the work of the German Carol I, who had taken a poor Ottoman backwater and horse-whipped it into a state. After all, Romania was rich in black earth, mineral resources, shale gas, and perhaps offshore energy deposits. Constanța, Geoană said, was "under-utilized" as a container port, connecting as it did the Black Sea with Central Europe via the Danube. Romania surely had possibilities, the former foreign minister went on. It had, for example, prevented Peter the Great from achieving his goal of erecting a Slavic continuum south to the Mediterranean. Yet, in the same breath, Geoană admitted that the momentous conversations between Reagan and Gorbachev in the late 1980s were about the fate of Central Europe only. The Balkans were not even discussed, but rather relegated to a geographical category where Russia would always have a substantial say. In fact, one could argue that Russia was not an impediment to NATO intervention in the Balkans in the 1990s only because Russia under Yeltsin was weak at the time. And that situation would not obtain under Yeltsin's successor.

I TOOK A WALK in Herăstrau Park, not far from Geoană's office, where amid the little stone bridges and flower beds, while passing briefly through Bucharest in the summer of 1973, I had observed Romanian families strolling arm-in-arm in their Sunday best: the women in dresses and the men in jackets and ties. *Yes, it was a Sunday. I now remember!* The early 1970s were just before Ceaușescu retreated further into Stalinism, and Romanians had not yet lost all hope. Now forty years later there was again hope, as young people zipped by on Rollerblades and mountain bikes, and fashion had lost all traces of an Old World formality which the Communist era had ironically preserved. In the center of the park I came upon a plaza, around which were arranged massive stone busts of postwar Europe's founders: Jean Monnet, Robert Schuman, Konrad Adenauer . . . The sculptures, which had the monolithic, minimalistic style of Easter Island heads, were powerful and mythic in their effect. These were the liberal gods which offered a respite from history for this Latin nation in the Balkans. United Europe meant not only the end of war: it also meant a world of modern states—with all their impersonal and legal norms, which offered protection for everyone as a sovereign individual—rather than a world of ethnic nations with age-old disputes, which had been the curse of Romania all along. That, even more than prosperity, was the underlying raison d'être of the European Union to which Romanians so aspired. The direction was clear. But would geopolitics and the actions of men allow? More to the point, would the democratic West— for so much of Romanian history so far away—remain vigilant?

Chapter III

LATIN BYZANTIUM

I**N 1981, WHEN I ARRIVED IN COMMUNIST EASTERN EUROPE AFTER** six years of never venturing beyond the Mediterranean, it wasn't only the different landscape and climate—to say nothing of the political oppression—that shocked my sensibilities, but the books I had brought with me to read. One of them was *Buddenbrooks*, by Thomas Mann, which I had read in Central Europe after traveling through Romania and the rest of the Balkans. *Buddenbrooks*, with its cozy, sumptuous backdrops of "heavy red damask," "stiff massive sofas," "flaming candles," "gilt candelabrum[s]," and "good heavy food" served with "full-bodied wines" amid "dim grey gothic façade[s] . . . shrouded in rain," further invigorated the stark yet intimate wintry settings in which I suddenly found myself.[1]

The novel's acute psychological insights, particularly the way in which Mann shows the protagonist Thomas Buddenbrook sliding by degrees into a state of depression, led me directly to Mann's fictional masterwork, *The Magic Mountain*. Among that book's treasures is the encyclopedic and eccentric mind of one of literature's great humanists, Ludovico Settembrini. Settembrini, arguably Mann's most abundant philosophical creation, recounts the story of the French philosopher Voltaire's revulsion at the 1755 Lisbon earthquake.

Voltaire, expounds Settembrini, "protested in the name of reason and the intellect against" the "scandalous dereliction of nature" that flattened three-quarters of the Portuguese capital and left perhaps tens of thousands of people dead. "You are astonished? You smile?" Settembrini goes on, sensing the incredulity of the other characters—not to mention that of the reader—at the notion of protesting an act of nature. But as Mann in the voice of Settembrini famously explains, Voltaire's denunciation of a natural event had a serious moral purpose: Voltaire would not accept that humankind must give in to fate. "Nature is force; and it is slavish to suffer force, and to abdicate before it. . . ." For the acceptance of any kind of force—natural, geographical, cultural, ethnic, economic—over the direction of society is an affront to "human dignity."[2]

Nor was Voltaire unique in his opposition. In 1953, in a lecture that would be published the following year under the title "Historical Inevitability," the Oxford scholar Isaiah Berlin condemned as immoral and cowardly the belief that "'vast impersonal forces'"—again geography, natural resources, ethnic characteristics, and the like—determine our lives.[3] Berlin had fascism and Communism in his sights, for the way in which they sought to deny human beings, in the words of Berlin biographer Michael Ignatieff, "their right to moral sovereignty."[4]

What in our day gives especial poignancy to Voltaire's and Berlin's frontal attacks on fatalism is the blunt, irreducible fact that the Nazi Holocaust is still only one lifetime removed from our own—a virtual nanosecond in the scheme of things. Thus both intellectuals and policymakers have a responsibility before history: a responsibility not to succumb to fatalistic arguments rooted in, for example, geography and ethnic characteristics.

To be sure, Hannah Arendt's words on this matter from *The Origins of Totalitarianism* deserve to be quoted in full:

> Racism may indeed carry out the doom of the Western world
> and, for that matter, of the whole of human civilization. When
> Russians have become Slavs, when Frenchmen have assumed

the role of commanders of a *force noire*, when Englishmen have turned into "white men," as already for a disastrous spell all Germans became Aryans, then this change will itself signify the end of Western man. For no matter what learned scientists may say, race is, politically speaking, not the beginning of humanity but its end, not the origin of peoples but their decay, not the natural birth of man but his unnatural death.[5]

And so, in the spirit of Thomas Mann's Settembrini, of Voltaire, of Isaiah Berlin, and most crucially of Hannah Arendt, to think of Romanians as mere *Latins* is the doom of Man.

But at the same time, that surely cannot be the end of the argument. Of course, to *degrade* individuals by assigning them such broad categories—Latins, Slavs, white men, whatever—certainly justifies the fears and admonition of those humanist philosophers. As Berlin writes, in his reproach to the historians Edward Gibbon and Arnold Toynbee, "nations" and "civilizations," while they exist, are not as "concrete" as the individuals who embody them.[6] Individuals not only count morally to a greater extent than groups, but the very existence of the former is not inherently problematic like that of the latter. Groups, civilizations, and other mass human assemblages are either artificially constructed to some degree or other (by nationalist ideologues, for example), or in any case are not so clear-cut as they seem, owing to the subtle and not-so-subtle influences upon them of other groups and civilizations over considerable stretches of time.

And yet to say, for instance, that there is no such thing as a distinctive Latin Romanian culture, with its own language, music, art, architecture, poetry, predominantly Orthodox Christian faith, as well as common hopes, dreams, and fears, all anchored to a shared historical experience by way of a specific geographical setting, is also a sacrilege. Just as to deny individuals the right to moral sovereignty denies their humanity, so it is to deny their right to express themselves through a common material culture and national character—however vaguer and more problematic that character might be compared to the mil-

lions of individual ones. The foreign policies of every state are all
unique because the characteristics and historical experience of each
state are as well. So not to be able to generalize to a reasonable extent
in these matters immobilizes observation. It would make us all mute.

For example, note this passage from the Cambridge-educated Romanian art and architecture critic Sherban Cantacuzino:

> National traits are determined by race, climate and topogra-
> phy. Frequent raids and invasions have made Romanians tough,
> brave and resilient. Political instability, the uncertainty of what
> the future holds, has made them intensely resourceful and prac-
> tical, but also wily and corruptible. Romanians are neither mys-
> tical nor dreamers by nature. Hence Romanian art does not
> suffer from an excess of fantasy, but is firmly rooted in rational-
> ism. . . . Architecture is generally a response to practical needs
> and is hardly ever extravagant; decoration, with the one excep-
> tion of the painted churches, is rarely done to excess.[7]

Perhaps Cantacuzino, a Romanian himself, is generalizing too
much about his own people. But how else is he to bring the reader to
grips with an utterly original architectural style rooted in a particular
national experience? Patrick Leigh Fermor called Romania "the most
idiosyncratic society that I had ever encountered," one of "splendour
and remoteness." Lucian Boia, a professor of history at the University
of Bucharest, as recently as 2001 observed that in Romania "there is
still a strong emphasis on the nation and the national state (just as
there was in the West until not so very long ago)."[8]

I should note that I write these words while listening to one of
George Enescu's two Romanian Rhapsodies, written in 1901, sum-
moning up with their distinctive folk rhythms, exactly as the Romanian composer intended, all the beauty and grandeur of the Romanian
landscape. The music recalls to me the fields of Wallachia in all their
vivid immensity, complete with the bright orange hues of the turnips
in spring. Enescu's music makes me think of, among so much else that

I distinctively associate with Romania, the pure vegetal dyes and biblical settings of the painted monasteries of the Bukovina, and the original mix of Oriental and Occidental styles that constitutes the unique enchantment of Brâncoveanu architecture. I think of the earthy and vigorous smell of *țuică* with its evocations of interbellum Bucharest café music. I think of the scenery on the northern and western slopes of the Carpathians, with their texture of oil brushstrokes, where the Occidental styles in architecture and much else predominate, as we are now in former Habsburg Central Europe. I know that it is on the southern and eastern slopes of the Carpathians where the Oriental influence is stronger, with its richly detailed carpets and icons—and the Phanariot costumes of the local boyar families—as we are closer to the world of the former Byzantine and Ottoman empires. For me Romania is aesthetically a last remnant of Byzantium in ways that even Greece, more a child of Ottoman despotism, is not.

These are all partly fatalistic and romantic generalizations that are less real than the individual characters of the 21 million or so Romanians who inhabit both sides of the Carpathians, and who will in their very persons frequently not conform with such a condensation of reality. The dilemma, therefore, is how to generalize without going too far, and yet at the same time to describe honestly what one has experienced—and draw conclusions from it—without being intimidated by a moral reprimand. I have failed in this regard in the past, and have struggled for years trying to find the right balance. And I am more and more unsure of myself as I get older, even as I know that there is a vast distance between describing obvious cultural peculiarities and provoking the specter of both racism and essentialism.

Indeed, the willingness to delineate the contours of Romanian culture and experience is more necessary than ever, since the country still exists, albeit to a lesser and lesser extent, in the dreary shadow of Communism. For it was Communism that ground down regional differences within Romania into the same oatmeal, even as it cut the country off from the West, creating stereotypes about the population that did not previously exist and intensifying the least attractive cultural characteristics. The Communists were the ultimate essentialists, it turns out.

Elias Canetti, the late Bulgarian Nobel laureate in literature, in his book *Crowds and Power* recognized the existence of national characteristics and consequently identified "national crowd symbols": the *sea* for the English, the *dikes* for the Dutch, the *forest* for the Germans, the *revolution* for the French, and so forth.[9] In 1990, an expert on Romanian folklore at Cuza University in Jassy, Adrian Poruciuc, suggested to me that during the worst of the Ceauşescu years the "utmost pride" of a Romanian was to provide food for his family, so that *the family seated around the humble table* was the Romanian crowd symbol during the period of late Communism.[10] "Because Ceauşescu denied us food, he had to be executed," another Romanian friend told me in 2013, recalling those dark days. The degree of humiliation that Romanians suffered under Ceauşescu was such that their very identity, my friend said, was reduced to the ugly concept, *At least we're not Gypsies.* Communism had been both the preserver and instigator of group animosities.

Thus, to see Romania in the immediate aftermath of nearly a half century of Communist-cum-Stalinist rule, as I did in the spring of 1990, was to see an entire population struggling to recover their self-respect as individuals, for it is only through elaborate and healthy individual identities that a national character worthy of the name can be realized. And that is not a contradiction: stability and civilization must come from the increasingly numerous and complex relations within the more autonomous elements of a society, as the nineteenth-century French philosopher Alexis de Tocqueville indicated.[11] Individual personalities and group characteristics need not be at odds: the latter can exist in a positive sense without diminishing the former. So as Romania becomes a society of rich individualism, a new crowd symbol will perforce emerge.

Still, crowd symbols of the kind Canetti meant are myths, which, in turn, are rooted in powerful and distorted generalizations, so it is right to be wary of these symbols. "To forget . . . and get one's history wrong, are essential factors in the making of a nation," wrote Ernest Renan in the nineteenth century, "and thus the advance of historical studies is often a danger to nationality."[12] The more history people know, the greater the danger to national myths, in other words. Reinhold Niebuhr, writing in the twentieth century, argued along similar lines. He wrote that since the claims appealing to an individual's emotion and to his mind are incompatible, "and can be resolved only through dishonesty," nationalism in order to be successful requires "self-deception."[13]

Myth, forgetfulness, and self-deception suffuse the national memory of Romanians, as they do those of other peoples, but maybe more so in the Romanians' case because the legacy of Communism—and particularly that of the Ceauşescu variety—was really one of national fascism: a national fascism that had to contend with a late medieval, early modern, and modern history of being a mere group of weak principalities eventually cobbled together as a nation. This was unlike more formidable powers such as Poland and Hungary to the north and northwest, and the adjacent Balkan kingdoms of Serbia and Bulgaria to the west and south.[14]

Ceauşescu's national fascism was an intensification of his predecessor Gheorghiu-Dej's own national Communism: an ideological orientation which stood in opposition to the Moscow-based Communism of most of the other ruling Communist parties of Eastern Europe in the early decades of the Cold War. Whereas the other East European parties were led by men and women who had spent World War II in exile from their home countries in Moscow under Stalin's supervision, in Romania the power struggle was won by those like Gheorghiu-Dej and Ceauşescu, who had spent the war years in prison inside Romania itself, and who therefore distrusted those other Communists who returned after 1945 from the Soviet Union. To Gheorghiu-Dej and Ceauşescu, the Moscow-based Communists were seen as *cosmopolitans* and *Jews*; not altogether Romanian, that is.

It may not be entirely an accident of personalities and the unpredictable outcomes of closely fought power struggles that gave Communism in Romania an unprecedented nationalistic and fascist element. The idea of the ethnic nation, rooted in geography, the rural peasantry, and Latinity, has always run deep in Romanian intellectual and political life—from poets to Communists—and cannot be so easily dismissed. Indeed, Latinity especially became a pronounced element during the nineteenth-century age of nationalism, as the Habsburg and Ottoman empires weakened and the Romanians, linked to the Slavs (who partially surrounded them) by virtue of the Orthodox Church, required a means to differentiate themselves from not only the Slavs but also from the neighboring Hungarians.

It is telling that whereas intellectuals in the West—particularly in France, England, and America—have tended to inhabit the left of the political spectrum (with variations, of course), with a distinctive passion and proclivity for advancing human rights and cosmopolitanism, Romanian intellectuals over the course of the past two centuries have demonstrated in a marked number of cases a disposition to occupy the philosophical space on the right, with an emphasis on myth, the ethnic nation, and the agricultural life of the soil. The late-nineteenth-century "national poet" and staunch conservative who resented foreigners, Mihai Eminescu, and the deeply eclectic twentieth-century philosopher of religions Mircea Eliade are the obvious examples of this tendency; the composer George Enescu, with his humanistic concern for Jews and Gypsies, and the playwright Eugène Ionesco (Eugen Ionescu), with his demonstrated horror at the rise of the fascist Iron Guard, are the antithesis. The poet Eminescu railed at "heavy-throated" Bulgarians and "hook-nosed" Greeks, even as he was a notorious anti-Semite.[15] Eliade—the prolific novelist, essayist, and pathbreaking philosopher of religious experience who spoke and read numerous languages—became thoroughly smitten with the fascist and violently anti-Semitic Iron Guard leader Corneliu Zelea Codreanu. Eliade in 1937 called the Iron Guard, or more precisely the fascist Legion of the Archangel Michael, "mainly a spiritual movement, meant to bring about the *new man* and pursuing our *national redemption*. . . . The young Legionnaires," he goes on, "alongside other wonders achieved through sacrifice, dedication, and creative will, have also laid the foundations of a Romanian elite. . . ."[16]

It is important to note here that Eminescu, Eliade, and other conservative thinkers were not faux or vulgar intellectuals. Such men were the epitomes of erudition and artistry. What Isaiah Berlin was to English philosophy in terms of rank, Eliade was to Romanian philosophy. It's just that one was a liberal humanist and the other a conservative nationalist reactionary for significant parts of his life. The historian Lucian Boia summarizes the phenomenon nicely in his balance sheet on the eve of the Communist takeover in 1945:

> Overall, Romania inclined towards the Right. It was a predominantly rural world, both literally and symbolically speaking, and the peasants, with their smallholder mentality, were not easily tempted by left-wing ideologies. Paradoxically, even the Left showed apparently "rightist" inclinations.[17]

To be sure, the interwar period of the 1930s saw a trio of famous intellectuals, Eliade, Emil Cioran, and Constantin Noica, fall under the sway of the fascist right, though it is important to note that all three of them would morally evolve and experience varying levels of remorse for the views that they held as young men. Perhaps the most interesting case was Noica, a protean personality, who, as his disciple Gabriel Liiceanu explains, would celebrate the study of Greek, Latin, and European civilization in general in order to escape the vulgarity of Communist ideology, and also to enrich the development of Romania's own indigenous culture.[18] But here, too, even when they are not being specifically right-wing, there is still that particular emphasis on national culture more than on cosmopolitan values which has made Romanian intellectual life unique.

An axiomatic text for comprehending the intellectual experience system under which Romanian intellectuals operated until deep into the twentieth century may be Mircea Eliade's *The Romanians: A Concise History*. It is a comparatively little-known and short work, only sixty-two pages in my cheap and smudgy English-language translation. It is a product of Eliade's immature period in his mid-thirties, before he evolved into the great universal philosopher that he was to become. Eliade published the little book in 1943 in right-wing dictator Francisco Franco's Spain, at the time he was living in dictator Antonio Salazar's Portugal as a diplomatic representative of Romania's fascist Iron Guard and Antonescu regimes. Eliade had been based as a Romanian diplomat in Great Britain, but when World War II broke out and other Romanian diplomats in London defected to the side of the Allies, Eliade make the deliberate decision to move to philosophically congenial, dictatorial Portugal, where he could safely represent the interests of pro-Nazi Romania. After the war, Eliade lived in Paris and in 1956 eventually settled at the University of Chicago, where he became professor of the history of religions. His short history of the Romanian people, with its romantic and sympathetic tone, could almost have been employed by Ceaușescu as the latter turned to national fascism. (Though Eliade never returned to Romania following World War II and was rabidly attacked by the new Communist regime, Ceaușescu did make some unsuccessful overtures to him.)

While elements of Eliade's history have been attacked as credulous (for example, he claimed that the pagan god of Romanian antiquity Zalmoxis had eased the way for monotheism), his book is a useful if quirky primer for coming to grips with why Romanians have as a people felt themselves different, heroic, and oppressed. Like many nationalistic histories—not *that* different from the schoolbooks I grew up with—with Eliade there exists the tyranny of a pattern. Many of the historical figures he describes seem consciously working in the direction of a future nation-state, whereas in truth they were, in part, chieftains and warlords bent on self-interest, overwhelmed by contingency and quite understandably without a limpid view of the future. This is where, as Ernest Renan suggests, further historical research may lead to a healthy decline in nationalism among Romanians.

To view Romanian history with the young and immature Eliade as a guide accomplishes two main tasks: it provides the reader with an overview of the Romanian past, however brief and somewhat distorted, even as it illuminates the context in which many twentieth-century right-wing Romanian intellectuals have had their own national identity shaped.

Eliade is both brilliant and dangerous. I discovered him the way I discovered so many other Romanian writers, originally through a love of the Romanian landscape. A traveler's journey can be not only spatial but also historical, literary, and intellectual.

ELIADE'S SETTING IS WHAT Edward Gibbon identified as the new Roman province of Dacia, conquered and incorporated into the empire by Trajan at the beginning of the second century A.D., and whose natural boundaries were the Dniester River in the northeast, the Euxine or Black Sea in the east, the Lower Danube in the south and southwest, and the Tisza River in the northwest. It was a territory which roughly configured with what would become Romania at the greatest extent of its territorial expansion and claims (minus the southern Dobrudja in modern-day Bulgaria, which lies south of the Lower Danube). The new Roman province with its "rich harvests," in Gibbon's words, "was neither strong enough to resist, nor rich enough to satiate, the rapaciousness of the barbarians," namely the Goths and "Scythian hordes." And so the indigenous Dacians, whom Gibbon labels as "industrious . . . more settled barbarians," once having achieved their independence, entered into an alliance with Rome against "the savages of the North."[19]

Eliade here adds a layer of pivotal, perhaps quasi-historical myth: that the "Geto-Dacians," as he calls them, were not so much settled barbarians as themselves remnants of the large Thracian family who may have migrated from elsewhere, "deeply anchored in the ancient history and old religions of Hellas," and benefiting from the high quality of ceramics, oil, wine, and luxury items, as well as the advanced level of administration and urbanization that were some of the gifts of Greek city-state culture. Eliade quotes Herodotus, who called the

Getae or Dacians "the bravest and most righteous among the Thracians." And it was these inhabitants of the shadow lands of classical Greece who interbred with the classical Romans to form today's Romanians.[20]

Here, early on, is an example of Eliade's selective recounting. For while quoting Herodotus on the bravery on the indigenous Geto-Dacians, Eliade neglects to mention other descriptions of Herodotus, about how the Geto-Dacians, in the words of the scholar Vladimir Tismăneanu, "considered agricultural work to be humiliating and found idleness as a most pleasant experience." This causes Tismăneanu to label such nationalistic histories as Eliade's a "fetishization and idealization of the past."[21]

The Roman conquest of Dacia in A.D. 102 had been a close-run affair, with Decebalus, the "heroic" Dacian king as described by Eliade, inflicting "huge casualties" on Trajan's forces both north of the Lower Danube and south of it in Moesia (northern Bulgaria). Decebalus became a Roman "client prince" with a Roman garrison headquartered in Dacia. A second Roman-Dacian war in A.D. 105–106 led to Dacia's complete subjugation as a Roman province. "Until then Dacia had inclined towards the Hellenic East; from now onwards, she began to turn to the West," writes Eliade rather triumphantly. "The Dacian population merged with Roman colonists" and "vulgar Latin" became the universal tongue of the inhabitants. Thus were the Romanians not to be part of the Germanic, Slavic, and proto-Turk morass of savage peoples; instead they were destined to emerge as remnants of the Greater Mediterranean classical world of Romans and Greeks: closer in spirit and culture to Italy and Spain, say, than to neighboring Serbia and Bulgaria.[22]

However, the story line is not so simple, something I learned upon further research. To wit, as the late historian Vlad Georgescu summarizes: "the Romanian people is the product of a long process beginning with the Romanization of the Dacians, ending with the Romanianization of the Slavs, and taking place over an area extending both north and south of the Danube."[23] The Romanians are a mixture, like so many peoples, and lack the pure origin that Eliade's history appears to ascribe to them.

Eliade does present a region in turmoil that, nevertheless, preserves a Latinate story line of sorts amid the constant flow of tribes. "The barbarian world of the Goths was in full movement," he writes, leading to continued attacks, predominantly from the north, into Roman Dacia. The Emperor Aurelian decided upon a strategic withdrawal from the province in A.D. 271–272 to the more defensible, southern shore of the Danube in Moesia. Following the legions southward across the Danube were the civil servants and the wealthy. But the "Daco-Roman peasants and shepherds remained in their lands," just as they had during the invasions of the Indo-European Cimmerians and other barbarians, writes Eliade. "The forest is a brother to the Romanians," goes a popular saying that had its roots with the Daco-Romans who hid in the dense woods from the barbarians.[24]

The classical world endured inside the besieged forest, helped by the civilizing mission of the Roman army for nearly two centuries and by the Roman road network. One senses Eliade's joy in his rendition of all the key Latin-influenced words that came to define the Romanian language as well as indicating the early roots of Christianity here, despite the dark centuries of divorce from the Roman West: *biserică* (church) from the Latin word *basilica*; *Dumnezeu* (God) from *Dominus Deus*; *înger* (angel) from *angelus*; *răposa* (to pass away) from *repausare*; and so on. It was Roman colonists who brought Christianity to Dacia as early as the second century, according to the Roman writer Tertullian. Eliade suggests that Rome had been attracted to Dacia in the first place partly because of the province's Greek cultural influences. And now with Rome itself gone, even as Dacia had retained Rome's cultural riches, the province turned next to that rising "Rome of the East"—Byzantium—for succor against the savage hordes. To Eliade, the "secret rhythm" of Romanian history was the fusion of the two Romes in the ethnic homeland.[25]

Certainly, here is a thrilling and atmospheric truth: Romania does, indeed, constitute a unique blend of a Latinate language and an East-

ern Orthodox Church; the sound of Italy alongside the icons and frescoes of Greek Byzantium. One thinks of Ravenna—that Italian city
glorified by its Byzantine art and heritage.

Romanian, Eliade claims, is the only Romance language "to have
preserved the enclitic article: instead of *el* lobo, *del* lobo, *al* lobo (*the*
wolf, *of the* wolf, *to the* wolf) one says in Romanian lup*ul*, lupu*lui*, etc.
just like in Latin—lup*us*, lup*um*. . . ." Such a phenomenon, he tells
us, is central to the "miracle" of Latinity, especially as Romania was in
large measure cut off from the West throughout the Middle Ages and
into the early modern era, and was subject to Slavic and other migrations that influenced the language.[26] (But here, as well as in other
places, Eliade does not have it quite right, since Bulgarian, Albanian,
and Turkish all have word-final definite articles, too.)

For the Romanians, between late antiquity and modern times, were
to incessantly suffer the fate of a "frontier people," defending their territory "against the barbarians and all the nomads coming from the
East." Local and regional rulers emerged, *voivodes*, tasked to make war
and dispense justice. Following the Tartar invasion of 1241, we begin
to learn of two principalities, larger than *voivodates*, taking form: Moldavia, located between the Carpathians and the Dniester River, encompassing today's Romanian province of Moldova and the
independent, former Soviet Republic of that name; and Wallachia,
located between the great bend in the Danube in the west and the
Black Sea in the east, including the regions of Oltenia, Muntenia, and
northern Dobrudja, though the geographical labels have often varied.
It was a gradual, tortuous, and obscure process that is even today not
sufficiently understood by historians. Through the thirteenth and fourteenth centuries, despite the movements of Hungarian and Polish
armies against the Tartars, Romanian *voivodes* such as Dragoş and
Bogdan in Moldavia, and the Basarabs (of Cuman origin) in Wallachia, were able to carve out the beginnings of these principalities,
marking a development in political formation beyond the medieval
micro-kingdoms. Eliade avows that these two Romanian principalities

entered modern history as rescuers of the West, defending Latin civilization and Christianity "against the Slav-Turanic threat" from the east. The Romanians would "anonymously bleed," so that Western Europe had the "necessary respite" to prepare for future hegemony.[27]

The limitations of this thesis are obviously numerous. For example, one could well argue that the Russians, pressured by the Mongol Golden Horde, served a purpose for Northern Europe no less important than what the Romanians did for southeastern Europe. One could also say that the rise of the West was in any case owed to a vast array of internal factors: the Renaissance and later on the Enlightenment and Industrial Revolution. The West wasn't so much saved by Romania as the West was a cultural phenomenon in and of itself. Romania was a footnote to the rise of the West, not a central element to it.

But for Eliade, Romania's preeminent role in saving the West is prologue for his larger mission statement:

> There are nations whose role in history is so obvious that nobody has ever thought to question it. But there are also less happy nations, who perform quite disagreeable missions without anybody noticing it. A discreet obscure role like the one played by the Daco-Romans' descendants, the Romanians . . . Ignored, or misunderstood at the best, the life of these nations is more intense. In addition to its tragism, their history is transfigured, one may say, by a permanent divine presence. . . . Incessantly attacked, they can only think while defending themselves. Their history . . . is a permanent war, for centuries on end, for their own survival. In each battle they risk everything: their right to life, to religion, to their language and culture.[28]

In other words, not only have the Romanians suffered more than other European peoples, but their suffering has created a mystical martyrdom in their souls. This is not too far removed from what Eliade would later write in *The Myth of the Eternal Return*: that as the terror of history grows worse, ahistoricism and archetypal myths take over.[29] According to this logic, it is not going too far to suggest that as a people, the Romanians are like the savior on the cross.

Just as the savior died to save men's souls, in Eliade's telling the Romanians have been the protagonist in the equivalent of a long, drawn-out passion play to save the West from the Asiatic hordes. For it turns out that the greatest trials of this martyred, classical people lay ahead of them in the twentieth century, not behind. Thus does Eliade, the erstwhile champion of the fascist Iron Guard (founded in the late 1920s as the Orthodox Christian Legion of the Archangel Michael), introduce us to the almost five-century-long struggle of the Christian Orthodox Romanians against the Muslim Ottoman Turks—that "Islamic colossus" trying to penetrate the heart of Europe.[30]

The saga of the Romanians' violent contest against the Turks is told by Eliade mainly through the exertions of the great *voivodes* and princes—Mircea the Old, Iancu de Hunedoara, Vlad III ("the Impaler"), Stephen the Great, and Michael the Brave—some to whom Eliade devotes considerable space, while others he breezes past. These are names that I began to come across during my first extended visit to Romania in 1981, and which became more and more familiar to me over the course of the ensuing decades, as though characters in my own life.

Mircea, of the House of Basarab, is called "the Old" (Mircea cel Bătrân) both because of his long reign (1386–1418) and posthumously to distinguish him from a grandson, Mircea II, as well as from others of the same name who ruled later. Eliade calls Mircea the Old "one of the greatest sovereigns the Romanian people ever had," who fortuitously held the reins of Muntenia (the heartland of Wallachia) just as the Turks were advancing into the Balkans and toward the Danube in the last two decades of the fourteenth century. Mircea's policy of trying to forge a Christian alliance against the Muslims led him to send a Romanian contingent to fight alongside the Serbian Knez ("Prince") Lazar at the Battle of Kosovo Polje in 1389, which saw the defeat of the Serbs and the beginning of their subjugation by the Ottoman Turks for almost four and a half centuries. Turkish Sultan Bayezid I Yildirim ("the Thunderbolt") followed up his victory over the Serbs with one over the Bulgarians in 1393. But the exposed and outnumbered Romanians under Mircea the Old managed to defeat the Turks under Bayezid at Rovine in Wallachia on May 17, 1395, one of the most important dates in Romanian history. Too exhausted to capitalize on the victory (if that's really what it was), and quickly under renewed attack, Mircea concluded (in the Transylvanian city of Braşov) an alliance with the Hungarian King Sigismund of Luxembourg, and consequently the forces of the two Christian sovereigns managed to keep the Turks on the far side of the Danube. But the "Christian League" soon broke up and in 1397 an Ottoman army crossed the Danube and attacked Mircea's forces. That year, and again in 1400, Mircea's peasant army repelled the Turks. In 1417, the Turks were back across the Danube, and Mircea, an aged man who would die the following year, was forced to pay tribute in order to preserve Wallachia's internal freedom. And yet as Vlad Georgescu concludes in his own history, published in 1984, more balanced than that of Eliade: because of Mircea's fighting and maneuvering, "Wallachia survived as a political entity at a time when the Turks were liquidating the czardoms of Bulgaria and Serbia."[31]

The rhythm was thus established. As vassal states of the Ottoman sultanate, unlike Serbia and Bulgaria, which were directly ruled from the Bosphorus, the Romanian lands could not hope to remain truly independent or even semi-independent for long. Their great *voivodes* were sometimes great less because of outright victories than because of their constancy, political ingenuity in forming temporary alliances, and endurance by way of their interminable military maneuvering against the Muslim enemy.

Nevertheless, Iancu de Hunedoara, the Transylvanian *voivode*, defeated two Ottoman armies in 1442 and then moved southwestward into the heart of the Balkans, where he defended the fortress at Belgrade against Mehmet II in 1456.[32] (This halted the Ottoman advance into Central Europe for more than three-quarters of a century.) In that same year of 1456 when Iancu died, Vlad III, a grandson of Mircea the Old, ascended the throne of Muntenia, giving him influence over the surrounding region. Vlad's sobriquet became Țepeș, "the Impaler," because of the way he tortured his personal enemies and captured Turks alike. (Under the name Vlad Țepeș Dracula — "son of the Dragon" — he became the stuff of Gothic legends that had as their origin his extreme cruelty and strong sense of justice. However, *Dracul*, "the Dragon," referred not to anything cruel, but to an honorary feudal order to which Vlad's father had been recruited by Sigismund of Luxembourg.[33]) In any case, Vlad III was fierce beyond all imaginings, a "doughty champion" of Orthodoxy against Islam and Roman Catholicism. In 1462, he annihilated an entire host of Turks poised at the Danube to attack Wallachia. In painting Vlad as an implacable foe of the Turks and another hero in the struggle of Orthodox Christianity against Islam, Eliade conveniently neglects to mention that Vlad himself owed his throne to the Turks, who had favored him over his brother. Moreover, Eliade might have included the alliances with the same Turks made by Vlad's father, Vlad II Dracul, which the elder Vlad strayed from only because of the strength and unity of other Christian nations in the region like Hungary and Poland. Vlad II was also, like his son Dracula, utterly ruthless toward the Muslims, but he was clever and at times a subtle politician as well. Because the Turks enjoyed the semblance of permanence, countering them required not only war but long bouts of innovative diplomacy.[34]

Yet Eliade's account, while slanted, is by no means entirely propaganda. For here was the desultory torture and bleeding of the civilian peasantry by armies in an almost permanent state of conflict, the armies themselves stopped only by their own experience of hunger and disease.[35] Romanian history really is, after a fashion, an unending tale of bravery and martyrdom. It was the late medieval European condition writ more extreme by the very absence of a thematic variation: the most desperate maneuvers and subterfuges, both violent and not, against the Muslim Turks.

Whereas in Wallachia and its environs there were Mircea the Old,

Iancu de Hunedoara, and the two Vlads, among quite a few others, obviously, in Moldavia there was Stephen III, or Stephen the Great (Ştefan cel Mare), who ruled for nearly half a century, from 1457 till 1504. Stephen the Great, too, practiced the deft diplomacy required by the tragic realism of his age. His alliances with both Roman Catholic Poland and the Muslim Turkish sultanate brought him into conflict not only with the Catholic Hungarian monarch Matthias Corvinus but also with fellow Romanian-speaking Wallachia, an ally of Hungary. The notion encouraged by Eliade and other nationalist historians that Romania was an inevitable geographic project toward which the various medieval and early modern *voivodes* were always working is rather one-dimensional: survival amid such chaotic conditions and shifting alliances often leaves limited room for grand conceptions.

Nevertheless, Stephen was probably the greatest of the medieval *voivodes* because of his organizational abilities. He centralized bureaucratic power and built a military machine in Moldavia that allowed him to fight a legendary forty wars during his long reign and prepared him for his epic confrontation with Ottoman Turkey.[36]

Eliade notes at the outset that the Byzantine Empire fell to the Turks in 1453, only four years before Stephen began his reign. The world of Eastern Orthodox Christianity was left utterly unprotected since the Greeks, Serbs, and Bulgarians were already under Ottoman domination, even as Russia was exceedingly weak (with its vast geography subject to power struggles between Moscow, Novgorod, Lithuania, and Poland). In this maelstrom only the Romanians, and in particular the Moldavians, had preserved their autonomy. "It was Stephen's intention," writes Eliade, "to revive the glory of Byzantium," and recommence the Crusade among the Muslim infidels. Stephen, writes Eliade, sent the Christian princes of the Balkans and Central Europe a letter announcing a recent victory and declaring: "'We have faced the foes of the Christian world. . . . We have trampled them under foot and we have put them on the edge of our sword, for which blessed be Our God.'" Fearing a much more considerable Turkish attack, Stephen then pleads, "'send us your chieftains to help us against

the enemies of the Christian world. . . .'" Eliade finds this to be proof
of Stephen's consciousness of a "historic mission." The truth may be
more complicated. Stephen clearly recognized the mission of defending Christianity against Islam, and saw Moldavia as a "bulwark for
Hungary and Poland," even as he was later to fight Poland and spend
his last years trying to buttress the frontiers with his own Christian
neighbors. But that is not quite the same as working toward a vision of
Romania—a union of Moldavia, Wallachia, and Transylvania—as a
unique national and legal entity. Eliade's story is not necessarily wrong.
But his aim is more inspirational than elucidatory. As the authors of *A
History of Romania*, published by the Center for Romanian Studies in
Jassy, say, the idea of Romanian unity "was totally alien" to the minds
of the medieval and Renaissance eras.[37]

Witness Michael the Brave (Mihai Viteazu), who ascended the
throne of Muntenia in 1593. By the time he was assassinated in 1601,
he was the first Romanian-speaking prince in history to rule all three
principalities—Wallachia, Moldavia, and Transylvania—if only for a
few months in 1600. The maps of the age show the three principalities
bordered by Poland to the northeast, the Austrian Empire to the northwest, and the Ottoman Empire all the way from the southwest across
to the southeast. But these maps barely address the dangers he faced.
For the portraits of Michael the Brave show a resplendent prince with
an immense, forward-thrusting turban and a knowing gaze that reduces the word "cunning" to a paltry attempt by the modern Western
mind to comprehend unfathomable layers of calculation. A figure of
the late Renaissance, Michael might arguably have been the fullest
expression of what Machiavelli, a father of the Renaissance, meant by
a true prince.

Eliade approvingly quotes Michael's statement about making "this
poor country of mine" into a "shield for the entire Christian world"
against Islam.[38] Eliade follows with this observation: that without Romanian political unity, nothing permanent could be built in Central
and Eastern Europe. And yet behind Michael's lofty undertaking lay
almost a decade of bloodshed and excruciatingly complex diplomatic

intrigue that reduces the very idea of history to a near-meaningless welter of suffering and quasi-anarchy—a series of events where a discernible direction is often hard to detect. Though Eliade tries to find an inspirational message in all of this, the problem is that Michael's career manifests a Machiavellianism limited to pure technique, with insufficient hint of a greater good to be achieved.

Consider:

Born in 1558, Michael rose to become a leading boyar, or feudal personage, buying up villages and acquiring the throne of Wallachia in 1593 by providing the Ottoman sultanate with the requisite bribes. The next year he initiated a campaign against the same sultanate by inviting Ottoman creditors to a litigation, then locking the doors and burning the building down. This was followed by a general massacre of Turks in Wallachia. In response to Michael's raids as far south as Adrianople in Thracian Turkey, the sultan's troops invaded Wallachia in 1595. Michael's overreach forced him into an alliance with the Hungarian ruler of Transylvania that allowed the Hungarian to subjugate neighboring Moldavia. Nevertheless, the alliance helped Michael defeat a Turkish army at Călugăreni, between Bucharest and the Danube in Muntenia. Yet the tactical victory was not enough to stop Michael's retreat north toward the Carpathians, in the face of an advance by the Ottomans that saw them take Bucharest. But with reinforcements from Hungarian-controlled Moldavia and Transylvania, Michael was able to force the Turks southward. The Ottomans, now preoccupied with a war against the Austrian Habsburgs, made a temporary truce with Michael in 1598. The Poles meanwhile had invaded Moldavia, toppling the Hungarians there and removing Moldavia from the anti-Ottoman alliance. The alliance completely collapsed when the Hungarians made a deal with the Austrians over Transylvania. So Michael, rather than continue to fight the Turks, began to negotiate with both them and the Austrians for recognition of his right to retain the throne of Wallachia. But the Turks wanted too much tribute and so Michael made an alliance with the Austrians instead. Then the Poles, who held sway in Moldavia, forced the Hungarian rulers in

Transylvania to break their alliance with the Austrians. This led, through more convolutions, to a deal between Christian Transylvania, Christian Moldavia, and Muslim Turkey. Michael then entered negotiations with the Turks, even as he plotted with the Austrians to topple the Hungarians in Transylvania. Michael's successful invasion of Transylvania was secured at the Battle of Selimbar, near Sibiu, in 1599. In 1600, now in charge of both Wallachia and Transylvania, Michael invaded pro-Polish Moldavia. The victory there allowed Michael to claim the unity of all three core-Romanian principalities. But later the same year, the Austrians defeated Michael in Transylvania and the Poles defeated him in Moldavia. Michael responded by entering into negotiations with the Austrians. The Hungarians in Transylvania, fearing a deal between Michael and the Habsburgs, assassinated him near Cluj in 1601.[39]

Romania, in this reading, emerges from the travails of history as an even more intense version of early modern Europe itself: nothing is ever secure and more bloodshed always lies in wait. If European history is a nightmare, then that of Romania is doubly so. The very unswerving energy of Michael the Brave—operating for years on end at levels of stress that would immobilize the average Western politician in the twenty-first century—was the mere requirement of any warlord of the age. And if Michael as a late Renaissance man could not conceive of a unitary Romanian state, his accomplishment, nevertheless—and however short-lived—gave Romanian speakers of later eras a vision of what was politically possible. In that regard, Eliade and other historians have it right.

Eliade marches on through the early modern and modern eras, and, amid all the numbing complexities, the travails and dismemberments of the ethnic homeland never cease. (It is a history that, as I would learn more about it from other authors, would continually fascinate me, and which I will explore in greater depth in later chapters.) In 1775, the Habsburg Austrians acquired from a weakened Ottoman Turkey northern Moldavia, which they renamed the Bukovina, or Bucovina (from "great forest" in Ukrainian). Then, in 1812, the Russians took the eastern half of Moldavia from the Turks, which they "abusively" called "Bessarabia," after the Basarab *voivodes*. With Moldavia torn away and Romanians thus humiliated, the Wallachian revolutionary Tudor Vladimirescu suddenly appeared in 1821 to lead a successful rebellion against the hated Phanariots: Greek princes appointed by the Ottoman Turks as local administrators, who stood accused of exploiting the Romanian peasantry. (These Greeks were named for the Phanar, or "Lighthouse," district of Constantinople from which they had originated.) It was the dominance of these Greeks that had so far helped delay the development of a Romanian national identity. And yet a generation later, the Moldavian-born boyar Prince Alexandru Ioan Cuza united Wallachia and Moldavia after Russia was defeated in the Crimean War and had lost parts of Bessarabia. But because of weak administration and the intrigues of Romania's princely families, at that moment Romanians wisely put their destiny in the hands of a no-nonsense foreign ruler, the German Carol of Hohenzollern-Sigmaringen, whose dynasty would rule Romania until the Nazi and Communist eras.[40]

As for the era of Nazi domination, Eliade, remember, is writing from the vantage point of 1943, as a diplomatic representative of Antonescu's fascist-trending regime. Eliade thus portrays Romania's military alliance with Hitler as "defending Christian and European assets against Euro-Asiatic mysticalness." For the enemy now is "Slav imperialism"—the successor to Turkish imperialism—and taking back Bessarabia from the Soviet Union with Hitler's help constituted nothing less than correcting a historical wrong. In other words, Romania is once again the tip of the spear of the West against the East.[41]

Eliade concludes his *Concise History* with a flourish about the miracle of Orthodox Christianity, the foundation myths of Romanian spirituality, the general artistic genius of the Romanian people, the Byzantine and Gothic monuments of Romanian religious architecture, and the triumph of Romanian folk culture—the upshot of an archaic and rural peasantry that has survived through the middle of the twentieth century. On the last page he lauds Liviu Rebreanu, Romania's "greatest contemporary novelist," for writing an epic about a Transylvanian peasant, "the eternal peasant," as Eliade puts it.[42] Of course, it would be Communism—the very consequence of the Nazi-fascist military onslaught into Bessarabia and beyond for which Eliade was a cheerleader—that would finally destroy the Romanian peasantry and its folk culture that Eliade so adored.

ELIADE IS NOW PROPERLY under attack. Early-twenty-first-century Romanian intellectuals, such as Horia-Roman Patapievici and Vladimir Tismăneanu, are understanding of the brutal, difficult, valiant, and tragic whirlpool of the past from which Romanians have emerged, and they are also cognizant of the brilliant material culture that has emerged from that past—an authentic confection of the Roman and Byzantine, exactly as Eliade proclaims. Nonetheless, these contemporary intellectuals have greatly distanced themselves from Eliade's feverish and mystical patriotism. Tismăneanu, born in Braşov of Romanian-Jewish parents and for decades an academic in the United States, probably provides the best synthesis of a healthy, respectable nationalism in his 1998 book, *Fantasies of Salvation: Democracy, Nationalism, and Myth in Post-Communist Europe*.

Leaning a bit on the ideas of the early-twentieth-century German-Jewish intellectual Walter Benjamin, Tismăneanu explains that "all societies need foundation myths, and this is a fact of civilization no one can or should deny." Without, for example, such myths that imply a common cultural experience rooted in geography, "humanity risks sliding into atomized uniformity and barbarous regimentation." Though civil society would seem to offer the remedy, even civil society is not "intractably benign," because of the tendency to homogenize culture and opinions. Tismăneanu then offers up Isaiah Berlin's comment that nationalism is "a response to degradation and a search for dignity."[43]

Yet, as Tismăneanu goes on, Romanian nationalism has had its dark sides. Eliade is part of a long and rich tendency to mythologize the Romanian past, by concentrating on the superheroic struggles of a Christlike, peasant *folk* population against Muslims, Slavs, and other Asiatics. From here it may be only a short way to anti-Semitism. Indeed, in the aftermath of the Cold War, and for years following, radical-populist nationalism and anti-Semitism hovered dangerously in the Romanian intellectual firmament. This was evident by the renewed interest in the far-right and racist writings of the interwar philosophers Nae Ionescu and A. C. Cuza.[44] Tismăneanu links this to a larger, Balkan phenomenon:

> The intensity of ethnocentric populism in Southeastern Europe, especially compared to the northern part of the post-communist map, is not simply the consequence of political manipulations exerted by skillful demagogues. To understand it one has to look into local traditions, the role of national religions (especially the Orthodox Church). . . . Balkan cultures . . . have always had a problematic relationship with the concept of universal individual rights, tolerance of alterity, admission of ethnic diversity. . . . This is not to deny the existence of liberal and pluralist traditions, but simply to acknowledge their pre-cariousness. . . . But whereas in Poland, for instance, the demy-thologizing exploration of the past has been a major endeavor of the intellectuals, in the Balkans the trend has been to cover up the shameful pages of national history and to fabricate new messianic, self-indulging fantasies.[45]

Tismăneanu quotes the philosopher and literary critic George Steiner as calling nationalism "the venom of our age. . . . By proclaiming himself a Ghanaean, a Nicaraguan, a Maltese a man spares himself vexation." Steiner goes on: "He need not ravel out what he is, where his humanity lies. He becomes one of an armed, coherent pack." Tismăneanu emphasizes that "there is nothing intrinsically wrong with national pride. The tragedy occurs when this natural sentiment ceases to mean just 'love for the little platoon we belong to in society' (Edmund Burke), and is exacerbated into an ideology of hostility, hatred, and envy."[46]

The tension within me reading these words was vast: *Communal pride is good, yes, for gazing at the quantities of gold-leaf icons, at the Byzantine-Gothic-Baroque-Brâncoveanu architecture, at all the darkish and chiseled faces in the streets of Bucharest, so individualistic and yet so encompassing of a unique history and geography, I knew that to deny such a thing as a Romanian national and, again, yes, ethnic identity was to deny reality itself. And yet I also knew that to get carried away with such an emotion and observation was to deny an even deeper, more material, and less corruptible reality—given the history of the twentieth century—that of all the individuals I saw and had ever encountered in Romania, and how each encapsulated his or her own moral and vividly complex personal universe.*

I think now of the Yale historian Timothy Snyder, who outlines the flexible, early modern nationalism encapsulated by the career of nineteenth-century poet Adam Mickiewicz in his academic classic, *The Reconstruction of Nations: Poland, Ukraine, Lithuania, Belarus, 1569–1999.* Mickiewicz, writes Snyder, saw Lithuania "as a land of many peoples but of an ultimately Polish destiny." Never having set foot in Warsaw or Cracow, Mickiewicz nonetheless became a "medium" for Polish nationalism; and while he never envisioned a Lithuania separate from Poland, his writings were utilized by Lithuanian nationalists. However, technically speaking, as Snyder notes, Mickiewicz would in today's terminology be counted a Belarusian. Then there was the protean Polish statesman and military leader in the interwar period, Józef Piłsudski, who, Snyder says, "never quite chose between Poland and Lithuania," even as he spoke the "folk Belarusian of the countryside." Piłsudski was buried in Cracow's Wawel Castle in 1935 alongside Polish kings; his heart was cut out and buried next to his mother in Wilno, the Lithuanian capital. For instead of the "settled 'facts' of geography," Snyder documents a wealth of cultural and linguistic interchange, teeming with intricate and overlapping identities in northeastern Europe. Herein are identities far too subtle to fit within the ethnic straitjackets demanded by modern nationalists, who have rejected the elastic definitions of early modernism—of which Mickiewicz, for one, was an exemplar—and turned instead to illusions of group purity and "inborn national traits" that have led, ultimately, to genocide and ethnic cleansing. The fact that the ethnic cleansers have usually been former Communist apparatchiks is not ironic, Snyder tells us, for it is an outgrowth of their desire to retain power, this time by setting group against group. Communism, I repeat, by pulverizing individual identities in favor of the mass, was essentialism in action, and so easily lent itself to the politics of ethnicity. The attraction of the postmodern European Union, in spite of all its difficulties, constitutes a desire on the part of the peoples of the former Communist states— from the Baltics to the Balkans—to escape the strictures of modern nationalism and enter a world of individual rights beyond ethnicity.[47]

Snyder's thesis is helped by the fact that the region of northeastern Europe (Poland, Ukraine, Lithuania, and Belarus) about which he writes is more or less flat, with relatively few natural borders, and is predominantly Slavic, encouraging the movements of people and thus of fluid identities. The mountainous Balkans, with a geography less conducive to such constant human to-ing and fro-ing (even as it is on the path of Eurasian trade routes), and populated as it is by a mixture of Romance speakers, Hungarian speakers, Turkic speakers, Greek speakers, Albanian speakers, and Slavic speakers, might be somewhat less friendly to Snyder's message. Yet the one place in the Balkan Peninsula where war actually broke out following Communism's demise was in Yugoslavia, almost exclusively among Slavic speakers—rather than between Slavic speakers and others. Moreover, identities between Romanians, Hungarians, Jews, and others are not always so clear-cut as they seem. In any case, Snyder's overarching idea is that group identity—and war and peace—depend foremost on human choices and contingencies which "escape national reasoning."[48]

The timeline from Mircea Eliade's *The Romanians* to Timothy Snyder's *The Reconstruction of Nations* is one that passes through the colossal and cursed chasm of Holocaust, Communist totalitarianism, and ethnic cleansing. Whereas the former book is riddled with an imprecise and mystic nationalism, the latter is laced with a nuance and clarity that eviscerates hard nationalist categories. But while the second book is visionary in the best sense of the word, the power of the first book cannot be denied because half-truths and three-quarter truths still contain much truth. It wasn't a question of balancing both books as I traveled throughout Romania, because one was clearly superior to the other. It was a question of searching in the course of my journey for the fading of one sensibility, and the hopeful, imminent arrival of another.

Chapter IV

THE BĂRĂGAN STEPPE

T HE FOG PARTIALLY OBSCURED A FLAT AND LIMITLESS PANEL OF cereal cultivation, the colors of which manifested the indeterminate darkness of an engraving. The poplars and black locusts grieved. Here and there was a backdrop of shacks and scrap-iron construction reminiscent of Africa. A river crossed the plain that was less water than an eternal movement of nutrient-rich soil. The very immensity of the flatness was a revelation. For I was in the easily breachable path of empires, so much so that the Latinate words, surviving as they did, constituted a miracle. It was a Sunday morning. I was listening to Orthodox hymns on the radio: the rhythmic monotony intensified the beautiful loneliness of the landscape. I noticed horse-drawn carts and a few bent-over old women wearing black kerchiefs: a solitary rumor of Turkey. Soon the fog began to lift, revealing a long and solemn horizon to which only a Pasternak could do justice.

I crossed the Bărăgan Steppe, the utter minimalistic essence of Wallachia, where there is not a single landscape feature, just awe-inspiring emptiness, roaring winds that have traveled all the way from Siberia, and black soil punctuated here and there by a primitive water well: a twisted diagonal wooden pole pivoting on a vertical one, like those I had seen in the Nile Delta. On the Bărăgan Steppe, the Com-

munists in the early 1950s had sent more than forty thousand pre-
sumed regime opponents, often at the beginning of winter, to be
stranded with no shelter. You were left to die, in other words. And if
you survived, you got to write letters home that were almost never
posted by the authorities.

A friend told me this about her great-uncle:

> You fight with the Germans against the Russians in the east
> in Transdniestria, where you are sent to the front lines because
> you have a Jewish wife. Then, because Romania switched sides
> during World War II, you are sent to fight against the Germans
> and the Hungarians in the west in Transylvania. You suffer all
> the deprivations of a soldier on some of the bitterest fronts of the
> war. And for what? After the war you are deported to Bărăgan
> because you are an intellectual.

On a forlorn and badly paved road on the Bărăgan Steppe, I came
upon a cross so worn by time and winds that the Cyrillic was practically unreadable. (Until the mid-nineteenth century, Romanians wrote
in Cyrillic, a legacy of the Greek and Russian influences, another reminder of the miracle of Latinity.) I imagined that the cross signified
the vaguely defined area where in 1395 the *voivode* Mircea the Old
defeated the Ottomans in the great Battle of Rovine, a battle which,
alas, proved indecisive, as the Turks would return to rampage across
Wallachia and demand tribute. But according to some sources, the
battle took place near the Argeș River, which would put it very far to
the west of where I was standing.[1] I was totally confused. I remembered what a historian at Cuza University in Jassy, Florin Platon, had
told me: "Romanians celebrate only their heroes, their charismatic
personalities [Mircea the Old, Stephen the Great, Michael the Brave,
and so on] because the exact places where they fought are often un-
known." In fact, between Bucharest and the Danube, in the extreme
south of Wallachia, on another trip, I would come upon another
gnarled Cyrillic cross, this one beside a busy highway, commemorat-

ing Michael the Brave's defeat of the Ottomans in 1595 at Călugăreni — another indecisive victory. But again, where precisely this battle, involving many thousands on each side, was fought is not altogether clear. I saw only dust, chickens, garbage, and Gypsy children. Still, I was on a flat plain, and the Ottoman army had been marching north from the Danube, probably close to the modern highway. Observe the geography well enough and the howl of the trucks disappears, I told myself.

WALLACHIA: LAND OF THE VLACHS — the name that Germanic peoples gave to the Romanians.[2] Because Wallachia is flat, it was always infinitely *invadable*. And considering the transportation technology of earlier ages, it was vast — over 300 miles by 100 miles — with a near-aquatic, swampy landscape far in the east, so that invaders often foundered in it. Patrick Leigh Fermor saw Wallachia as "monotonous, forlorn, and rather beautiful," with, nevertheless, a feeling of "profound melancholy and hopelessness."[3] In A.D. 251, the Roman emperor Decius was lost with his entire army fighting the Goths in the marshes of the southern Dobrudja, in eastern Wallachia just over the Romanian border in modern-day Bulgaria.[4] (In the same area, in A.D. 680 and 708, Byzantine armies met similar fates at the hands of the Bulgars.[5]) The Goths, in turn, were besieged here by Huns, Visigoths, Avars, Cumans, and Pechenegs, as well as by other tribes and war bands, most of them originating from the eastern steppe as far away as Turkic-Mongol Central Asia. Thus were the Balkans ravished from eastern Hungary all the way southward to Bulgaria in the early Christian centuries. These invasions occurred just as the capital of the ancient world's greatest empire was formally transferred in A.D. 330, from Rome to Constantinople, completing a process that shifted imperial authority, with all of its infrastructure and other instruments of stability, from the central Mediterranean to the very outskirts of the Balkans, providing, therefore, more coherence to southeastern Europe. For the rugged and fertile area just to the northwest of Constantinople itself, as far as the Lower Danube—Thrace, Moesia, and the southern Dobrudja—and roughly corresponding with modern-day Bulgaria, would come under direct Byzantine authority, even while the area of modern-day Romania, though closer to Constantinople than to Rome, was still a bit too far afield for direct imperial rule.

Wallachia, on the northern side of the Danube, the area where I now traveled, was therefore a boundary region, in which the northern Dobrudja was most directly affected by the military might of Byzantium to the south. The map of the Byzantine Empire during the rule of Justinian the Great in the sixth century shows the Danube as the northernmost imperial border. Only the Dobrudja, of all the historic regions of Greater Romania—located between the now northward-flowing Danube and the Black Sea—was a sovereign territory of Constantinople. The same holds true for the map of the empire in the eleventh century, at the time of the death of Basil II Bulgaroctonus (Basil "the Bulgar-Slayer"). In that eleventh-century map, we see that north of the Danube lay the Kingdom of Hungary and the Turkic-speaking Pechenegs. Not only was Romania yet to be even thought of, but also yet to be born were the principalities of Wallachia and Moldavia, from which the modern state of Romania would much later emerge.[6]

Roman and Latin Dacia certainly lived on in terms of a rich linguistic and cultural orientation, but they disappeared in the early medieval era as a political one. Dacia and the Romanians crop up only here and there in Byzantine histories, for example, in reference to the origins of emperors Constantine the Great and Leo I, even though the exact locations of their births were inside present-day Serbia and Bulgaria. But all of these geographical orientations, as I shall explain, are deceptive.

I CONTINUED TO LISTEN to the Orthodox hymns on the radio, the most inspiring and evocative religious music I know. These hymns can conjure up an entire civilization for me. While the territory of present-day Romania lay just outside the confines of Byzantium, Byzantium itself remains central to Romania's historical and cultural experience in a way that no other empire ever has been—even those that have actually overrun or occupied Romania. The Soviet Union may have embedded its ideology and belief system into the material and political world of Romania for decades, but it is a legacy that the Romanians simply want to escape. Byzantium, on the other hand, has provided Romania with a cultural and religious identity that, while unhelpful in some aspects, has also proffered the Romanian people stores of spiritual beauty, aesthetic abundance, and geopolitical inspiration.

Romania is a fusion of Roman Latinity and Greek Orthodox Christianity, so that ancient Rome and Greece live on, however vaguely and indirectly, inside the Romanian soul. But this Romanian fusion is itself the by-product of a Byzantine one. The great Russian-born Byzantinist who taught in the former Yugoslavia, George Ostrogorsky, writes, "It was the integration of Hellenistic culture and the Christian religion within the Roman imperial framework that gave rise to the historical phenomenon which we know as the Byzantine Empire."[7] Robert Byron, the early-twentieth-century British travel writer and historian, put it succinctly: "the three spheres, Western, Oriental, and Hellenic, were respectively identified with the stable, the transcendental, and the cultural elements of the new [Byzantine] civilization," providing it with a signal "vitality."[8]

Robert Byron is key to understanding Byzantium and its porous affect on Romania. He died tragically in 1941, at age thirty-four, when the Germans torpedoed the ship he was taking to Egypt. By then he had already published some of the best and most exquisite travel literature of the century, *The Station* (1928), about Mount Athos in Greece, and *The Road to Oxiana* (1937), about Persia and Afghanistan.[9] But it was as a historian, and particularly as a revisionist art historian, that he may have wielded his most serious influence. *The Station*, which details the life of Eastern Orthodox monks in the richly decorated monasteries of Greece's Mount Athos Peninsula, was the first of a trilogy of sorts about his obsession with Byzantium. *The Byzantine Achievement*, published the following year, in 1929, is a historical polemic about how the medieval Byzantine Empire, not the city-states of ancient Greece, represents the most noble legacy of Greek culture; and therefore, Gibbon's argument in *The Decline and Fall of the Roman Empire* that Byzantium embodies a degenerate historical tendency is plain wrong. In 1930, Byron published *The Birth of Western Painting* (with David Talbot Rice), which argues that Byzantine art and iconography, by way of Giotto and El Greco, played a pivotal role in the development of Western art.[10] Byron, along with Talbot Rice and English historian Steven Runciman, as well as others, pioneered the reconsideration of Byzantium as a spiritual and temporal triumph, something which, as it happens, has infused Romania's own related culture and historical experience with an especial purpose and legitimacy.[11]

At the same time that Byzantium, as Byron notes, "evolved, in painting and mosaic, a technique of color and delineation, which envisaged the experiences of the soul as none has before or since," the empire also stood for more than eleven hundred years as a "solitary bulwark" of the West against "the peoples of Asia" (in particular, against the armies of Persia and Abbasid Baghdad). Byzantium itself was, in a critical sense, Eastern, and not only by virtue of its location. As the English historian John Julius Norwich puts it, in terms of a governing mentality, whereas "the Venetians were cynics . . . [t]he Byzantines were mystics." Then there is Byron's broad description of a civilization that, in fact, recalls specifically Hagia Sophia in Constantinople: "The superstructure was Roman, and the cupola Asiatic." Even beyond the blend of West and East, we are clearly dealing here with a culture of extraordinary combinations. Byzantine art was monotonously sensuous even as it was austere, and with an irresistible splendor that "dumbfounded," revealing a civilization that encompassed at once stirring liturgies and fierce doctrinal debates over the nature of Christ and the possession of the True Cross. "As spiritual legacy," Byron is able to write, "the Byzantine intellect has left the world the definitions of the seven Ecumenical Councils, which at present form the basis of almost every variation of Christian belief."[12]

Despite the internecine wars between the various Orthodox Christian nations within southeastern Europe, "it was only by the imitation of Byzantine institutions, the assumption of Byzantine titles and the borrowing of Byzantine culture," writes Byron, "that the conscious nationalities of Bulgars, Serbs and Rumanians, were evolved and were able to withstand the extinction threatened by Turkish enslavement." Without the legacy of Byzantium, that is, Romania simply could not have survived. Byzantium's cultural power and attraction, in this regard, Ostrogorsky explains, was itself based on a "tenacious awareness of the [Roman] classical achievements" that it had been the Byzantine Empire's duty to preserve. Indeed, it was Romania's Byzantine heritage, in addition to its Latinity, that filled its late medieval and early modern *voivodes* with stores of inspiration that, in turn, fortified the obligations of religion, culture, and national or subnational group.

What could better stimulate group passion, both martial and religious, than the collective memory of the icon of the Virgin borne on a chariot through the streets of Constantinople, while the monarch himself (John II Comnenus), returning triumphant from the battlefield, walked behind it, "carrying a cross"?[13] The emperor was so powerful as to be otherworldly, and yet he was a slave to the Virgin Mary, herself made aesthetic and magical by the beauty of a painting. It is from such ceremony, and the retention of it in the mind of generations of followers, that the strength was found to repel centuries of invaders.

Byzantium's other gift to Romania was its tradition of ingenious national survival amid powerful geopolitical forces based on the Eurasian steppe, the Iranian plateau, the Mesopotamian plain, and the Danube frontier.

The scholar and security expert Edward N. Luttwak writes that "the Byzantine empire relied less on military strength and more on all forms of persuasion—to recruit allies, dissuade enemies, and induce potential enemies to attack one another." And when they did fight, Luttwak goes on, "the Byzantines were less inclined to destroy enemies than to contain them, both to conserve their strength and because they knew that today's enemy could be tomorrow's ally." Unlike Napoleon,

Clausewitz, and other military strategists to this day, the Byzantines accepted "the impossibility of decisive victory." Their strategic advantage was "psychological," according to Luttwak: "the moral reassurance of a triple identity [again, the Hellenic-Roman-Orthodox fusion] that was more intensely Christian than most modern minds can easily imagine."[14] The fact that Romania throughout much of its history has been an intensely Christian nation which has mastered the arts of survival against greater geopolitical forces, often coming from the East, cannot be divorced from this Byzantine heritage. For it was only in the latter half of the eighteenth century that Romania began moving away "from the patriarchal traditions of the Byzantine-Orthodox South-east toward the dynamic innovations of the West," begins the historian Keith Hitchins in *Rumania 1866–1947*. A hundred years on, in the latter half of the nineteenth century, Romanian politicians were still torn between conservatives who adhered to the Byzantine tradition and liberals who pined for the West (though it was the West at the time which stood for nationalism based on ethnic identity).[15]

Nor can the Romanian style of leadership on occasion be divorced from Byzantium even in the twentieth century. Here is Ostrogorsky, the Byzantinist: "Removed as it were from the earthly and human sphere, he [the emperor] stood in direct relationship to God and became the object of a special cult that was both political and religious." This cult was enacted daily in impressive pomp and ceremony, reflected in the many portraits of "the Christ-loving Emperor," in the honors bestowed on him, and so forth, all reflecting the "imperial absolutism" which defined the Byzantine system.[16] If one thinks of Marxism-Leninism as a replacement for Orthodox Christianity, then Ceauşescu's relationship to his subjects, his style of public leadership, and the nature of the political system under him are vaguely similar to those of a Byzantine emperor. Communism is itself indirectly derived from Byzantium. Remember that the conversion of Russia to Orthodox Christianity more than a millennium ago represented a religious and political victory for the Byzantine state. And Bolshevism, moreover, was an Orthodox form of Marxism, according to the early-twentieth-century Russian intellectual Nicolas Berdyaev. For it underscored "totality" and the impossibility of compromise, just as Orthodoxy did in Christianity.[17]

A dominant fact of Byzantium is, to be sure, its overwhelming religious mystery, which has enshrined the empire in indestructible memory, even as it has provided believers with reserves of spiritual sustenance against the constant blows of fate. The Romanians were invaded, and invaded again, and plundered and ground down as a nation—as I had witnessed firsthand during the Cold War—and their communal survival through it all was due, in some measure, to the legacy of Byzantium as transmitted through their own Orthodox Church. The miseries I witnessed in 1980s Bucharest will at some point fade away; Byzantium never will.

But how hard it must have been in those final imperial centuries to persevere! Michael Psellus, an advisor to successive Byzantine emperors, is already conscious of the process of decline in his eleventh-century *Chronographia:* "neither Athens, nor Nicomedia, nor . . . the two Romes," he writes, "glories any longer in literary achievement. The golden streams of the past, and baser silver, and streams of metal more worthless still, all are blocked and choked up. . . ."[18]

And there are, of course, the haunting notes of the turn-of-the-twentieth-century Greek from Alexandria C. P. Cavafy, the great poet of cultures and empires in decline, and of the very method of memory itself. In one poem, Cavafy writes of Theophilos Palaiologos, a kinsman of Constantine XI Palaiologos, the last emperor of Byzantium when it finally fell to the Ottoman Turks in 1453. "I would rather die than live," Theophilos says as Constantinople is besieged. Cavafy writes:

> *how much of the pathos, the yearning of our race,*
> *how much weariness . . .*
> *your six tragic words contained.*[19]

FROM BUCHAREST I CONTINUED to drive northeast through central Wallachia, or Muntenia, as it appears on some maps. After a few hours, the monumental flatness ended with a slight heaving of the earth: an occasional broad, rolling hill signaled what English speakers have called Moldavia, and what the inhabitants themselves have called Moldova. I will take the liberty to stick with the name Moldavia when referring to eastern Romania, since it carries the benefit of not confusing this region with the separate independent state of Moldova, a former Soviet republic, lying alongside Romania's eastern border.

The road was good, with spanking-new gas stations, minimarts, modern light industry, and much construction. Wind farms and the latest center-pivots for irrigation competed with the ancient horse carts or *leiterwagens* for my attention. Even this, the poorest region of Romania, was in the midst of change and development. Instead of the monotony of corn and cereal fields, there were now, too, wineries, apiaries, and animal husbandry. Metal Russian-like onion domes glinted through the last of the late-morning fog. The poplars had thinning manes of late autumnal gold. Mistletoes, a parasite actually, hung from mature tree branches. Elsewhere, rows of young black locusts had been planted. Then, surprise after surprise, with each turn yielding another vast panorama of cultivation rising steeply off valley floors oceanic in their dimensions.

I spotted a group of beautiful horses in the middle distance. Moldavian horses were especially valued by the Ottoman Turks, who comprised the foremost imperial element in both Moldavia and Wallachia for centuries in late medieval and early modern times. The Ottomans had blown up fortresses, leveled churches, and in a general way ravished the countryside. Having very briefly discussed Byzantium, let me now consider the Ottoman Turks, whose history, even in Romania, is more nuanced and complex than often supposed.

WHEREAS THE BYZANTINE EMPIRE generally ended at the Lower Danube (the current border for most of its length between Romania and Bulgaria), the Ottoman Turkish Empire which succeeded it, while also employing the Danube as a natural northern frontier, often ruled indirectly over Wallachia, Moldavia, Bessarabia, and Transylvania as vassal states, administered by submissive *voivodes* or ethnic-Greek Phanariots (after the Ottomans had stopped trusting the native Romanians). Moreover, Timişoara (the Temesvár of the Hungarians), in the western Romanian region of the Banat—to the southwest of Transylvania and west of Wallachia—was in direct Ottoman hands from the early sixteenth century during the reign of Suleiman the Magnificent to the early eighteenth century, when it was captured by Prince Eugene of Savoy, in service to the Habsburgs. The Ottomans also held at certain periods river ports on the northern bank of the Danube like Giurgiu and Turnu. And so while the Byzantines were fellow Orthodox Christians who culturally inspired the Romanians, and were in most instances not a direct threat to their lands, the Ottomans periodically invaded and overran Romanian territory, and perennially demanded subservience, even as they represented a hostile world religion. Romanian *voivodes* and boyars often ruled, as I said, at the pleasure of the Ottomans (even if Ottoman suzerainty was limited to the payment of a nominal tribute up through 1877).[20] And yet the Ottoman Turks were not the monochrome terrorizing beast, lacking in all cultural and political refinements, that a mythmaking Romanian historian such as Eliade might intimate.

For the Ottomans constituted nothing less than the inheritors of the Greek and Roman classical tradition, by way of the Byzantines, ruling as they did from the Second Rome, or Constantinople. (Over time, they began to refer to the place as Istanbul, a corruption of the Greek phrase *I-stin poli*, "to the city.")

The Turks had migrated westward over the course of the centuries from deep inside Central Asia, converting to Islam at the end of the tenth century as their contacts, both direct and indirect, with the Arabs intensified. By the middle of the twelfth century the Seljuk Turks established a polity in Asia Minor (Anatolia) at Konya. This Seljuk state was known by the other Muslim powers farther to the east as the "Sultanate of Rum," or Rome, because of its relative proximity to Byzantine Constantinople—seen as the "ultimate imperial prize." But Seljuk authority began to crumble during the Mongol onslaught in the mid-thirteenth century, when Asia Minor became a maelstrom of competing Turkic bands. Of the small principalities of "march warriors" that materialized out of this vortex, one led by a certain Osman gradually gained ascendancy. Osman's legitimacy increased with his defeat of a Byzantine army in 1302 near İznik (Nicaea) by the Sea of Marmara. His extended tribe would later be known to the West as Ottomans, a Latin corruption of *Osmanlis*. Ultimately, an Ottoman imperial state would emerge over roughly the same territorial expanse as the Byzantine Empire—stretching from the Balkans to the Middle East and North Africa: *from the Danube to the Euphrates*, as it were, at the height of its power. In the words of historian Bernard Lewis, this new empire would contain "echoes of Islamic jurisprudence, Greek philosophy, and Persian statecraft."[21]

If this sounds comparable to the fusion of ancient Greek, Latin, and Orthodox Christianity achieved by the Byzantine state, it is. The Muslim army of Mehmet II ("the Conqueror") that toppled Byzantine Constantinople on May 29, 1453, after a fifty-seven-day siege did not extinguish the Byzantine Christian tradition, but rather transformed and invigorated it, helped along by Greeks, Albanians, and Slavs in its service. Like the Byzantine imperium, the Ottoman sultanate was a "government by God," albeit Muslim instead of Orthodox Christian. The new Ottoman palace in Constantinople—the Topkapı Seraglio— would symbolically be built atop the old Byzantine Acropolis, thus representing continuity rather than a break in the historical tradition. For the Ottoman Empire, rather than merely a rampaging host, also represented an extraordinarily cosmopolitan civilization. The late University of Chicago historian Halil İnalcik calls it a "true 'Frontier Empire' . . . treating all creeds and races as one." Mehmet II, who conquered Constantinople while still in his early twenties, had grown up speaking six languages: Turkish, Greek, Arabic, Persian, Hebrew, and Latin. Mehmet consciously modeled himself as the civilized heir to Roman and Byzantine emperors, inviting the Italian Renaissance painter Gentile Bellini to Constantinople in order to paint his portrait. Ottoman soldiers and administrators hailed from the western Balkans, Poland, and Ukraine; the harem at Topkapı numbered women from Greece, Russia, and Circassia: the Ottoman system provided the possibility of rapid social advancement for those taken initially by force away from their families, however obscure their origins. As the historian Arnold J. Toynbee puts it, the Ottomans "served a positive political purpose by providing the Orthodox Christian World with the universal state which it was unable to achieve for itself."[22]

It is Lord Kinross—the Scotsman John Patrick Douglas Balfour—in a classic book dedicated to the English travel writer Freya Stark, who provides the most memorable summary of this imperial history. In *The Ottoman Centuries: The Rise and Fall of the Turkish Empire*, published in 1977, a year after his death, Kinross observed that the crucial result of Mehmet's conquest was the replacement of a weak, near-death, and decentralized Byzantine state with a vigorous and centralized one. The Ottomans "had everything to gain" from the "hatred" of the Orthodox Christians of the Balkans for the Roman Catholic Church in the West, and for the "hatreds" between the Serb, Bulgarian, Greek, and Romanian Orthodox themselves. "It meant that each race . . . was disposed to prefer Ottoman rule to that of its neighbors—and above all to that of the [Catholic] Hungarians."[23] Thus, to say that the Romanians constituted the Western and Christian fortress against the Muslim menace, as traditional Romanian historiography (particularly that of Eliade) often put it, is far too simplistic. The Ottomans were, at least to some degree, a balancing force against Romania's immediate neighbors. The Turks, especially in the eighteenth century, integrated Romania not only into an Oriental Anatolian world, but more specifically into the wider Orthodox world of the Balkans. For example, Greek, not Turkish, became the language of high culture in Wallachia and Moldavia, as the principalities were under the direct rule of the Ottomans by way of the Greek Phanariots.[24]

The Turks crafted a system of *millets*, or self-governing religious communities under a patriarch or other leader, responsible, in turn, to the central Ottoman authority. Within Istanbul's walls resided not only the Islamic authority, but also the Greek and Armenian patriarchs and the Jewish chief rabbi. Lord Kinross calls the state of affairs a "Pax Ottomanica."[25] Because this system worked so well for centuries, it would be the drawn-out decline and eventual breakup of the Ottoman Empire following World War I that would ignite so many ethnic, religious, and national conflicts in the Balkans and the Middle East. The Middle East, in particular, in the early twenty-first century is still unable to find a solution to the demise of the Ottoman Empire.

Of course, the cruelties of these Ottomans are almost beyond imagining. The stability of the dynasty was assured by the edict of fratricide—the younger brothers of the new sovereign strangled with a silken bowstring—which continued for about a century and a half after the conquest of Constantinople. The hideous practice of castration, which existed for a time for the sake of maintaining a palace corps of eunuchs, was inherited from the Byzantines. Victories over the Catholic Hungarians sometimes resulted in mass beheadings (ten thousand supposedly in one case) of the defeated army. Lord Kinross writes of the Ottoman retreat from Central Europe: "The Turkish troops set fire to their camp, massacring or burning alive all their prisoners from the Austrian countryside, except those, of both sexes, young enough to qualify for the slave market."[26] This Ottoman military machine was supported by an elite force of Janissaries (*Yeniçeri*, or "new soldiers"), which consisted of Christians in the defeated nations taken away from their parents at a tender age and forcibly enslaved and converted to Islam. The Janissaries fought, as Gibbon put it, "with the zeal of proselytes against their *idolatrous* countrymen."[27]

This at times cruel and hardy Ottoman soldiery was in the end limited by the fact that it, in Lord Kinross's words, was "essentially a summer force," whose horses could not survive the harsh winters of Central Europe.[28] The sultan's military aggressions had the character of nomadic seasonal wanderings: an inheritance of the Turkic past. Despite the urbanity of Constantinople, the empire was in another sense a "vast encampment," nearly continuously at war, in the words of the scholar Paul Coles.[29] This may be partially why, while capturing Buda and Pest in 1526, they failed to take farther afield Vienna in 1529, and had to retreat through the Balkans all the way back to Constantinople.

Perhaps worse than the premeditated cruelty was the anarchy unleashed in the fringes of the Turkish Empire. The Ottoman Porte would cede authority to local warlords, or *ayans*, whose own military forces the Porte would often play against each other. The result was that, especially toward the end of the eighteenth century, the inhabitants of the Wallachian countryside were for long periods terrorized by bandits and rebellious Janissaries.[30] The weaker the Ottoman Empire got in its later centuries, in a way the more dangerous it became.

The cardinal fact about the Ottoman Empire for a place like Romania was that the economic heart of the Porte's rule was here in the Balkans, not in central Anatolia, the Levant, or North Africa. The Danube was a waterway of commerce, and Wallachia and Moldavia were breadbaskets. So even while the various Romanian principalities and lands were ruled only indirectly by local warlords, the Porte rarely took its eye off the area.

And yet it is important to remain aware of a pivotal fact, as the historian Keith Hitchins writes: "By recognizing the sultan as their suzerain and by paying an annual tribute, the Rumanians [often] avoided an occupation by Ottoman armies and the Islamization to which the South Slav lands had been subjected."[31] This is primarily why when Romanians gaze across the Danube at Bulgaria to the south and Serbia to the southwest they see *the East*.

I STOPPED OFTEN ON the road. Focşani, owing to its position near the border of Wallachia and Moldavia, was briefly considered as a capital of the new Romanian state after Alexandru Ioan Cuza had united the two principalities between 1859 and 1861 (later to be known as the Regat). Now Focşani was a typical small town of the new Moldavian countryside: its historic buildings renovated, neat beds of flowers planted along the central square, masses of cars everywhere, and a rash of construction and new signage. New bridges and malls were making this muscular landscape less lonely and haunted, even as fires raged in the fields, deliberately set by farmers in order to clean the earth.

Ceaușescu's Communism officially collapsed in the last weeks of 1989, and when I had traveled extensively throughout the Romanian countryside only four months later in April 1990 to do research for *Balkan Ghosts,* I witnessed a landscape of human and material devastation that had been accumulating for forty-two years. Even in the late 1990s, much of this countryside was still an economic disaster zone, with only a few major cities pulsating with life. In Romania a form of neo-Communism had followed Communism and so it wasn't until almost 2000 that real reforms started to happen. But now in 2013 it was almost a quarter century since Ceaușescu had fallen, and much of the bleakness I had seen on previous visits was dissolving like the dawn fog.

I walked into a bar cum coffee shop near the central square in Focșani. It was Sunday and every table was packed with young people. The air was filthy with cigarette smoke and incomprehensible music blasted. Most of the customers had smartphones. The women were fashionably dressed with expensive hairstyles and were sipping exotic fruit concoctions. The men, who mostly looked like slobs, were the smokers, sipping coffee or simple alcoholic drinks. Actually, the crowd was not dissimilar to young people everywhere. The clothes, hairstyles, and smartphones, not to mention the cigarettes, indicated some disposable wealth, even if the women, for instance, were making stringent economic sacrifices for the sake of their appearances, a phenomenon especially common in the former Soviet Bloc and the Mediterranean. This whole scene might have suggested a low-grade cosmopolitanism, but it was a form of cosmopolitanism, nonetheless. Ceaușescu had encouraged a kind of debased, lumpen folkishness, with archaic, polluting factories destroying the landscape and the government television channels dominated by peasant dance groups. It was a world that, by the looks of this bar deep in the countryside, had been completely eviscerated. There was a big display of Western newspaper mastheads near the entrance. Even if no one here could read them, the display indicated an aspiration toward life beyond Romania's borders.

I continued northeast to the town of Bârlad, where I would spend the night in one of the handful of new boutique hotels that had lately sprung up. I had a deep and abiding interest in this town. But first there was this surprise: the Museum Vasile Pârvan, a vast treasure-house of art exhibited in the most loving, meticulous displays: the requisite Roman-era artifacts, Oltenian rugs, and Byzantine icons, of course, along with such fine objects as Delft porcelain, gleaming nineteenth-century Biedermeier desks and cabinets, and Oriental silk-screens. The museum, starved of all funds during the Communist decades, was kept together by a small and dedicated staff as an act of aesthetic resistance, and was now flourishing. Beyond the neoclassical museum building I saw a town center still in the act of definition, with dazzling flower beds, new traffic signals, one or two little baroque gems, and the odd two- or three-story Plexiglas structure, as well as many empty derelict spaces. The old people, like elsewhere in Wallachia and Moldavia, bore intimations of Ottoman Turkey in their dress; the young, as in Focşani, looked like hipsters everywhere. But it was the area a bit beyond the center with which I was particularly interested.

For beyond the small center Bârlad was merely a big, overgrown village, into which you stepped back decades. After many inquiries, I finally found Griviței and Hotin streets. Here I found something between a bleak, provincial Russia, as expressed in the pages of Dostoevsky and Gogol, and the pseudomodernity of a Turkish *gecekondu*, which translates literally as a "built-in-the-night" shantytown that can serve as a way station en route to the lower middle class. Stray dogs and chickens proliferated in streets and alleys running with mud. There was the anarchy of rusted corrugated iron, crude breeze blocks, and rotting wooden planks; hastily constructed outhouses stood alongside brave attempts at pergolas. Low, nearby hills revealed more such architectural chaos. I saw a single evidence of Old World civilization: a small stone structure with a neoclassical façade that had been chipped and smashed up and was now covered in rusted wire mesh.

It was somewhere on these neither-nor streets of a town that was really a sprawling village where Gheorghe Gheorghiu-Dej—Romania's first Communist dictator, who had smashed utterly a society and particularly its bourgeois elements—had grown up in the first decades of the twentieth century. The exact house or houses associated with his past were somewhat of a mystery, as Ceaușescu, after he had assumed power, removed all remnants of his predecessor and benefactor here. History had been erased rather than properly remembered: nobody in the area mentioned or claimed any knowledge of Gheorghiu-Dej.

Clearly, the semi-urban landscape just beyond the center of Bârlad had undergone repeated metamorphoses in the course of a century and much more. For example, Cuza himself, the first modern ruler of the United Principalities (whom I will deal with later in this book), had come from Bârlad. But Cuza was of a wealthy and cultured boyar family and was educated in Jassy and Paris. Bârlad itself was historically a crude backwater. Walking these streets I had the sense that Gheorghiu-Dej was a man who had come from nowhere—from no real articulated cultural tradition—and whose legacy was to reduce a whole country to the nothing that he himself was.

Let me explain.

AS TRAGIC AS ROMANIAN HISTORY has been, the Communist epoch raised suffering to an unprecedented level.

The end of World War II had given Romania little or no respite. From early 1944, the Western Allies recognized that the war inside Romania and the peace that followed, therefore, was "Russia's business." In October 1944, British prime minister Winston Churchill conceded to Soviet party chief Joseph Stalin a "90 percent" interest in Romania. By early 1946, the Red Army "quartered ... between 600,000 and 900,000 men" in the country. "This bleak state of affairs was primarily the consequence of geography," writes British historian

Hugh Thomas in *Armed Truce: The Beginnings of the Cold War 1945–1946*. "A place between two totalitarian empires, the German Nazi one and the Soviet Russian, is unenviable."[32] The humanitarian consequence of such geography during the early phases of the Cold War was simply appalling.

The late New York University historian Tony Judt tells us in *Postwar: A History of Europe Since 1945* that Romania "saw perhaps the worst persecution, certainly the most enduring" in the emerging East Bloc. He cites the example of the Danube–Black Sea Canal project in the Dobrudja, where prison and slave labor numbered in the tens of thousands, of whom "thousands died and whose numbers don't include those deported to the Soviet Union." Moreover, "physical and psychological torture" was rife in various "experimental" prisons.[33]

The story of Romanian Communism and its two guiding lights, Gheorghe Gheorghiu-Dej and Nicolae Ceauşescu—arguably two of the most ruthless men in the history of the second half of the twentieth century—is neatly documented in Dennis Deletant's *Romania Under Communist Rule*, a book I had read just before embarking on my journey through Wallachia and Moldavia in the autumn of 2013. The dry, academic style of the author, a professor at the University of London's School of Slavonic and East European Studies and more recently at Georgetown, makes the subject matter that much more powerful—and chilling.

Indeed, the Communists had to be particularly pitiless precisely because Romania, as we know from the history of its intellectual life through the 1930s, was a culture in which the right exerted greater influence than the left. Idealism, an emotion which the Communists were traditionally expert at manipulating, had been the particular province of the Romanian right during the interwar years. Moreover, Romania, a predominantly agricultural country, lacked much of an indigenous working class out of which the Communists could form a base. Thus cruelty was a method used to overcome a weak starting position. It was a starting position made more tenuous by the fact that, in the first half of the twentieth century, Romania had occupied what was considered Hungarian, Bulgarian, and Russian territory. This made neighboring Communist parties doubly suspicious of their Romanian colleagues, who, consequently, were under even more pressure to prove themselves.[34]

This was all prologue to the life of Gheorghe Gheorghiu, born in Bârlad in Moldavia in 1901. At eleven, he was sent to work as a porter in the gritty Danube port of Galați, before taking jobs in timber and textile mills, and then as an electrician in a railway yard. Military service as a sergeant came next. As Deletant lays out the numbing details, what emerges is a coarse lesson in youthful survival in backbreaking and filthy jobs, an existence alien to that of the bourgeois, toward which young Gheorghiu naturally developed an utter lack of understanding and compassion. He would soon inculcate in his very person the essence of class resentment and hatred. It was accusations of "Communist agitation" that led Gheorghiu in 1931 to be transferred from the railway yards at Galați to those at Dej (in Transylvania), which afterward became the suffix attached to his name in Communist lore. We next see him at a mass meeting of railway workers in Bucharest in 1932 where he is elected to the Central Action Committee. The following year there are violent clashes between the railway workers and the regime of King Carol II, by which time Gheorghiu-Dej is in prison, sentenced to twelve years of hard labor.[35]

In 1936, Gheorghiu-Dej and other Communists were thrown together at the Doftana prison in Câmpina, in northern Wallachia, near the foothills of the Carpathians. Here, between 1936 and 1938, Gheorghiu-Dej bonded with the young agitator Nicolae Ceaușescu, barely twenty years old at the time. In Doftana, the prisoners "were allowed visitors, food parcels, money, and reading materials." More crucially, letters were smuggled inside. This permitted Gheorghiu-Dej to be in contact with other members of the Romanian Communist Party Central Committee, to which he was elevated in absentia. Gheorghiu-Dej was clearly a leader who, writes Deletant, "cultivated an avuncular image, being addressed as 'the old man'" even though he was only in his mid-thirties. He was the quintessential Communist that one associates with Party myth: a rough-and-tumble blue-collar worker, certainly not one of the Romanian intellectuals who had studied at the Comintern school in Moscow. Indeed, Doftana prison would turn out to be a proving ground for the homegrown, *national* Romanian Communists who would later decimate the so-called *Moscow* Communists—those who had lived outside Romania in the interwar period and World War II. (Gheorghiu-Dej, for example, lived in various prisons during World War II, including Târgu Jiu in Oltenia, where he met up again with Ceaușescu, Chivu Stoica, and Gheorghe Maurer—the latter two of whom would later hold high positions in both the Gheorghiu-Dej and Ceaușescu regimes.)[36]

Gheorghiu-Dej took power in Romania at the end of 1947, upon the forced abdication of King Michael (King Carol II's son) and the declaration of the Romanian People's Republic. The previous three years after the end of World War II had witnessed a cynical charade of convoluted political transformations in which the West pretended to care about Romania's future and the Soviet Union pretended to be merely following the dictates of the population, even as the Kremlin was, register by register, working toward a totalitarian outcome. Churchill had been optimistic in expecting that Stalin would be satisfied with 90 percent of Romania's destiny: Stalin got it all. Gheorghiu-Dej, the avuncular railway yard worker, would be the skull-crusher.

A single, mass Communist Party movement soon replaced the traditional interwar and postwar political parties, tainted as they were by democratic and traditional values. The new mass party refused members of the "former exploiting classes," as the mass party became a vehicle for implementing Stalinism across the board in industry, agriculture, banking, mining, and transport. The Party soon abolished private landholdings. "This permitted the liquidation of the remnants of the old landowning class and of the 'kulaks,'" writes Deletant, a reference to anyone who used hired labor or lent out equipment, regardless of the size of his property. Peasants were organized into massive collective farms. Total censorship of newspapers, books, and the arts reigned. The Greek Catholic or Uniate Church, with its links to the West and to the pope, was forcibly merged with the Orthodox Church, as the latter came under the control of the regime and the new Securitate. By the early 1950s, hundreds of thousands of Romanians were incarcerated in forced labor camps for political reasons. By the early 1960s, a network of camps was established in the Danube Delta where tens of thousands of prisoners were made to work waist-deep in water cutting reeds, with specially trained dogs nearby to bite them if they faltered.[37] Such small details illustrate the magnitude of the human disaster more than do the statistics.

Thus were centuries of history, national life, and cultural traditions ground up into dust within a little more than a decade, something Gheorghiu-Dej deemed necessary in order to eliminate rightward tendencies in Romanian society. The only way for an ordinary Romanian to survive under Gheorghiu-Dej was, as the saying went, to *keep your mouth shut.*

From the beginning of Gheorghiu-Dej's rule, an unoriginal brutality was the key ingredient. In 1946, Communist Party general secretary Ştefan Foriş, an ethnic Hungarian who had long run afoul of Gheorghiu-Dej, "was battered to death with an iron bar in the Communist Party headquarters." Foriş's mother was then murdered, and her body weighted with stones and dumped into the Criş River in Transylvania.[38] Like Stalin's murder of the czar's family in 1918, and the murder-mutilation of Iraqi prime minister Nuri Said in 1958 (which ushered in nearly half a century of military dictatorship in Baghdad), Foriş's killing signaled the dawn of an utterly remorseless era.

Foriş's demise was part of an ideological and factional purge within Romania's Communist ranks that culminated in 1953 with the arrest of Ana Pauker, Gheorghiu-Dej's foreign minister from 1947 to 1952. Pauker, from an orthodox Jewish family in Moldavia, was a fellow Stalinist who headed the Romanian Communist Party's Muscovite faction, as she had spent World War II in Moscow. With Pauker's arrest, Gheorghiu-Dej's victory over the Moscow wing, with its cosmopolitan aura, was total, though it must be said that Gheorghiu-Dej's own *national* faction included Jews and ethnic Hungarians. The intricacies of such factional struggles were rarely clear-cut, and often involved the most personal of motives. Because of Stalin's death and subsequent pressure from Moscow that resulted in a measured reduction of intraparty violence, Pauker was not executed, and lived the remainder of her life in seclusion in Bucharest.

By strengthening internal security controls—in other words turning Romania into a complete secret police state—and by acting as Moscow's most trusted ally while the Soviets brutally suppressed the Hungarian uprising in 1956, Gheorghiu-Dej was able to survive Khrushchev's de-Stalinization while remaining at heart a Stalinist. The Soviets rewarded Romania for its support against Hungary by withdrawing all of their troops from Romania in 1958. But given the fact that Romania was flanked on most sides by loyal Soviet allies and by the Soviet Union itself, this was much less of a risk for the Kremlin than supposed. Gheorghiu-Dej thus established a pattern that his successor, Nicolae Ceaușescu, would demonstrably exploit: Romania would be Stalinist in ideology, totalitarian in its levels of repression, and nationalist in its appeal to the emotions of its population. (It is no irony that Ceaușescu, according to the historian Vlad Georgescu, "was secretly obsessed with the ultranationalistic Iron Guard . . . while believing passionately in orthodox Stalinism."[39])

Gheorghiu-Dej died on March 19, 1965, still the Party leader and dictator therefore. Three days later Ceaușescu became first secretary of the Romanian Communist Party. Ceaușescu was the third of ten children, born in 1918 to a peasant family in Oltenia, among the most backward of Romanian regions. Like Gheorghiu-Dej, he left home for manual labor at the age of eleven, becoming a cobbler. But to perhaps an even greater extent than Gheorghiu-Dej, Ceaușescu represented the lumpen urban peasantry, the scholar Florin Platon told me recently. As a teenager, Ceaușescu joined the Communist Party and was jailed four times in the 1930s. He rose in the Party ranks and was captured by the authorities in 1940, after having been convicted in absentia: very much the biography of Gheorghiu-Dej. Ceaușescu, too, was an unusually skilled leader in his own right, regardless of the somewhat pathetic figure he cut in old age on the brink of his execution.

But whereas Gheorghiu-Dej supported the Soviet invasion of Hungary, Ceaușescu, only three years into his rule, opposed the 1968 Soviet invasion of Czechoslovakia. Ceaușescu's seemingly brave stand on Czechoslovakia was rooted not only in his fear that Romania could face a similar fate at the hands of the Soviets, but in his requirement for social control by an appeal to nationalist sentiment. The acclamation at home that greeted his denunciation of the Kremlin's move "left an indelible mark upon him," writes Deletant, "and whetted his appetite for the excesses of the personality cult."[40]

Ceaușescu's 1971 visits to China under Mao Zedong and North Korea under Kim Il Sung constituted a turning point. Rather than being repelled at those two totalitarian systems, Ceaușescu and his increasingly powerful wife, Elena, were suddenly envious of the mass mobilization and perfectly choreographed pageants in celebration of the tyrant that characterized Mao's and Kim's leadership style. The Ceaușescus henceforth embarked on a methodical plan to turn Romania into an Eastern European version of North Korea. A key feature of this plan was *systematization*, a crackpot scheme to reduce the number of Romania's villages by half by the year 2000, requiring the destruction of thousands of them. The map of Romania itself would be emptied of names, and replaced with spreading rashes of work camps and industrial and agricultural combines. Though systematization was only in its early stages by the time the Ceaușescus were executed in 1989, the very concept embodied much of the dehumanizing and maniacal aspects of their Stalinist ideology.

This all went hand in glove with their national fascism, as exemplified by Ceaușescu's 1984 call to the female Romanian populace: "breed, comrade women, it is your patriotic duty." Women of childbearing age were subject to regular examinations to make sure they were not using contraceptives, and childless couples were made to pay punitive taxes. It is estimated that more than ten thousand women died from unsafe and illegal abortions because of those directives.[41]

All of this occurred while the Ceauşescus were directing the construction of their veritable Stalinist-cum-Thousand-Year-Reich City of the Dead in the heart of Bucharest. *Bigger, bigger,* the Ceauşescus kept demanding of the architects in the mid and late 1980s, regarding the Pentagon-size house where they expected to live, and which they were never to live in.

I CONSIDERED THE TOWN of Scorniceşti worse than Bârlad. Here there was no museum that had salvaged a beautiful tradition from a ravaged past; no new street lighting, or new and restored buildings. There were only weather-stained cement walls, scrap iron structures, and barracks-style apartment blocks patrolled by goats and stray dogs on a dreary, bumpy plain in Oltenia: a dirty, unkempt, deserted world of weeds and rust and potholes. The soccer stadium looked like a ruin from antiquity. I was in Nicolae Ceauşescu's hometown.

In one yard, I spotted a large white statue of Ceauşescu that looked like a cheap, mass-produced suburban lawn sculpture. It was the house of Emil Bărbulescu, Ceauşescu's nephew. He maintained the property as a private tribute to his late dictator uncle, who had been executed nearly a quarter century before. The middle-aged Bărbulescu, in old jeans and a cheap blue sports jacket, walked up to me with a limp and spoke in a gravelly voice. Despite the limp, there was a certain stocky and wiry toughness about him, indicating an agile and perhaps mean aggression. His small, shifting eyes and feeble, pasty features provided a vague resemblance to Ceauşescu in his later years.

Bărbulescu took me inside a small house on the property: a typical, folkloric peasant dwelling, with a handsome wooden roof and a whitewashed façade renovated in the 1970s. It was beautiful, and out of place in the general surroundings. Inside there were traditional weavings and rugs beside an old Oltenian stove that provided heat on both sides of a wall. Handsome wooden beams dominated the ceiling. The place was caked with dust. Bărbulescu pointed to an ancient black-and-white picture that evoked a daguerreotype, with the words "Maria and Andrei" above it. The photo showed a woman with a traditional scarf and a man with a fur cap, their dress heartrendingly evocative of Turkish Anatolia. The couple was crooked with age, wearing startled expressions, for this was a time long past, when the act of photography itself was an amazement. "The late president's grandparents," he told me. Bărbulescu would refer to Ceaușescu often as the "late president," for as he explained to me, the title of president began with Ceaușescu, since Gheorghiu-Dej was only general secretary of the Communist Party and before that there had been kings. He pointed to another photo, "Alexandrina and Andruță," Ceaușescu's parents: the poorest of peasants, they seemed.

He pointed out a large and naïve painting of Ceaușescu's first arrest at the age of thirteen. The future dictator would spend years in prison with the likes of Gheorghiu-Dej, I was told. It was a heroic life, according to the hagiography which Bărbulescu maintained. One photograph especially fascinated me: a clear facial shot of Ceaușescu taken in 1950 or 1951, when Ceaușescu had been in his early thirties. In the years leading up to Ceaușescu's downfall, and particularly afterward, the tyrant had appeared to the world as merely old, pathetic, and out of touch. But Ceaușescu was seriously ill by then. In this photo, the mystery of how he had risen from the lumpen peasantry to the heights of power in a Communist state was solved. It was a photo of a young, tough, commanding, and almost charismatic leader, with strong features, handsome and formidable in his way.

I was taken to a larger house next door, still on the property, also deliberately decorated in the folkloric manner. Bărbulescu had laid out pretzels, mineral water, and soft drinks for me. It was a gray day and he did not turn on the light in the house. We talked in the semidarkness.

Bărbulescu had been the Securitate commander in Oltenia during his uncle's reign, and so he saw Ceaușescu often, whenever the tyrant came here to hunt. "The former president was always polite, never angry, often sad. He always looked worried, preoccupied. He could not live in the moment." Truly, the tyrant knows that all men are his enemies, and thus he must try if possible to satisfy the needs of those around him, or else increase the risk of a horrible fate.[42] Ceauşescu was indeed a lonely man—but he was not stupid. He was wise enough to always worry.

Bărbulescu told me a story.

Ceauşescu had asked one of his ministers how many tons of cereal there was in the national reserve. The minister said 30 million tons. Ceauşescu replied: "I'm not stupid. I'm a peasant. If you tell me you have thirty million tons, it means that you have only sixteen million tons." Then Bărbulescu explained: "In fact, my father, who worked in the ministry, told me that there were only eight million tons. When my father tried to tell the truth to Elena [Ceauşescu], she got so angry that she nearly threw a bottle of mineral water in his face."

While Ceauşescu had the wisdom to know how precarious is the position of the tyrant, in his last years he was not in charge, Bărbulescu confirmed. Ceauşescu's wife, Elena, was. And Bărbulescu confirmed the opinion of many others that Elena Ceauşescu was "violent, always angry, and yet naïve." Bărbulescu said: "It was not a problem to occasionally tell Ceauşescu the truth. But it was not a good idea to tell Elena the truth. And in the last years, she was always with him."

Then Bărbulescu spoke of the 1989 revolution. In his mind it was not a revolution at all, but a Soviet coup d'état. "There were thirty thousand Russian agents in the country. [Mikhail] Gorbachev was an agent of the CIA." This was nonsense—or an utter exaggeration at best. It may be true that throughout much of the Cold War, the Soviet intelligence establishment harbored a deep distrust of their ostensible Romanian comrades, owing not only to Ceauşescu's relatively independent foreign policy, but also to the potentially destabilizing population of ethnic Romanians in next-door Soviet Moldova.[43] Moreover, the Russians were instrumental in helping to encourage the more liberal Communists who took power upon Ceauşescu's downfall. But the uprising was at the end of the day, despite all of these factors, by and large a popular event.

Bărbulescu went on:

The country had done "very badly" since 1989. "We have lost our dignity, and as a military man I am concerned with dignity and honor. We have been brought low on our knees. Romania was a real country during much of the Ceaușescu era, with good relations with both China and the United States" despite Romania's membership in the Warsaw Pact. "A powerful Russia is never good for Romania. Russia will try to impose itself again. Ceaușescu did his best to maneuver from a weak geographical position. Who knows what Ceaușescu might have achieved had he stayed in power! Look at all the apartment buildings he put up! Though, freedom of speech and movement is a big plus now, I admit."

As self-serving and delusional as his sermon was, Bărbulescu's fear of Russia constituted, nevertheless, a common thread throughout Romanian history: Ceaușescu's determination to wrest a bit of freedom from the Kremlin by playing off great powers represented, in fact, the tradition of Romanian *voivodes*, kings, and dictators going back centuries.

"This house where we are sitting—where he would come to visit and hunt—was always the former president's real home: not the great big House of the People in Bucharest where he never lived." And in a sense what Bărbulescu said was true. Ceaușescu was a peasant to the end. And at the end he was very ill, so his fate was in the hands of another vindictive peasant, who was not nearly as shrewd: his wife.

A FEW DAYS LATER I was inside the protocol offices of Ceaușescu's summer residence on the Black Sea, at Neptune (the Communists gave such idiotic names to their make-believe resorts). A former member of Ceaușescu's diplomatic detail let me inside. The house was a vast square, surrounding a courtyard where there had been a fishpond. Beyond the building on all sides, seen through bulletproof glass, was a forest of birch, oak, and pines. The spacious hallways gave onto meeting and banquet rooms. Despite the carpets (made during the Ceaușescu era) and wall fixtures of recent years—current Romanian presidents occasionally used the facility—a close inspection indicated how both tasteless and expensive the construction was: with hard angles and inferior stone. Ceaușescu's office was maintained somewhat as it was, with a desk too large to be at all credible. Beside it was a table with the complete works of Lenin, Marx, and Engels. In an adjoining room the tyrant had met with Arafat, Nixon, and other world leaders. Nothing builds tension, I have found, more than grandiose isolation: a place where you are forcibly enclosed amid luxury and pristine scenery in order to debate, receive orders, and take important decisions. I could imagine the suffocation, the proverbial elephant bearing down on your chest. I had been to Camp David once: Camp David, with its simple and tasteful small cabins made of wood actually reduces stress, however stressful the meetings there are. This place, however, emanated frightening power. Ceaușescu had built this retreat in 1967, two years after becoming general secretary of the Party—not for him the resort of Gheorghiu-Dej next door with its swimming pool, bowling alley, and other amusements. Ceaușescu, the utterly ambitious and barely educated workaholic, needed a place for serious business. And yet really, how different was this place from the summer retreats of other autocrats? Not very. It wasn't completely out of proportion—like the Pentagon-size House of the Republic in Bucharest. This retreat was still *him*; the House of the Republic built in his last years in power was *her*.

ALEKSANDR SOLZHENITSYN WRITES THAT nations who worship youth are doomed, while those with ancestor cults last for ages.[44] In Romania, I especially valued the old people. They had real stories to tell. They had actually experienced the past, and were usually, therefore, not afflicted by false nostalgia for it like so many young people (even if a former regime and family crony like Bărbulescu was an exception).

Thus, I found myself in a traditional home in the Muntenian countryside near Bucharest (often there was no geographical direction to my travels, swiveling and crisscrossing the landscape as I did by train and automobile). It was an evening of țuică, cold cuts, roast pork, homemade wine, and Turkish baklava. Albums of black-and-white family photos were proudly displayed while Romanian music—a mixture of classical and folk melodies—played in the background. The woman had a smile that triumphed over decades of worry and despair; the man wore an iron-willed gaze, clouded nevertheless by difficult memories.

He remembered a small boy, himself, placed between two plow horses by his peasant grandfather in eastern Muntenia. He never forgot how he laughed and how happy he was then. But one day the Communists came—the early Gheorghiu-Dej period, it was. They said matter-of-factly that the peasants had to hand over all their tools to the collective. "My grandfather cried as they took his tools away. They were his tools, his most prized possessions, the objects that most defined him and that he had collected over the decades, that he had taken care to keep in a certain order. For a peasant, his tools are everything."

He added: "Gheorghiu-Dej was characterized by sheer brutality which crushed the population. Then Ceaușescu provided the North Korean element." Such analysis was unnecessary, though. It was the relatively commonplace image—merely an aside—of a once-happy boy watching his grandfather humiliated that revealed the true depth of what happened, making the much greater horrors, with all of their immense scale, suddenly and vividly imaginable.

"YOU HAVE TO UNDERSTAND," Ion Iliescu, Romania's former president, told me, "Ceaușescu was a very limited person, he had only a primary school education." And so over time, as he established himself in power, Ceaușescu "promoted only the most obedient" Communists: never those who were likely to disagree with himself and his wife. This set the stage for the 1980s, when the regime reduced the entire population to sheer "degradation." In December 1989, after the

Ceauşescus had ordered troops and police to fire on protesters in Timişoara and Bucharest, "the popular decision was made to execute them." There was "no question" about it, Iliescu told me about his own role in the decision.[45]

Iliescu, a reformist Communist (to the extent that any existed during the Ceauşescu era), had served as president from 1990 to 1996, and again from 2000 to 2004. The long tenure made him the most important historical figure in post–Cold War Romania as of this writing. Iliescu's backpedaling and repeated postponement of institutional reforms during his first stint as president has caused him to be attacked within Romania for keeping the country backward at a time when other former Warsaw Pact states in Central Europe charged ahead economically, in the heady years following the collapse of the Berlin Wall. Under Iliescu, Romania, in the first half of the 1990s, did not so much become a capitalist state as a liberal Gorbachevian Communist state, after having been a Stalinist state for decades—especially since the Ceauşescus' visit to North Korea. This all followed from the reported help that Mikhail Gorbachev's Soviet Union provided in the autumn of 1989 to Iliescu, the late Silviu Brucan, and other reform Communists opposed to the Ceauşescus. Because of the unrepentant Stalinism of the Ceauşescus, Romania's revolution constituted the only one in Eastern Europe that year that the Soviet Union implicitly supported. Bărbulescu had a point in this regard, even if he wildly exaggerated.

The other interpretation is that Iliescu's very go-slow approach, combined with his emphasis on regime security in the early 1990s, saved Romania from becoming a version of Yugoslavia next door, whose ethnic civil war was coterminous with Iliescu's first six years as president. Rulers often succeed less by accomplishing anything specific than by preventing even worse things from happening. Sustained violence against ethnic Hungarians in Transylvania, and indeed "general anarchy," as Iliescu told me, were distinct possibilities for a Romania that had few usable institutions, dozens of new political parties, and severe urban and rural poverty in the wake of the Ceauşescus' 1989 execution. The worse the tyranny, the worse the power vacuum that must follow. Iliescu thus saw his role as primarily holding the country together: what Romania required was less a democrat than a transition figure. Remember that the essence of enlightened conservatism according to Edmund Burke is *pacing*—that is to say, gradual change preserves society better than sudden disruption, even if such disruption has a moral basis.

Instead of Václav Havel, the Romanians in 1990 got Iliescu: a Communist Lyndon Johnson of a sort, a scheming politician who is no thinker—but also no ideologue; a man who is not particularly interesting to talk to, as I found out, a man who is full of evasions, but who understands power and what buttons to push. A philosopher-king Iliescu is not. He studied hydropower engineering in Moscow in 1949. His father was also a Communist, imprisoned along with Gheorghiu-Dej and Ceauşescu by the pro-Nazi regime in Romania during World War II. When I tried to get Iliescu to admit that the veritable Soviet occupation of Romania following World War II was arguably the worst tragedy to befall Romania in its history, he answered that "it could have been worse": Moscow, he said, would have been even more brutal had Romania not "switched sides" to fight for the Allies in the wake of the ouster of the military-fascist regime. I was doubtful. One might well argue that because Romanian troops had fought so fiercely alongside the Nazis at Stalingrad, in addition to occupying what had previously been Soviet-held Bessarabia—not to mention parts of the Soviet Union proper in Transdniestria and the Odessa region—Stalin would, in any case, not have been impressed by Romanian second thoughts toward the end of the war. In Stalin's eyes, Romania remained an enemy combatant. It was that simple. Moreover, given the sheer destruction wreaked on Romanian society by the Communists in the late 1940s and 1950s, really, how could things have been demonstrably worse for this country?

And yet Iliescu was sometimes worth listening to. At eighty-three, he was vibrant and elegant in manner and appearance: a veritable life force, younger than his years, clearly enjoying his newfound legitimacy as the working-class elder statesman, a man who had been a force against anarchy in the 1990s and a force for reform in the 2000s, when he returned as president.

Iliescu had been a little boy during the interbellum rule of Carol II. While Carol II is almost universally acknowledged to have been corrupt and, in conventional terms, immoral, with distinct authoritarian tendencies, Iliescu took pains to mention that the monarch did have a first-rate intellect. The second Carol was also a vaguely populist king whose very foibles and love affairs brought him closer to the Romanian people than Carol I—a Prussian-style cold fish, albeit the great leader who had built the Romanian state. As for Ion Antonescu, the militaristic disciplinarian who allied himself with Hitler and then began perhaps to have second thoughts after Stalingrad, Iliescu nevertheless thought that Antonescu—who had met ten times with Hitler in Germany, Austria, and East Prussia—was simply far too compromised politically to turn against the Nazis, even if he had wanted to. The actual switch in favor of the Allies had to be carried out by the successor regime. Don't take the revisionism about Antonescu seriously, Iliescu warned me.

By the late 1940s, Antonescu had already been executed and Iliescu was a young man in Moscow, which despite the totalitarian political climate of Stalin's final years, was a feast in terms of animated late-night discussions on science and culture. Iliescu clearly, even at this late date, did not want to wholly condemn the now-defunct Soviet Union.

He labeled Ceauşescu "a Stalinist who never would have been tolerated by Stalin himself" because of Ceauşescu's maverick foreign policy by the dismal standards of the East Bloc. Leonid Brezhnev, who became Soviet Party leader in 1964, "tolerated Ceauşescu though he didn't like him, because Brezhnev knew that" Ceauşescu's own Stalinism constituted insurance against Romania trying to leave the Warsaw Pact.

Was Iliescu worried about the decline of the European Union and NATO and the rise of Vladimir Putin's hydrocarbon-rich Russia? (Remember, this was still a few months before the outbreak of the Ukraine crisis, so the answer wasn't that obvious.) "No. Putin is not Stalin. He is not even Brezhnev. And Europe is not the Europe of the 1930s, or even of the 1950s. Geography may now even be a benefit to Romania," he went on, "because we are close to the Middle East and are therefore useful to the Americans."

THE TRAINS IN ROMANIA continue to take you back: to a world of iron and dust, a world of bad oily smells, of old people with shopping bags and damaged expressions, and of beggars and hawkers in rags from an earlier era that recall the freeze-frame poverty of Communism, even as budget airlines have proliferated for domestic travel here. The old infrastructure is not being improved so much as new infrastructure is overtaking it.

This time I am en route straight east from Bucharest to Constanţa. Outside my window is a perfect mathematical surface, lacking a hillock or other blemish, neatly sectioned into cereal fields; so exposed is it to the sky that an intimation of the unfathomable distances of the heavens is your reward for looking at it. Only Mesopotamia, perhaps, represents such a fecund and exposed path at the crossroads of empires. On every journey I am repeatedly heartbroken by this Wallachian landscape.

In eastern Wallachia, the west-to-east-flowing Danube abruptly turns north and splits into two main channels. I encounter the first channel at Feteşti. It is an understated and ashen-blue announcement of a new terrain, with swampy oak and beech forest on the opposite bank. The second channel soon appears, another panel of water in terrifying slow motion.

The train stopped at Cernavodă and I recalled another train journey, in November 1981. I had taken a day trip from Bucharest to observe the building of a nuclear plant here. It was a disorienting landscape of mud without paving: my memory of it is in black-and-white. Workers in light clothes despite the outside temperature, with hopeless expressions, coated in grime, had descended from their shifts to line up for stale bread and other scraps of food in the wintry chill. Body odor mixed with the scent of plum brandy. I had a hint of Gheorghiu-Dej's and Ceauşescu's gulag: the massive Danube–Black Sea Canal scheme built with the prison labor of hundreds of thousands. That was another day, barely a week after I had left Israel, when I had felt that the media was missing the story of where history was really being made.

Beyond Cernavodă, still heading east, low sculptural hills appeared, like extended limbs, alleviating the flatness: Dobrudja, Scythia Minor, roamed by various Tatar and Bulgar bands, and violated by Byzantine, Ottoman, and Russian armies. Dobrudja was once home to the Getae, a Thracian people close to the Dacians, and also to the Iranian-related Scythians. Turkish mosques with simple, rocket-shaped minarets marked the landscape along with the silver domes of Orthodox churches. Ottoman Turkey had ruled this region from 1417 to 1878, following back-and-forth direct rule by Bulgars and Byzantines.

At Constanţa I felt both the faintly lugubrious sensibility and stimulating confusion familiar from other Black Sea ports which I had visited over the decades—Varna in Bulgaria, Trabzon in Turkey, and Batumi in Georgia—places with a seedy and faded elegance, hovering on an uneasy tectonic plate of sorts between an overbearing Russia and a volatile Near East. Constanţa brought to mind Romania's relative geographical proximity to the Turkish-Arab-Persian-Afghan world and thus its geopolitical usefulness to the United States, as Iliescu had put it. Indeed, Romania had been prominent as a staging post for various American military expeditions throughout the 9/11 decade (as well as a location for CIA "black sites" or detention centers). Romanian leaders deep down did not fully trust NATO, and thus required a special security relationship with the United States for protection against Russia.

Constanţa constituted a hinge point in Romania's development. In the autumn of 2013, it was in the process of destruction, abandonment, and massive urban renewal all at once. The effect was a backdrop for a war movie, with drills and saws substituting for machine guns. Downtown streets were impassable and a thick film of dust coated everything, especially around the famous statue of the Roman poet Ovid, who was sent here (then the ancient port of Tomis) in exile in A.D. 8 by Emperor Augustus.[46] There were few places to gather and eat as much of the city center was boarded up. This was progress, though. For with significant deposits of energy offshore, a massive modern port complex, a world trade center being built, and development money from the European Union, such engineering mayhem was necessary for the sake of the reborn, pulsing city that I knew in a few years would be unrecognizable to me.

Piercing this chalky mass of a vast construction site were the minarets and scintillating silver domes of Turkish and Tatar mosques and Greek and Romanian Orthodox churches. In particular, dominating the skyline was the poured concrete grand mosque, built in Egyptian-Byzantine style, and dedicated to the Muslim community by Carol I in 1913. For Constanța was historically a cosmopolitan port city of minorities, very much a mini-Alexandria or mini-Smyrna.

For example, in 1878, when Romania received the northern Dobrudja as part of a peace settlement following the Russo-Turkish War,[47] 55 percent of the population was Turkish or Tatar, according to Gelil Eserghep, the president of the Democratic Union of Tatars in Romania. The Tatars—of which only 45,000 are left in Romania—originate from northeastern Mongolia, and descend directly from Genghis Khan through the Golden Horde. Eserghep, whom I met in Constanța one evening, had a stereotypical round dark face and vaguely Mongolian features. He regaled me about a city in the late nineteenth century—and even prior to World War II—of Greeks, Armenians, Jews, Germans, Bulgarians, and others like himself, almost all of which has been lost: the Bulgarians leaving after the population exchanges of 1940, when the southern Dobrudja reverted from Romanian to Bulgarian hands; the Germans leaving after World War II; the remnants of the Jewish community leaving throughout the Communist period; and so forth. But the urban renewal which presently made the city virtually unlivable would ultimately lead to a return of a rich, multicultural life, he predicted. It wouldn't be like a century ago, yet Constanța would certainly return part of the way in that direction.

Serin Turkoglu, a leader in the Turkish community, told me a parallel story: of how Communism had destroyed the communal life of the thirty-two thousand ethnic Turks in Dobrudja, making it a crime to teach Turkish or to publicly teach the Muslim religion; whereas now Islam and Turkish can be taught in schools several hours per week. The danger now, she said, was that precisely because Turkish culture could be so openly expressed in Constanța, the younger generation lacked the intense memory and appreciation of it that she had harbored throughout the Cold War. "They are less interested in traditions than in global culture, which offers everything and diminishes everything at the same time."

I headed south in a taxi to Mangalia, another nondescript architectural monstrosity born of nearly a half century of Communism, near the Bulgarian border by the Black Sea. There was only one lovely building in the whole town: the Esmahan Sultan Mosque, built in 1573 by a granddaughter of the Turkish sultan Suleiman the Magnificent. It is marked by a minaret and interior pillars made of finely cut stone, with a cobbled roof and intricately worked wood, and decorated with spotless ruby carpets. Surrounding the edifice was a poignantly overgrown Turkish cemetery. The entire structure had been renovated just a few years before. It was not big or dramatic, but perfect in its way. A group of about twenty men speaking Turkish gathered outside before the noon prayers.

If Romania had a usable future it would have to emanate from such an authentic aesthetic, I thought: beauty is in line with freedom; ugliness with repression. I looked forward to returning to Constanța in a few years.

NO LONGER BY THE BLACK SEA, I was now at Giurgiu, where the energetic fury of the wide Danube flowed west to east. On the opposite bank was Bulgaria, the Ottoman and Turkic-Slavic heartland, whose history Romanians were relatively ignorant about, so obsessive were they concerning their own past. The ugly industrialization on both sides of the river indicated not modernity but poverty compared with the present-day, lavish nineteenth-century opulence of Budapest, with its numerous stately bridges, more than seven hundred miles upriver. I spied the ungainly bridge that I had walked across forty years before from Romania to Bulgaria, as part of my first foray into Central and Eastern Europe. Because it looked exactly as I had remembered it, the years fled and for a moment I was twenty-one years old again with a backpack.

Giurgiu was a city of harsh, painful rectangles: Communist-era concrete dormitories where the bulk of the population lived, interspersed with the occasional stolid, one-story square house that evoked not Europe but Anatolia. Amid this wounding spirit of debased urbanization, I was dumbfounded by the sight of the steep, layered roof work of a traditional Gothic church from the Maramureş, a region at the other end of Romania, in the extreme north near the Hungarian and Ukrainian borders. The pinewood construction was so soft on my eyes. Was this a dream vision, an optical illusion?

I approached through a weedy morass between concrete buildings. Walking up the steps of this wooden jewel I encountered a priest in the black, sleeveless wool vest and cassock of the Orthodox Church. He had a short stylish haircut and a tightly clipped black beard with hints of snow. His expression had the forgiving, moderating clarity associated with the Enlightenment. He thus appeared, in my own terminology, as *modern*—and young! His name was Liviu Mihai Dinu, and he had, as he told me, taken a lead in organizing the building of this church, which was affiliated with the local hospital. He explained that Giurgiu, ravished as it had been by Turkish invasions and easy prey to the planning schemes of Communists in nearby Bucharest, had no architectural identity, "nothing to look at in order to lift the spirit. What was required," he went on, "was something purely of Romania. And what was more typical of the country than the building style of the Maramureş, with its Gothic-inspired roofing that suggested the West," the direction Romanians always yearned to go! (In Moldavia, too, Gothic elements in the otherwise Byzantine architecture spoke of inspiration from the West.[48]) Indeed, the church here was a rebuke to Giurgiu's otherwise architectural enslavement. The construction had taken place between 2006 and 2008, under the direction of Maramureş artisans. I looked up at the roof and remembered how one of Dostoevsky's characters in *The Idiot* had equated Europe with the sight of a Gothic cathedral.[49] And it was Gothic monasteries in the heart of Europe, moreover, which had preserved the classics of ancient learning— the Western Canon—throughout the dreary centuries until the Renaissance.

In front and to the left of the oak-wood iconostasis was a neo-Byzantine icon with hints of modernist abstraction of the baby Jesus and the Mother of God, painted in the 1930s by Costin Petrescu, the celebrated artist who also executed the circular mural in the Athenaeum in Bucharest. In the late 1940s, when the Communists came to power, the icon was taken from the hospital and removed to the local cathedral for safekeeping—in the cathedral it was harder for the Communists to confiscate. But now the icon is back in the hospital's possession and thus able to be displayed in this church, Father Liviu explained to me.

Just beyond this fantastic church, the spiritual urban violence of the Communist 1950s and 1960s still predominates, intermingled with the neither-nor architecture of later periods. But the church was a beginning. True modernity—true liberation, in Romania's case— requires a return to sanctified tradition. The young cleric's genius was his understanding that the way forward could only come by building a bridge to a less morally defiled past. Proper aesthetics inform a people's ethical character. These layered Gothic roofs (like the roof of the renovated Ottoman mosque in Mangalia) signified such modernity— the same as that which shone in the cleric's eyes. What was, in fact, primitive was the sea of concrete outside, built deliberately to erase the past.

Chapter V

THE GREAT CEMETERY OF THE JEWS

DUST COATED THE MIGHTY TABLELAND OF MOLDAVIA, MAKING it appear faraway and ancient. Heading north, this epic landscape crumbles into dizzying folds, bearded with fir, spruce, and beech, as the name Bukovina indicates. The houses and yards are prim, with decorative wooden and metal roof designs hanging over the gutters like lace, providing a hint of the civilizing influence of Transylvania and Austria-Hungary. Just as the birches and cypresses are rare, so, too, was the signage in Polish and Ukrainian. Yet it existed: suggestions of empires past and borders nearby.

I came to the monastery of Putna, close to the border with Ukraine. The region of Bukovina was split between a northern part inside Ukraine and a southern part inside Romania. Romania had held the entire territory between the two world wars; but then, on the eve of World War II, Stalin annexed the northern part, a move facilitated by his non-aggression pact with Hitler.

Putna is called "the Jerusalem of the Romanian People." It was founded in 1469 by Stephen the Great as the foremost of the thirty churches and monasteries he is reputed to have established during his prodigious forty-seven-year reign (1457–1504). Putna holds his tomb, as well as a princely necropolis belonging to the Muşatinii dynasty of boyars. When I had first visited Putna in the spring of 1990 it was like a forlorn jewel hidden in a forest, with barely twenty monks. Now the grounds have been meticulously landscaped, and an area has been cleared for an immense parking lot to hold tour buses. About one hundred monks occupied the place.

In 1990, I had experienced the final aftershocks of Gheorghiu-Dej's Decree 410, issued in 1959, which emptied the monasteries of three-quarters of their inhabitants, so that the monks could be "integrated" into "socialist society." But since the downfall of Communism, Romanian monasticism has gradually undergone a rejuvenation. The newly modernized museum, among its fifteenth-century icons and late medieval embroidery in magenta and gold, proudly displays an early-sixteenth-century map depicting Stephen's *voivodedom* at the height of its territorial magnificence, with both northern Bukovina and Bessarabia incorporated within it. To the south lay the Ottoman Empire; to the north the Kingdom of Poland and the Grand Duchy of Lithuania; and to the west the Kingdom of Hungary. In fact, the Romanian Orthodox Church, in a discreet way, of course, is an emotional proponent of Romania Mare, "Greater Romania," with all of the lost territories restored. Historically, Romania's has been a national church, not a universal one. One should not forget that hundreds of Orthodox priests were unambiguous enthusiasts of the fascist Iron Guard in the interwar and World War II eras.[1] In a biting general criticism of the Eastern faith, the mid-nineteenth-century Russian intellectual Vissarion Belinsky writes that the Orthodox Chuch "has always been the bulwark of the whip and the handmaid of despotism."[2] Yet as I had learned over the decades—and not only in the former Byzantine and Ottoman Balkans, but in other parts of the world besides—while the past must heavily inform the present, the future will not necessarily follow from it. Institutions and cultures evolve in oblique and surprising ways. The Romanian Orthodox Church was certainly prone to change, that is.

The monastery church in Putna, which I recalled from almost a quarter century ago as especially mysterious and gloomy (I had actually required a flashlight to see the frescoes), was now amazingly bright and glittering with gold leaf. It was as though Byzantium itself had been reborn, with the emperors and saints appearing to move almost. Was this the same church? I asked myself. Was my memory confused? "The whole interior of the church was restored and repainted between 2001 and 2010," one of the monks, Father Dosoftei, informed me, noticing my interest.

Father Dosoftei, from Oltenia, was in his late thirties. He had the pale soft skin of a baby and a long black stringy beard beneath his stiff, cylindrical black hat. We fell into conversation and he asked if I would join him for cake and mineral water at one of the nearby guesthouses which had also been restored—as well as returned to the monastery—in the years after 1989.

"I have much to tell you," he began. "How to say . . ." He was breathing in and out in short breaths, evincing frustration in trying to express himself. "The Communists destroyed the landscape, but deep down they destroyed nothing. It is only a matter of recovering the tradition. Tradition and modernity cannot exist one without the other. You can only build from the past."

This was prologue to his rousing defense of Eastern monasticism, which is contemplative rather than active in spirit, he admitted, and traces its roots back to St. Anthony in the third century A.D., and who had lived as an anchorite in the Egyptian Thebaid (the desert of upper or southern Egypt). "For the eternal truth of God's Will is that you are never alone, even as a hermit in the desert," Father Dosoftei told me.

He explained that while Western monks, Franciscans, for instance, are often actively engaged in doing practical good works for the community, Eastern monks have a role that is just as functionally moral and universal.

"We are monks not for ourselves but for everybody else. By meditating on all the facets of spiritual love we can rescue meaning from the past and give hope to the generations yet to come. My ancestors who died in the two world wars and in the Middle Ages can be helped by my moral life now."

His mind and words raced:

"Dostoevsky understood; Rousseau did not. Man is by nature not wholly good. He must actively and deliberately cultivate what is good in him. So I must meditate. This all goes back to the different natures of Christ, God, and Man. Man must cultivate the God-like good in him. And if you are a man in power, you must always protect the weak—that is the essence of love. . . .

"The problem is that good and evil can coexist like the different strands of a thread. Therefore, we must look at faith and sacrifice as merely tools to achieve love. If suffering and sacrifice lead only to hate [as in the early careers of Gheorghiu-Dej and Ceauşescu], then they lose all meaning. Suffering must lead to forgiveness: that is the strict logic of Christ." My mind, by way of analogy, fixed momentarily on Camus's *Rebel*, in which the philosopher states that rebellions happen when sacred traditions of the past have been discarded, but that the rebel's cause only becomes legitimate when he assumes the responsibility to create a new moral order out of his own suffering, one that is more just for the individual than the previous order.[3]

"I am concerned with the spiritual essence of people," Father Dosoftei went on. "In 1989, it turns out that people wanted liberty to do good things—and bad things. Yes, thousands of boys wanted to become monks. But thousands of girls became prostitutes and thousands of others became thieves. So I must work at prayer. Liberty has to have an ethical purpose. You must always be willing to sacrifice to achieve God's love."

He spoke of the Miorița ("The Little Ewe"), a Romanian folk legend, in which a shepherd knows that to accept death is to lose one's fear of it. Yet there was nothing folkloric about Father Dosoftei. He was beyond national characteristics and concerned only with the universal. Such is how the Orthodox Church here can change.

JASSY'S NINETEENTH-CENTURY METROPOLITAN CATHEDRAL was vast and yet claustrophobic, so jam-packed was it with evening worshippers, who, by the looks of their clothes and expressions, seemed crushed by the unrelenting vicissitudes of life. And they weren't all old either, for there were many young people as well. The resurgence of religion was not simply a reaction to decades of atheistic Stalinism, but to the frankly tough economic times Romanians were currently enduring, partly thanks to the crisis within the European Union. Nearby Greece, for example, which had never experienced Communism, but whose economy had virtually collapsed, was in the throes of an Orthodox revival. The frescoes of transfixed emperors, the thick incense, the hypnotic chants fostered a dream state that overwhelmed one. Orthodoxy's very magic will guarantee its survival.

Jassy appears on most maps nowadays as Iaşi, but the Germanic spelling may be more familiar to readers of old histories and travelogues. It is the traditional capital of Moldavia and the traditional hearth of Romanian nationalism, associated as it is with the 1859 union of Moldavia and Wallachia. It, too, nearly a quarter century following the fall of Communism, was in the throes of considerable urban renewal. Jassy's historic buildings were floodlit, even as so much of the skyline remained tragically strangled by the visual devastation of Communist-era construction. "Those buildings represent the 1950s, and those the 1960s," Florin Platon, a local historian, explained about the architecture that still made the central square ugly. "The horrors of the past live on. The archives are still disorganized, the Communist archives are in many cases closed. Our links to the past have to get closer in order to move beyond it," he told me.

"But my students at the university here are less nationalistic, more open to Europe, more cosmopolitan," he continued, as we eyed the young people at the café tables with their tablets and smartphones, some speaking French and Italian. "We may now be in the midst of a historic upheaval in people's attitudes, even if we cannot exactly define it, and even if the demons of the nationalist right wing in Romania should not be dismissed." He held out the hope that ethnic nationalism, as Romanians have known it in the nineteenth and twentieth centuries, can only henceforth appear in diluted form.

"Let's hope that Russia becomes weak," he summarized. Translation: Jassy and Moldavia are geographically close to Russia, and if Russia were to exert more and more pressure upon Romania, then the nationalist demons would have the possibility to reawaken. This conversation, remember, occurred in the autumn of 2013, a few months before the Ukrainian crisis would resurrect the very Russian threat he feared.

JASSY'S PROXIMITY TO THE PRUT RIVER, separating it from the now-independent former Soviet republic of Moldova, opens the window onto Russia and its unrestrained relationship with Romania throughout early modern and modern history. If, from the perspective of the two Romanian principalities, Byzantium was the inspirational power and Ottoman Turkey the rapacious one, then Russia has been the contradictory and complicating power, defining the Romanian heartland once and for all as both a victim and a battlefield of European imperial politics. However, it is only from the prospect of the twentieth and early twenty-first centuries that Russia appears altogether and vividly oppressive. This distorts somewhat the role Russia played in earlier eras.

Whereas Byzantium is now politically deceased, and postmodern Islamist Turkey both benign and still emerging—at least from a Balkan perspective—Russia remains the bully practically next door, and thus retroactively evil in too many Romanian eyes. But it wasn't always exactly so. I had to free myself of my Cold War memories to gain a more balanced view of Russia in the Balkans.

Greater Romania was partially occupied by Russia ten times since 1711.[4] After all, Romania, along with Poland, dominates Russia's western borderland, a borderland so much more prosperous for so long than Russia's own Asian frontiers. Whereas Poland constituted the invasion route through the North European Plain that so bedeviled and obsessed Russia for much of its history, Romania boasted a long border with Ukraine, which by 1900 was the Russian Empire's agricultural heartland.[5] For Russia, Romania was on the pathway southward via the Lower Danube and the Black Sea to the Mediterranean and Constantinople. Romania, in the Kremlin's eyes, was a buffer against Ottoman Turkey. Russia's appetite for Romania—particularly for Moldavia and Bessarabia (Moldova), next door to Ukraine—was thus considerable.

And yet Russia in its epic scope and landmass was the lodestar of Orthodoxy, the very lifeblood and protector of Orthodox Christians in the Romanian principalities. For Russian and Romanian peasants alike, the liturgy of the Orthodox Church, its music and icons, "were among the most stirring and beautiful experiences" of a person's poor and miserable life. This spiritual bond had political consequences, moreover. Dominic Lieven, government professor at the London School of Economics, provides the historical backdrop:

The conquest of Byzantium in 1453 by the Ottoman Turks was seen by Russia as God's punishment for Byzantine apostasy. Thus, "Russia was now beyond question the champion of the only true faith not only because it was the only remaining independent Orthodox state but also because its faith had proven purer and less prone to error than that of the Greeks." Indeed, the Russians had much earlier repudiated the decision of the patriarch of Constantinople to merge the Orthodox Church with that of the Western Catholics at the Council of Florence in 1439, which had been an upshot of Byzantium's desperate need for Europe's help against the encroaching Muslim Turks. In 1589, when the creation of the Moscow Patriarchate finally asserted the independence of the Russian Church from Constantinople, it represented the culmination of a long process of separation and rebuke to Byzantium. As the late British historian Hugh Seton-Watson put it, "Russia was now the only sovereign state whose official religion was Orthodoxy, its Tsar the only Orthodox autocrat." Moscow had truly become "the third Rome," following Rome itself and Byzantium. It followed, therefore, that the protection of Orthodox Christians in Romania and throughout the Balkans was now regarded as "a religious duty as well as a good policy for the securing of Russian influence in the peninsula," writes the late Indiana University historian Barbara

Jelavich.[6] For Romania, thus, it would seem that the Kremlin had replaced Byzantium's gravitational pull.

But it was more complicated than that. For as Jelavich explains, while the Ottoman Turks now ruled in Constantinople, or Kostantiniyye as they called it (preferring it to "Istanbul"), the Orthodox Patriarchate there still retained substantial sway over Christians in the Balkans, and this Constantinople Patriarchate happened to be dominated by Phanariot Greeks—the same Phanariots that dominated for about a century Romania's Danubian principalities.[7] The result was a constant interplay of Greek and Russian forces vying for influence in Wallachia and Moldavia, with the Greeks—as the ones far more numerous on the ground—gaining the upper hand. And the Greeks, remember, were representatives of the Ottoman Turks. The Danubian principalities were, as much as anywhere in Europe, burdened under not one but several layers of foreign imperial influence. Romania, if not pivotal to European history to the extent that France or Poland has been, was nevertheless a telling register of power shifts in Central and Eastern Europe. Bucharest offered a front-row seat to history long before foreign correspondents congregated at the Athénée Palace in 1940 to watch the Nazi advance.

It was Romania's spiritual, military, and political domination by great powers that began my own private literary journey, leading me over the years and decades, by twists and turns, to minor classics in some cases only tangentially related to Romania itself. For instance, there was Robert Byron's *The Byzantine Achievement* and Lord Kinross's *The Ottoman Centuries*. Lately I discovered Barbara Jelavich's *Russia and the Formation of the Romanian National State 1821–1878*, in one sense a difficult and compressed academic thesis, in another sense a delicious subtext for how Wallachia and Moldavia slowly and miraculously emerged into the sunlight, as if from under shallow water, as a function of the subtle play of tensions between Romanov Russia, Ottoman Turkey, and Habsburg Austria, and their common requirement for a buffer zone. Fortunate countries are heirs to empire; less fortunate ones constitute the outlying residue of such. It was the constraints upon imperial aggression that initially produced Romania. To wit, I look at maps of the nineteenth-century Balkans and see Wallachia and Moldavia in a striking lighter shade squeezed between the vast, darker shades of the sprawling Russian, Austro-Hungarian, and Ottoman empires.[8]

For Russia, the lands of the fellow-Orthodox Romanians were seen as both a staging area against the Ottoman Porte and as a source of agricultural supplies for their army: the grain fields of Wallachia and Moldavia had already been for centuries legendary among the Venetians and Turks. Jelavich documents the movements of imperial armies from Russia and Austria against Turkey into Wallachia and Moldavia in the 1730s, 1760s, 1780s, and 1790s. The Russian and Austrian invaders were looked upon not altogether negatively by the Romanian boyars, who saw them as a hedge against the hated Turkish-appointed Phanariots. Going back to 1711, when the prince of Wallachia, Constantine Brâncoveanu, and the ruler of Moldavia, Dimitrie Cantemir, concluded a treaty with Peter the Great, Russia had appeared often to Romanians as a necessary bulwark against Turkey. By 1829, according to the terms of the Treaty of Adrianople, Russian forces gained de facto control of Wallachia and Moldavia from the Ottoman Porte, and, by the standards and conditions of the time, introduced somewhat enlightened administration.

The larger truth, as Jelavich, Seton-Watson, and other historians intimate, is that Wallachia and Moldavia were for centuries the plaything of Russia and Turkey, with Austria and later Austria-Hungary having a critical role, too. (For example, in 1848, the Russian and Turkish militaries cooperated in invasions of Moldavia and Wallachia, as a response to a Romanian revolutionary uprising. The following decade, during the Crimean War (1853–56), Russia and Turkey fought a naval battle on Christmas Day, 1853, at Cetate on the Romanian side of the Danube in Wallachia.[9]) It was the Russian thrust into Moldavia and Wallachia, potentially en route to the Balkans, Constantinople, and the Mediterranean world, that had helped start the Crimean War. The Principalities of Wallachia and Moldavia were a marchland guarding the eastern Habsburg front, a front that the Western powers felt they had to defend. Russia's defeat in the Crimean War and its subsequent withdrawal from the Principalities further reinforced its enmity toward Habsburg Austria, a contributing factor to World War I.

It is in the mid-nineteenth century when we see the first concrete stirrings of modern Romanian nationalism, a theme that Jelavich elegantly captures in her academic saga of Russian influence. Nationalism in Romania quite simply meant *the West*. For despite the presence of the occupying Russians, few young Romanians were attracted to study in St. Petersburg. Whereas the older generation in the Principalities wore the national costume associated with Turkey and the East, the younger generation reflected Paris fashions, which went along with their fascination with the "liberal-national revolutionary doctrines of the age." French was replacing Greek as a second language, and the use of the Cyrillic alphabet was dying out. (Ironically, this was somewhat because of the Russian influence: the czar's officers spoke French and encouraged the Romanians to do likewise.) And whereas the older generation saw the Russian Protectorate as a somewhat benign rule by their Orthodox big brother, shielding them against the Muslim Turks, the younger generation began to look back to the Latin heritage of their people, associated with ancient Dacia and the Roman West. For nineteenth-century nationalism across Europe was also associated with the romantic movement, and in the case of Romanians this meant the rediscovery of their classical history.[10]

The leading edge of this tendency was the group of Romanian intellectuals who congregated in Paris and were branded by the experience of 1848, the year of liberal-romantic and political upheaval across Europe, which raised up the banner of nationalism against imperial rule. This Romanian generation first became known to me by way of the street names of Bucharest: Ion Brătianu, Nicolae Bălcescu, and General Gheorghe Magheru. The most important was Alexandru Ioan Cuza.

Born in 1820 to a family of Moldavian boyars in Bârlad, Cuza was educated in Jassy and Paris and held administrative positions in Galaţi,

where the Danube Delta region meets the Moldavian heartland close
to Bessarabia in the vicinity of Ukraine. Most important, though, Cuza
was, in Jelavich's words, a "forty-eighter," a young man defined by the
experience and meaning of 1848.[11] The uprisings of 1848, from France
to the Balkans, pitting bourgeois intellectuals and working-class radi-
cals against conservative regimes, were generally unsuccessful because
the conservative regimes held the institutional advantage as well as—
partly, at least—the moral advantage, for ethnic and national interests
eventually trumped universalist longings once the Metternichian system began to weaken.[12] And yet usually forgotten is the fact that Romanian independence was not only a child of infernally complex imperial
limitations and maneuverings (between Russia, Austria, Turkey, Great
Britain, and France[13]), but also of the liberal-national spirit of 1848,
even if Cuza himself did not actually take office until 1859. It was in
that year that Wallachia and Moldavia separately elected Cuza as the
prince of what would be known between 1862 and 1864 as the United
Principalities of Moldavia and Wallachia: the first real Romanian
state.

Cuza, in Jelavich's narrative, labored in office against an atmosphere of debilitating poverty, widespread disease, nonexistent roads
and schools, and de jure (albeit not de facto) Ottoman suzerainty, with
Russia and Austria always hovering nearby. The Lower Danube was a
sensitive crossroads between the Polish, Hungarian, Serbian, and Bulgarian lands. Cuza developed militaries in each of the two Principalities, even as he worked to unite them in practice through the
development of post, telegraph, and customs. Heavily influenced by
Napoleon and the French administrative tradition, Cuza's reforms
substantially eased the life of Romanian peasants. It was Cuza who essentially made Bucharest the national capital before his benevolent
authoritarian regime was toppled in a swift and orderly coup led by
liberal-radicals in 1866. (Helping the selection of Bucharest was its
commercial position on a main trade route between Habsburg Austria
and Ottoman Turkey, even as Jassy would be in an exposed location
only a few miles from the Russian border once Bessarabia was lost.[14])

With Cuza gone, Romania was once again at the brink of anarchy and at the mercy of three neighboring empires—Ottoman, Austrian, and Russian—even as none of them had the wherewithal or overwhelming interest required for actual occupation. There was, too, the prospect of continued fights and intrigues between the various boyar families—Ghica and Bibescu, Cantacuzino and Mavrocordat—that threatened to undermine stability.[15] It was in such circumstances that Carol I took power, the German import who would over the decades build state institutions and thus a governable polity. Under Carol's Prussian-like command, the sense of a link to the West only intensified among educated Romanians. As they gazed out at the southern bank of the Danube, in their minds that was where not only Bulgaria but the barbarous Orient commenced.

But while Carol's forty-eight-year reign—one year longer than Stephen the Great's—appears triumphant in hindsight, the first dozen years or so were an awfully tenuous affair for the prince. What undermined his stability were the extremely bad choices he faced, a factor of Romania's position on the map. Through much of the 1870s, Carol, and especially his liberal prime minister, Ion Brătianu, were pro-Russian. The demonization of Russia because of the Cold War obscures how much more nuanced were Romanian attitudes toward its giant fellow-Orthodox neighbor in earlier periods, when the Islamic threat was still existent. Yet Carol was now faced with the likelihood of Russian military intervention in the Balkans. This was in order to redress the Kremlin's territorial losses from the Crimean War and to take advantage of rising nationalism in Bulgaria and Serbia, so as to further weaken the Ottoman Empire. Though Russia's enemy was Ottoman Turkey and not Romania, Carol knew that the route of any Russian army toward Bulgaria and Turkey must pass through Moldavia and Wallachia. If Romania refused to cooperate with Russia, Russia would simply invade and annex the territory of its passing army; if Romania did cooperate she would face the hostility of Turkey and probably lose part of her territory anyway to Russia. For Romania, geography was once again a nightmare.[16]

Carol chose the barely lesser of two evils and gave right-of-passage to Czar Alexander II's troops to cross the Prut from Bessarabia into Moldavia. The Turks retaliated by attacking a Romanian settlement on the Danube, as Carol with little enthusiasm declared war on Turkey. Soon Romanians were fighting and dying alongside the allied Russians in northern Bulgaria. The 1877–78 Russo-Turkish War ended with a Russian victory and creation, though only temporarily, of a Greater Bulgaria that was a Russian satellite. As for Romania, it was forced to cede—just as Carol feared—the southern part of Bessarabia (the Turkish "Budjak") to Russia, even as Romania received the Danube Delta and northern Dobrudja as compensation. Given the circumstances, the forty-year-old prince had done as well as he could for his adopted country. In the 1880 peace treaty, Romanian independence was formally granted by the great powers. A year later, Romanian legislators proclaimed Prince Carol as King Carol. He would rule until his death two months after the outbreak of World War I.[17]

ACROSS FROM THE CAFÉ in the central square in Jassy where I sat with Professor Platon was the Traian Hotel. In *Balkan Ghosts* I had this to say about it:

> The scene in the lobby and adjoining restaurant was one of corroded grandeur: big, dark stains on the red and brown carpets; metal champagne buckets filled with phlegm and mountains of cigarette ash; men and women huddled in overcoats with greasy faces and cigarette-stained fingertips; a Gypsy boy going from table to table, begging. . . . The room [had] no soap, no toilet paper, and (as I found out) sometimes no water in the taps. I called the reception desk. I was told that toilet paper would be sent up immediately. Soap, however, was in short supply. I called room service. I was told that the restaurant was out

of red wine, beer, and mineral water. Only white wine was available—warm, since there was no ice.[18]

That was only four months following Ceaușescu's downfall. The Traian now boasted the latest fixtures and amenities, with remodeled bathrooms and a brand-new lobby in a pseudo-European global style. The service was of an international standard, even though it was not a chain hotel. Whereas in 1990 there was a depressed and decadent aura to the place, now it was simply sterile. The Hotel Unirea, next door, which I had once described as a "veritable flophouse," was now all gussied up in a Day-Glo garish style, with a rooftop restaurant.[19] Jassy was far from having become a trendy destination, stranded as it was in Romania's northeast, hard up against the border with Moldova, a country undermined by Putinism as well as by tensions between Romanians and Russians. There was still no Hyatt, Hilton, or Sheraton here. Cuza's city was very much a work in progress, an indication, yet again, of Romania's challenging geography. For Jassy to truly come into its own and more demonstrably retire the demons of the past, Moldova, which dominates Romania's long eastern border along the Prut—only ten miles from here—would itself have to normalize. And that was unlikely so long as Russia remained an illiberal state.

JASSY'S GREAT SYNAGOGUE WAS a furious construction site. I counted two dozen workers in hard hats, every one of them banging or drilling or scurrying around. Nobody was standing around chatting or drinking coffee, as construction workers are apt to do. The original building dated to 1580, and the latest one had its foundation damaged in a 1977 earthquake. Though almost the entire edifice was underneath scaffolding, the multitiered dome and Star of David, as well as some of the magnificent brickwork, peeked through. The project was being funded by the Ministry of Culture, with encouragement from the European Union. Next to the synagogue was a short marble obelisk of very recent vintage engraved with a burning menorah. The words in Romanian, English, and Hebrew read: "In memory of over 13,000 Jews, innocent victims of the Jassy Pogrom of June 28–30, 1941, during the Ion Antonescu regime. We will not forget!" Local traffic whirred all around, oblivious to the words. I was aware how alone I was.

The Jewish cemetery of Jassy occupies one of the highest spots in the city. It is quite literally vast, crowded as it is with graves for hundreds of yards in different directions. An old woman with a dirty ball cap, who seemed a bit deranged, helped by a gang of dogs, guarded the cemetery. It was so overgrown with weeds that, except for certain areas, it left a scandalously derelict and frightening impression. A virtual army of gravestones—wide rows and rows of them—marked the burial sites of local Jewish military heroes who died fighting for Romania in World War I. Adjacent were four long rows of massive cement slabs with Stars of David, symbolically marking the graves of the victims of the Jassy Pogrom. As a plaque read: the victims were starved and suffocated in the "train of death," and elsewhere "butchered" by frenzied Iron Guardsmen and others: ". . . the moon shall be confounded, and the sun ashamed" (Isaiah 24:23). Also nearby, amid the assemblage of mottled and weather-stained tombs of a whole Jewish civilization going back centuries here, was a monument of more recent vintage: of 36 Jews—15 men, 9 women, and 12 children—murdered in the Vulturi Forest nearby, during the 1941 pogrom.

While a Jewish cemetery like the one in Prague is constantly celebrated and memorialized by virtue of it being on the international tourist circuit, even as the synagogues and Jewish graveyards of the Kazimierz district of Cracow are now undergoing intensive restoration, this towering ruined city of *those who have life everlasting*, at least at the time of my visit, still demanded its just recognition.[20] With few survivors left, life in the great Jewish magnet of Jassy had been reduced to silence. As it was, I was alone here, just as I had been at the synagogue.

Next I went to the Jewish community center, a series of small, neat, and modern rooms with an adjoining small museum listing some basic

facts: 43,500 Jews lived in the city in 1921; 350 in 2013. Before World
War II Jassy had 137 synagogues; now there were two. However, the
end of Jewish life in Jassy came mainly during the Communist era,
when the regime charged the West in hard currency to *buy out* the
Jews who desired to go to Israel or elsewhere. And of course they
wanted to go—who wouldn't have wanted to leave the Romania of
Gheorghiu-Dej and Ceauşescu?

"Antonescu was not as bad as Gheorghiu-Dej," an elderly Jewish
woman, who had opened the museum for me, offhandedly and flatly
remarked. It was an extraordinary statement on the face of it, given that
Antonescu had killed hundreds of thousands of Jews during his World
War II pro-Nazi dictatorship. Yet the remark was also in a certain sense
understandable: Antonescu was, as we shall see, among the most am-
bivalent central personalities of the Holocaust. And he did not crush
Romanian society for nearly as long—and not nearly as recently—as
did Gheorghiu-Dej and Ceauşescu. And he did not do so nearly to the
same extent.

I had written about Antonescu's role in the Holocaust in *Balkan
Ghosts*.[21] But that was in the immediate aftermath of the Cold War,
some time before scholars could grapple with the archival material on
the subject that became available with the downfall of Communism in
both Romania and the Soviet Union. These archives and their excava-
tion add more precision, perspective, further documentation, and telling detail to my earlier account, as well as correcting my occasional
mistake. Of particular note are British academic Dennis Deletant's
*Hitler's Forgotten Ally: Ion Antonescu and His Regime, Romania 1940–
1944*, published in 2006 by Palgrave Macmillan; Radu Ioanid's *The
Holocaust in Romania: The Destruction of Jews and Gypsies Under the
Antonescu Regime, 1940–1944*, published in 2000 by Ivan R. Dee; and
Vladimir Solonari's *Purifying the Nation: Population Exchange and
Ethnic Cleansing in Nazi-Allied Romania*, published in 2010 by the
Woodrow Wilson Center Press. These are unjustifiably obscure books,
brought out by relatively small publishers. Deletant's book, for exam-
ple, retailed for ninety dollars at the time of this writing in late 2013. I

hope my summary of Deletant's work—as well as that of Ioanid's and others on the subject—gives these academic texts, founded on original sources, a far wider readership than they presently enjoy. Antonescu continues to be an undeservedly dim figure of the Holocaust, perhaps because his role, however spectacular, was somewhat contradictory and therefore has bedeviled an absolutely clear moral reckoning. Nevertheless, I believe such a reckoning is possible—something Deletant, Ioanid, and Solonari obviously believe, too.

MARSHAL ION ANTONESCU'S ROMANIA was Adolf Hitler's second most important Axis ally after Benito Mussolini's Italy, though one might easily consider Antonescu more formidable and useful from Hitler's point of view than Mussolini was. Antonescu contributed 585,000 Romanian troops to the Nazi invasion of the Soviet Union from June to October 1941. At Stalingrad, in late 1942 and early 1943, Romanian troops fought alongside the Germans and against the Soviets with a particular ferocity. Romania, rich in natural resources and lying on the southern path of the invasion route of Operation Barbarossa, supplied Hitler's war machine with critical stores of oil from the Ploieşti fields as well as other raw materials. Antonescu met with Hitler no less than ten times, mainly in Austria and East Prussia, between the fall of 1940 and the summer of 1944: from soon after the Romanian dictator assumed power until a few weeks before his overthrow (in a coup orchestrated by the young King Michael). "Far from being overawed by the Fuhrer," Antonescu often contradicted him to his face—perhaps the only person ever allowed to do so—speaking his mind fully about Romania's territorial interests for hours on end, so that Hitler came to respect him from the beginning of their relationship.[22]

Antonescu directly orchestrated, through deliberate starvation and "horrific acts of mass butchery," the deaths of up to 300,000 Jews in northern Bukovina, Bessarabia, and Transdniestria: the areas to the east and north of Romania with large ethnic Romanian populations (in the cases of Bukovina and Bessarabia) that Romanian troops captured from Stalin's forces in the first weeks of the Nazi-led invasion in 1941. But in Romania proper—Moldavia, Wallachia, and southern Transylvania—Antonescu kept up to 375,000 Jews from local slaughter and transport to death camps in German-occupied Poland. This was something that would not have happened had the fascist Iron Guard regime remained in power in Bucharest. For in January 1941, after tolerating the Iron Guard inside his government for the first five months of his rule, Antonescu decimated the Guard and hunted down the fascist Legionnaires.[23] The survival rate of the Jewish population under his direct civil, administrative, and military control—within the legal borders of Romania, that is—"was greater than that of any other Axis ally, protectorate or occupied area aside from Finland," writes the scholar and Romania specialist Larry L. Watts, in a recent unpublished monograph.[24] If you were a Jew within Antonescu's Romania proper you were more likely to survive World War II than if you had been living virtually anywhere else in Axis-occupied Europe. But, on the other hand, if you were a Jew in the areas that Antonescu's troops recaptured from the Soviet Union, there were few places worse to be during that period.

Antonescu's crimes against humanity are beyond adequate description. Deletant breaks down the figures based on the latest evidence: between 12,000 and 20,000 Jews shot by the Romanian and German soldiery in northern Bukovina in July and August 1941; 15,000 to 20,000 Jews murdered in Odessa in a similar manner by Romanian troops in October 1941; the deaths of at least 90,000 Jews from typhus and starvation in the course of deportation organized by Romanian troops eastward from Bukovina and Bessarabia into Transdniestria between 1941 and 1943; and the deaths of as many as 170,000 local Ukrainian Jews inside Transdniestria itself during the same period of Romanian occupation. (There are, too, the thousands of Jews killed within Romania's legal borders: for example, the Jassy Pogrom of late June 1941.) "These figures," Deletant writes, "give the Antonescu regime the sinister distinction of being responsible for the largest number of deaths of Jews after Hitler's Germany. . . ." (Keep in mind that the deportation of half a million Jews from Hungary and northern Transylvania to death camps in Poland occurred after the March 1944 German occupation of those territories. Romania was never occupied by Nazi Germany: it was an ally.)[25]

Typhus, starvation, and shootings on the bleak and freezing steppe of eastern Romania Mare and its shadow zone, in Bessarabia and Transdniestria—these facts do not begin to capture what the Jews actually experienced at the hands of Antonescu's Romanian troops. The victims' valuables were confiscated and in many cases transferred to the Romanian national bank. The victims were forced-marched; brutally bullied into trenches and ghettos filled with armies of rats and mice; beaten mercilessly; left to die of their wounds; doused with gasoline and burned. Old men, women, and children were numerous among those who suffered the worst atrocities. Young girls were regularly raped. The Romanian soldiery killed vast numbers of Jews "from infants in swaddling bands to old men with white beards." On one occasion in the Bessarabian capital of Chişinău in July 1941, after 551 Jews had been rounded up, "Women and children were shot first, followed by the men who were forced to push the dead bodies into the ditch."[26] In a memoir appearing in 1998, Israeli writer Aharon Appelfeld calls Romania Mare and beyond, from Bukovina to Transdniestria, "the great cemetery of the Jews," where, in 1941, mass death "was not yet industrialized and any means of killing was used."[27]

To wit, the American-Romanian scholar Radu Ioanid's study of this geographic sector of the Holocaust is more than a book, it is a document from Hell: a dry, factual, nausea-inducing account of the most bestial and intimate atrocities, committed in one village and town after another against the elderly and the smallest children by Romanian soldiers and civilians, with Antonescu's bureaucratic fingerprints everywhere apparent. As Marshal Antonescu confided to his Council of Ministers on April 15, 1941, after sporadic atrocities in Romania proper, and on the eve of the invasion of Bessarabia and Transdniestria: "I give the mob complete license to slaughter them [the Jews]. I withdraw to my fortress, and after the slaughter I restore order."[28]

The roots of Romanian anti-Semitism date to the westward migration of Ashkenazi Jews here in the nineteenth century and are inextricable from the agricultural-based, blood-and-soil Romanian worldview—the upshot of a vast peasantry—that helped characterize both local political and intellectual circles since the beginning of the modern era. Jews simply did not fit in, even as they were so ever present. They constituted the only significant minority in nineteenth-century Romania, and as a *middleman* trading and commercial minority in particular, were antipathetic to Romania's racially based nationalism, anchored as it was in rural traditions. As the anti-Semitic historian P. P. Panaitescu complained in 1940, "The Romanians . . . did not have a national bourgeoisie at any point in their history. Our bourgeoisie has always been a foreign one. . . ."[29] Jewish immigration into the Romanian lands from Russia and Austria-Hungary in the second half of the nineteenth century had dramatically increased their numbers, so that Jews constituted 14.6 percent of all urban dwellers. In Moldavia they were almost a third of the urban population, and in Jassy itself over 40 percent.[30] This also fed the anti-Semitism of the illiterate masses, "a crude kind of class hatred" against a minority "which busied itself with money," in the words of Hugh Seton-Watson. His father, R. W. Seton-Watson, also a historian, had once quoted a Romanian politician as saying, "Work, civilise yourselves, and you will rid yourselves of the Jews." Bessarabian Romanians in particular were prone to such attitudes, helped by the fact that nearly half the urban population between the Prut and the Dniester rivers was Jewish.[31] Such was the demographic, economic, and historical background noise to the 1941 Jassy Pogrom.

The Jewish *middleman* minority was seen by many in the local elite as a mass of hostile Bolshevik sympathizers. The Jews, to them, represented the evils of capitalism and Communism at the same time. This was during a period when Romania was in the course of losing the historic territories of northern Bukovina and Bessarabia to Soviet Russia. The political system, meanwhile, partly as a result of the impossibility of defending national borders against such powerful and traditional adversaries, was in the late 1930s descending into quasi-anarchy. In the midst of such chaos, blaming the Jews became the default emotion. After all, anti-Semitism, as the memoirist Gregor von Rezzori wrote about the interbellum period, was a Romanian tic, something the majority of the population easily internalized, making anti-Semitism frighteningly unremarkable. Carol II (despite his half-Jewish mistress), prominent politicians and intellectuals such as Octavian Goga, Nicolae Iorga, Nae Ionescu, A. C. Cuza, and, of course, Antonescu himself, were all publicly committed anti-Semites.[32] (There were, it must be noted, Romanian intellectuals who defended the Jews at a time when the country and much of Europe were hurtling toward anti-Semitism: Mihai Ralea and Lucian Blaga come to mind, the latter of whom supported an "ecumenical framework" that would be friendly to minorities.[33])

The Jassy Pogrom was the signature event in which territorial loss, war and imminent territorial recapture, nationalist rage, and anti-Semitism all coalesced. Deletant says that "*at least* [his italics] 4,000" were killed during the few days the pogrom lasted, but such was the confusion and sheer blood-rage that figures as high as 12,000 "have also been advanced." If they were not deliberately rounded up and shot en masse, thousands of other Jews of Jassy died in sealed death trains, where they were packed without water, food, or air in the midst of the summer heat and driven around the Moldavian countryside for days until most expired. Again, women and children were numerous among the victims. And this was in addition to other, smaller pogroms occurring around Moldavia at the time that Ioanid painstakingly documents (complete with the names of the individual victims). The context for such aggression had come from Antonescu, whose government was not shy about making overtly anti-Semitic statements, even as Antonescu himself publicly deplored the mob actions that characterized the events.[34] German troops, then on the ground in Jassy, also played a critical role in the pogrom.[35]

Who was Antonescu, really?

A French assessment of him in 1922, when Antonescu was forty and a military attaché to Paris, stated: "A well-tried intelligence, brutal, duplicitous, very vain, a ferocious will to succeed . . . an extreme xenophobia, [these are] the striking characteristics of this strange figure."[36] To read Deletant, Hitchins, and others, we can say that Antonescu was a realist, militarist, nationalist, and authoritarian, who had no use for parliamentary democracy. But neither was he strictly fascist: he purged the fascists from his regime early on and had a disdain for pageants and parades. He believed in order, but not as a prerequisite to freedom, only as an end in itself. His support for Hitler was heavily determined by the calamitous international situation he inherited from Carol II and Romania's tragic position on the map between Nazi and Stalinist empires. Antonescu made the cold calculation that an alliance with Germany was simply the best option for regaining territories that Romania had lost to the Soviet Union. As Antonescu reportedly told journalists a few days after Pearl Harbor: "I am the ally of the Reich against Russia; I am neutral between Great Britain and Germany; and I am for the Americans against the Japanese."[37] But at the same time, Antonescu could also say that "Europe has to be liberated once and for all from the domination of Free-Masons and Jews."[38]

If not a proponent of the Final Solution itself, Antonescu was among the twentieth century's great ethnic cleansers.[39] He spoke about the need to "purify" and "homogenize" the Romanian population, and rid it of "Yids," "Slavs," and "Roma." (Antonescu's deportation of the Roma people to Transdniestria—where some 20,000 died of disease, starvation, and cold—was not a result of German pressure, but something he had initiated on his own.) One of Antonescu's ministers stated that the circumstances of German military successes provided Romania with a unique opportunity for a "complete ethnic unshackling." Antonescu himself saw the Jews as a "disease" and as "parasites," in Deletant's language, "to be cleansed from the body of Romania."[40] The deportation of Jews from the quasi-historical Romanian lands of Bukovina and Bessarabia to Transdniestria, a region where Romania had few historical claims, should be seen in this light.

And yet it cannot be forgotten that Antonescu kept, by some statistical reckonings, the largest number of Jews away from the Final Solution in Axis-dominated Europe. He did so in large measure because of "opportunism" and extreme nervousness as to his own fate, as the Soviets and the Western Allies began to tighten the noose on Hitler's war machine.[41] The end to deportation and mass murder in Transdniestria and the decision not to send Romanian Jews from inside the country to death camps in Poland were all actions taken *after* the Nazi defeat at Stalingrad, when Antonescu began to realize that Hitler might not, after all, win the war. Radu Ioanid might refer to this as "opportunistic mercy." Antonescu was more of a realist than a fanatical fascist, and so he was always sensitive to shifting geopolitical winds. There was also Antonescu's own proud and autocratic character. The idea of the Führer ordering him from abroad to give up *his* Jews did not sit well with him. As someone in direct contact with Antonescu at the time observed, the Marshal "did not like receiving orders; he liked giving them."[42] There was also pressure brought to bear upon Antonescu from Romanian intellectuals, from the queen mother, Helen, and from the National Peasant Party leader Iuliu Maniu to save Romanian Jewry. Again, this all must be seen in the context of Soviet and American victories on the battlefront.

Antonescu was toppled in a palace coup on August 23, 1944, just as the Red Army was already marching triumphantly into Romania. He was tried by pro-Soviet Romanian authorities, duly convicted, and executed in 1946 by a firing squad at Jilava Prison near Bucharest. Antonescu was a mass murderer without strictly being a fascist. The fact that he kept such an astonishingly larger number of Jews from death cannot erase the fact that he killed an astonishing number—in indescribable suffering. There is no moral ambiguity in that.

Georgetown University professor Charles King, an expert in these matters, remarked that the best thing which can be said about An-tonescu is that he was a conservative anti-Semite, not a millenarian one like an Adolf Eichmann or Alfred Rosenberg.

Upon Antonescu's removal from power, the Romanians switched sides in the war. For the remainder of the war Romania contributed more troops—538,000—to the Allied cause than any country except for the Soviet Union, Great Britain, and the United States. Romanian casualties against the Nazis in 1944–45 were some twenty-five times greater than those of Italy, another country that fought first for the Axis and then against it.[43] Of course, Romania's change of heart was a con-sequence of its need to regain all of Transylvania from Nazi-occupied Hungary. Self-interest dominates foreign policy thinking most of the time in most places. Yet rarely has national self-interest been applied so nakedly as by Romanian regimes during World War II, descending as it did to the level of sheer opportunism. It also bears repeating that the shamelessness Romania evinced during that war was, in turn, partly a function of its impossible geographical position, especially after Mu-nich, when Chamberlain abandoned Central Europe to Germany.

HE WAS AN ANIMATED SKULL with a loud voice, on account of his dif-ficulty hearing. He wore a pinstripe shirt under his suit and vest, with a red handkerchief in his breast pocket and a cane at the ready. Books littered his study, not only on the walls but on every flat surface—desk, chairs, and sofas. He had descended from boyars, and actually claimed a link to Vlad Țepeș Dracula: two brothers and twelve generations re-moved. Sunlight poured through the windows onto two half-burned candles, sitting atop another pile of books. The Romanian historian and philosopher Neagu Djuvara was ninety-seven years old when I visited him.

"My parents and I escaped St. Petersburg one day before the No-vember Revolution. I was a year old." He showed me the trace of a wound on his left forearm. "This saved me. I was wounded on the Odessa front in 1941 and sent to a hospital. Soon afterwards, my regiment was almost completely wiped out in the fighting" against the Russians, in support of the Nazis. "I had no knowledge at the time about what was happening to the Jews of Odessa," he quickly added, as though anticipating a question or accusation. He went on: "I was sent as a diplomatic courier to Stockholm the same day in August 1944 that the Antonescu government fell, so I escaped the Russians again and the Communist regimes that followed."

Djuvara had spent his nearly half century of exile in France and in Niger, where he taught and was an advisor to the government. He returned to Romania only after the fall of Ceaușescu, whom he labeled "a profound cretin, shrewd and illiterate, who nevertheless fooled de Gaulle and Nixon."

Djuvara's mind wandered. He talked of the infighting among the princely families in the nineteenth century and of the infighting among Romanian politicians today. It was hard to keep him on the same subject. But among his many digressions were the following:

"Antonescu was too proud of himself, too sure in his own opinions. That was an aspect of his downfall. He had an Albanian grandmother, Sultana, who must have been born sometime in the mid-nineteenth century, when there were quite a few Albanians in the country. No Romanian has such a name. Antonescu had red hair. He was stiff, stubborn, warlike, just like Albanians. It happens! A person gets a lot of his traits from one distant relative. Antonescu certainly did not have the weak, adaptable, compromising, wheeler-dealer nature common to Romanians. Thus, he was a calamity. His stubbornness and self-confidence was a factor in his sticking with the Germans longer than he needed to.

"Codreanu and the Legionnaires were not exactly fascists. They had a deeply religious coloration that the Nazis lacked. Thus, I had sympathy for them: they seemed so pure and honest. Aah, those were the times," he said with a sigh, as though asking for forgiveness for his extreme right-wing leanings as a young man, which had led to his attraction to the Iron Guard. The Legion of the Archangel Michael — which became the Iron Guard — had its beginnings in 1927 as a breakaway outfit of the National Christian Defense League. Prayer, mysticism, and authoritarianism, combined with an aspiration to a vitally pure ethic of sorts made the organization more like an Eastern Orthodox version of al-Qaeda than of the Nazi Party. And it had the same Eastern Orthodox version of a radical, intolerant Islamic emirate as its goal in order to replace the Romanian state.[44] Thus Djuvara's analysis has some merit.

"Carol II was both intelligent and immoral," he continued. "Carol hoped but did not expect that Britain and France would be strong enough to resist Hitler. Look, everyone made deals with the Germans back then," again, said in a somewhat complaining tone, as though asking for forgiveness. "None of us could have imagined in 1940—not me, not Carol, not Antonescu—that America would ever get involved in the war and would then go on to actually win it. No one could have imagined America as able to fight and defeat both the Germans *and* the Japanese at once. Only a Tocqueville could have imagined the latent power of the United States—but not any Central or Eastern European of the 1930s or 1940." This rang true. Again, I remembered what the late Communist Silviu Brucan had remarked to me before he died: that America was nowhere when the West deserted Central and Eastern Europe at Munich in 1938; that the American military did not appear in the real heart of Europe until D-Day.

"Mircea Eliade, I knew. He was a narrow nationalist even while he had a deep awareness of international, universal civilization. I didn't like him. Even as a young man, he was too sure of his own genius. Now, Emil Cioran was more of a genius than Mircea Eliade. I knew Cioran and liked him very much." It occurred to me that Cioran may have suffered from depression, guilt, and profound bewilderment throughout much of his life for supporting the Iron Guard as a young man precisely because he was not as sure of himself as was Eliade.

E. M. CIORAN MAY be among the most emblematic individuals for telescoping Romania's unsettling twentieth-century history, with ramifications for the twenty-first. Cioran is the subject of an intellectual biography by Marta Petreu, a Romanian-born editor, poet, and philosopher at Babes-Bolyai University in Cluj. Like the other books I have discussed, *An Infamous Past: E. M. Cioran and the Rise of Fascism in Romania* is as obscure as it is urgent. Cioran, born in 1911, was as brilliant and dazzling as he was immature and lacking in common sense. With the publication of his book *The Transfiguration of Romania* (1936) at age twenty-five, he became, in Petreu's words, "the first major representative of the 1927 generation [the generation associated with the founding of the Legion of the Archangel Michael] to be seduced by the ideology of the far right." As Cioran himself wrote following a visit to Nazi Germany, "If I like something about Hitlerism, it is the *cult of the irrational,* the exultation of pure vitality, the virile expression of strength, without any critical spirit, restraint, or control."[45]

Cioran despaired that whereas Nazi Germany was a first-rate country, his native Romania was a "second-rate country," a country which now required some sort of dynamic dictatorial regime to make it first-rate. He saw the national myth of the Miorița, accepting as it is of death, as encompassing all the passivity and fatalism that undermined the Romanian national character. The Miorița itself was evocative of Romania's pastoral and peasant folk culture, in which Romanians, according to Cioran, "lived . . . the life of plants." Cioran, as a young man in the heady fascist days of the late 1930s, wanted a Romania that would replace its passive agricultural model with one of full-bore industrialization in order to make itself into a great country. He longed for the end of capitalism and for a regime that would combine collectivization with right-wing nationalism. Petreu rightly points out the obvious when she observes that Cioran's vision was largely realized by Ceaușescu, who combined madcap industrialization, Stalinist-style collectivization, and a variant of national fascism that gave Romania, with its so-called independent foreign policy in the 1970s and 1980s, a measure of the international prestige Cioran so much craved for his country.[46]

And by ransoming off to Israel and the West so many Jews and ethnic Germans, Ceaușescu also achieved a degree of racial purity in Romania that the fascist movement of the 1930s, which included Cioran, had longed for. Though it must be said that Cioran did not share, in Petreu's description, the "obsessive" anti-Semitism of Iron Guard leader Corneliu Zelea Codreanu and others. Cioran called Jews only a "peripheral problem" for Romania, and not the cause of its misfortune. In his writings, he oscillates between admiration for and denunciation of the Jews. While not the disease they are for both Codreanu and Antonescu, the Jews are still traitors in his eyes. Cioran: "The Jews do not wish to live in a strong Romania, aware of its own identity." And there is his famous declaration from *The Transfiguration of Romania*: "If I were a Jew, I would instantly kill myself."[47]

Yet as Petreu painstakingly documents, Cioran was far more subtle and interesting than Mircea Eliade, Nae Ionescu, and other intellectuals who were simply smitten by the Iron Guard. Cioran admits at length that his Romania of the 1930s owes much to the nineteenth-century and early-twentieth-century modernizing influence of the liberal West. His plea for further modernization and subsequent industrialization, coupled with his relative lack of interest in Orthodoxy (and rural traditions in general), separates him from the blood-and-soil nativism of Eliade and the Iron Guard. In the 1950s, living in exile in Paris, and thoroughly bewildered by the results of the war and by the revelations of the Holocaust, Cioran declares, "*Metaphysically* speaking, I am a Jew." He cites the resilience and endurance of the Jews throughout history as constituting inspiration for himself to just go on living, despite his own damaged soul.[48] Cioran's very guilt, suffering, and inner turmoil throughout his entire life in exile raise him in moral stature above Eliade, who seems to have just shrugged off his earlier mistakes before continuing in his career as a consequential and prolific philosopher.

Cioran's later writing abounds in oblique and not-so-oblique evidence of recognition of his past sins. The former admirer of Hitler and of Codreanu's Iron Guard tells the world from his postwar Paris exile: "Any act of intolerance, of ideological intransigence, or of proselytism exposes the beastly core of all enthusiasm. . . . One can never stay far enough from the clutches of a prophet." And in what I consider his most perceptive realization, this former enfant terrible, who had once believed in "messianic nationalism," and who had called the temporizing liberal Iuliu Maniu a "distinguished, courteous weakling," now states: "One can only be a *liberal* out of exhaustion, and a democrat out of rational thought."[49]

In other words, liberalism and democracy, with all of their limitations, are what remains after every utopia and extremist scheme based on blood and territory has been exposed and shattered by reality. Hitler gone; Codreanu gone; Antonescu gone; whereas the noble statue of Iuliu Maniu reigns over Piața Revoluției in the heart of Bucharest, as it should. Rather than defend something grand and remote, like the marching masses or the ethnic nation, Maniu, like the hero of Kafka's *Castle*, represented the sanctity of the individual and his right to freedom and existence.[50] That is why, as prominent as he was, Maniu was out of fashion during Romania's terrible decades, and also why with all his flaws and mild prejudices he is, nevertheless, eternal. Dithering, temporizing, alas, too, a man of his time, Iuliu Maniu was the brave, decent, uncharismatic counterpart to the monsters he had to deal with.[51] As Father Dosoftei had told me at the Putna Monastery: "if you are a man in power, you must protect the weak—that is the essence of love."

Chapter VI

THE PONTIC BREACH

BETWEEN MY VISITS TO ROMANIA IN THE FALL OF 2013 AND THE spring of 2014, Central and Eastern Europe had undergone a geopolitical earthquake. In 2013, Romania had constituted a journalistic backwater—not so different from my visits there in the 1980s—and words like "Moldova" and "Transdniestria" were virtually absent from the news. When I told people I was researching a book on Greater Romania, they looked puzzled, since the headlines were clearly focused elsewhere, whether in Asia or the Middle East. "Why?" they asked. The conventional wisdom had it that Europe was strictly an economic story, having to do with an ongoing financial crisis in the European Union. For years I had passionately countered that the Russians, taking advantage of Europe's fiscal woes, were attempting to buy banks and electricity grids, oil refineries, and natural gas transportation networks, in addition to other infrastructure, even as they extended their energy pipeline network throughout the former Soviet satellite states. Meanwhile, a financially weakened Europe had less political capital to draw countries like Romania, Moldova, Serbia, Bulgaria, and Ukraine closer into its fold, in exchange for social and economic reforms. And I published articles in 2012 and 2013 specifically to that effect.[1] But I did not expect Ukraine in early 2014 to suddenly provide a new paradigm for Europe, overturning the previous one, which had reigned since the fall of the Berlin Wall in 1989.

It had all happened so quickly.

In response to popular demonstrations in early 2014 that eventually toppled the pro-Russian, elected government of Viktor Yanukovych in the Ukrainian capital of Kiev, Russian president Vladimir Putin dispatched special forces to the Crimean Peninsula on the Black Sea in southern Ukraine and in March 2014 formally annexed the territory, which was already home to the Russian Black Sea Fleet. Putin then lent a surreptitious hand to the takeovers of public buildings by pro-Russian gunmen in eastern Ukraine, even as he massed tens of thousands of troops near Ukraine's border with Russia. Having lost a pro-Russian regime in Kiev, Putin was intent on destabilizing the new pro-Western regime there, while also attempting to hive off parts of Ukraine's east. Thus did Ukraine settle into low-intensity conflict. Thus did Putin undermine the overarching assumption governing post–Cold War Europe—that Russia was contained.

After all, with the former states of the Warsaw Pact in Eastern Europe having joined both the North Atlantic Treaty Organization and the European Union, with the three Baltic republics of the former Soviet Union having done likewise, with Belarus nominally independent, and with Ukraine and Moldova (former Bessarabia) existing as buffer states between Russia and the West, historic Russia had been moved bodily eastward, neutering it in the eyes of the West. But Putin's rapid-fire aggression plainly indicated otherwise. Romania and Moldova/Bessarabia had suddenly become front-line states in what some dubbed a "new Cold War."

This so-called new Cold War was just as much about ideology as the old Cold War. Though the new Cold War erupted in 2014, it was best explained in a conversation in 1991 in Prague between the Polish historian and intellectual Adam Michnik and the late Czech president and playwright Václav Havel. With the Soviet Union about to expire and the Yugoslav war having just begun, Michnik remarked to Havel:

Communism was an ideology that in an extraordinarily simple way . . . was capable of explaining to any idiot the complexities of the world. It was enough to know a few formulas to be wiser than Plato, Heidegger, or Descartes. And here Communism collapsed, and along with it this simple way of explaining the world. There remained a vacuum. And don't you have the impression that into that gap is now entering a coarse and primitive nationalism? That those people who explained the world to themselves by using Communist categories are now doing it by using nationalist categories?[2]

Indeed, the nationalism that Putin employed to whip up the fury of the masses in Russia, in order to justify his actions in Ukraine, was not the nationalism of "emancipation," "human dignity," and "pride" of the kind that had motivated the revolutionaries in 1848 in Europe, for example. Nor, for that matter, was it like the Ukrainian nationalism of 2014, which yearned for a destiny with a freedom-loving, universalist West.[3] Instead it was a vulgar, exclusivist nationalism that in character was a direct descendant of Communist maxims.

This was all prologue to my latest visit to Romania.

"NATO'S ARTICLE FIVE IS LITTLE PROTECTION against Putin's Russia," Iulian Fota, Romania's presidential national security advisor, told me on my first morning back in Bucharest. With his clipped salt-and-pepper beard and hair, and his mournful expression, there was the air of the monastery about Fota. "Article Five protects Romania, Poland, and the other countries against a military invasion. But it does not protect against subversion," that is, intelligence activities, reliance on Russian natural gas, the running of criminal networks, the buying up of banks, strategic assets, and media organs to undermine public opinion. It does not protect against the funding of right-wing, anti-NATO, and anti-EU parties in each country, or the bribing of parliamentarians. "Putin is not an apparatchik; he is a former intelligence officer,"

Fota went on. "Putin's Russia will not fight conventionally for territory in the former satellite states, but unconventionally for hearts and minds. Putin knows that the flaw of the Soviet Union was that it did not have soft power. Putin knows that in this battle Gazprom is more useful than the Russian army. We began to tell our friends in Washington about all this some years ago. The Pentagon understood but your State Department was less interested. They thought we Romanians were being a bit paranoid."

Fota and I had been driving beyond Bucharest into a forest that ended in a clearing with a modernist, neoclassical villa. In the 1930s, the villa had once been the home of King Carol II's mistress, Elena Lupescu.[4] Now it was the headquarters of the Romanian domestic intelligence agency, the heir to the feared and hated Securitate of the Communist era. It was run by George Cristian Maior, who received Fota and myself in his office. Maior, who had studied law at George Washington University after Ceauşescu's downfall, spoke softly with the understated professionalism of a Beltway think-tanker. Romania, he told me, was back to being what it had been for so much of its Ottoman-era history, "a frontier state of the West facing the East." The Russians, he explained, were "applying active measures in the classical sense," a reference to the examples of low-cost subversion Fota had just talked about: a form of warfare containing attributes of both antiquity and postmodernism that made nineteenth- and twentieth-century conventional warfare, with its artillery and tank battalions, irrelevant. It was all about taking over countries from within. And because sowing confusion could be a deliberate tool of aggression in this kind of warfare, Russia's oh-so-suave foreign minister, Sergey Lavrov—who cut such a charismatic figure compared to U.S. secretary of state John Kerry and European Union foreign policy chief Catherine Ashton— seemingly contradicted himself from week to week, complaining about problems that he and his side had, in fact, just created.

After the chaos of Boris Yeltsin's rule, the Russians had simply rediscovered the czarist imperial tradition (one that Stalin himself had perfected), and "they now want Finlands everywhere," Maior said. During

MIRCEA THE OLD (1355–1418). Because of Mircea's fighting and maneuvering, in the words of one historian, "Wallachia survived as a political entity at a time when the Turks were liquidating the czardoms of Bulgaria and Serbia."

VLAD ȚEPEȘ DRACULA (1431–1476). Vlad's sobriquet became *Țepeș*, "the Impaler," because of the way he tortured his personal enemies and captured Turks alike. Under the name Vlad Țepeș Dracula—"son of the Dragon"—he became the stuff of Gothic legends that had as their origin his extreme cruelty and strong sense of justice. However, *Dracul*, "the Dragon," referred not to anything cruel, but to an honorary feudal order.

STEPHEN THE GREAT (1433–1504). He centralized bureaucratic power and built a military machine in Moldavia that allowed him to fight a legendary forty wars during his long reign and prepared him for his epic confrontation with Ottoman Turkey.

MICHAEL THE BRAVE (1558–1601). He ascended the throne of Muntenia in 1593. By the time he was assassinated in 1601, he was the first Romanian-speaking prince in history to rule all three principalities—Wallachia, Moldavia, and Transylvania—if only for a few months in 1600. A figure of the late Renaissance, Michael might arguably have been the fullest expression of what Machiavelli, a father of the Renaissance, meant by a true prince.

ALEXANDRU IOAN CUZA (1820–1873). In 1859, Wallachia and Moldavia separately elected him as the prince of what would be known as the United Principalities of Moldavia and Wallachia—the first real Romanian state. Cuza labored in office against an atmosphere of debilitating poverty, widespread disease, nonexistent roads and schools, and de jure (albeit not de facto) Ottoman suzerainty, with Russia and Austria always hovering nearby.

CAROL I HOHENZOLLERN-
SIGMARINGEN (1839–1914).
In his forty-eight-year
reign—one year longer
than Stephen the
Great's—this German-
born king literally built a
modern bureaucratic state
out of the ramshackle
contrivance of the
United Principalities of
Wallachia and Moldavia.
Thus, he is very much the
father of the Romania that
exists today, and his statue
graces the main square
of Bucharest.

Proclamation of the union between
Moldavia and Wallachia, 1859.

KING FERDINAND (1865–1927) AND QUEEN MARIE (1875–1938). The English-born Marie helped convince her husband, Ferdinand, the nephew of Carol I, to side with Great Britain, France, and Russia against Germany during the First World War. Though Romania was occupied by Germany, Germany's subsequent defeat led to the emergence of an enlarged Romanian state including Transylvania. Marie was known for her bravery in ministering to her troops and for a larger-than-life personality.

KING CAROL II (1893–1953). The dictatorial, corrupt, and undisciplined rule of Carol II, son of Ferdinand and Marie, helped along the territorial dismemberment of Romania engineered by Hitler and Stalin, though even a wiser ruler than Carol II probably would not have been able to prevent such loss of territory, given the desertion of Central and Eastern Europe by the West at Munich.

Ion Antonescu (1882–1946). The dictator of Romania during World War II, Antonescu was a militarist, nationalist, and authoritarian without being strictly a fascist. He was Hitler's most crucial foreign ally, contributing 585,000 troops to the invasion of the Soviet Union and meeting with Hitler ten times. He is responsible for the murder of 300,000 Jews, even as he kept a larger number from the gas chambers. In the words of one noted historian, he was a conservative anti-Semite, as opposed to a millenarian anti-Semite like Adolf Eichmann or Alfred Rosenberg.

MIRCEA ELIADE (1907–1986). He was arguably Romania's most famous intellectual and philosopher during the twentieth century. As a young man he, like other Romanian intellectuals, was attracted to the fascist cause. Romania is somewhat unusual in that its intellectuals, rather than being emotionally attracted to the left, have often been attracted to the right.

IULIU MANIU (1873–1953). An opponent of the Nazis when it was unfashionable and dangerous to be so, and equally an opponent of the Communists later on when it was also dangerous and unfashionable, Maniu was a liberal democrat to the extent that it was possible to be so in mid-twentieth-century Romania. He died in Sighet prison in northern Romania, a heroic victim of tyranny. His statue, along with that of Carol I, graces Bucharest's main square.

EMIL CIORAN (1911–1995). Deeply attracted to the fascists as a young man, he suffered from guilt and depression during his long exile in Cold War France. His tragedy was that he was brilliant and creative even as he was immature and lacking in common sense. Only in recognition of his intellectual failure did he achieve maturity. But at least he felt remorse, unlike the more confident Eliade, who in later life mainly shrugged off his earlier alliance with pro-Hitler forces.

GHEORGHE GHEORGHIU-DEJ (1901–1965). The Communist boss of Romania from 1947 until his death in 1965, he was at once avuncular and absolutely brutal. He decimated what remained of a middle class and bourgeois culture in Romania during the late 1940s and 1950s, reducing the country to the atmosphere and conformity of a prison yard. He represented the homegrown national Communists who purged the so-called Moscow Communists, those who had spent World War II in the Soviet Union.

Nicolae (1918–1989) and Elena Ceaușescu (1916–1989). A homegrown national Communist who took over at the death of Gheorghiu-Dej, Nicolae Ceaușescu mixed Stalinist-style central command economics and repression with a North Korean–style personality cult. By the time he and his wife were executed, they had reduced Romania to a level of poverty unlike any other in the Warsaw Pact. Though Ceaușescu himself was for decades a wily operator, in later years, as his health deteriorated, he relied increasingly on his less politically astute wife, whose decisions helped lead to their violent deaths.

チャウシェスク夫妻

Ion Iliescu (1930–) A lifelong Communist, he took power following the Ceauşescus' execution and gave the country stability in the early 1990s, even as he postponed necessary reforms. As a result, Romania lagged behind other former Communist countries in economic development, but one may argue that it also avoided the ethnic warfare of Yugoslavia and occasional bouts of anarchy such as those in Albania and Bulgaria. Iliescu typifies how Romania's 1989 revolution was less a revolution than a violent transfer of power from Communist hard-liners to more liberal Communists, who then paved the way for the authentic democracy of the late 1990s.

the Cold War, though Finland was capitalist and democratic, its foreign and defense policy was subservient to the Soviet Union—a form of capitulation based on geography: it did not entail the vast expenditures from the Kremlin that were required to keep the satellite states of the Warsaw Pact in line. Finlandization had constituted a successful form of empire in a way that the Warsaw Pact ultimately never did.

Maior continued: "We see the Russians buying influence with local medias and politicians in the region, and trying to take advantage of post-Communist privatizations," so as to establish commercial footholds. For example, Serbia was trying to get into the European Union, even though, as I was told, its banks, infrastructure, judges, and politicians were being purchased by the Russians, with Moscow and St. Petersburg oligarchs heavily invested in adjacent Montenegro.[5] The situation in neighboring Bulgaria was similar, though not quite as extreme. I thought of what Bernard Fall, a mid-twentieth-century French-American historian and war correspondent in Vietnam, had written: "When a country is being subverted it is not being outfought; it is being out-administered. Subversion is literally administration with a minus sign in front."[6] The Russians knew how to administer these borderlands of Europe from behind the scenes. But even with all of that, Maior emphasized, "we are not reliving the interbellum period. The United States is here and with us now, not like in the 1930s. And Putin is not Stalin."

Fota and I drove back to his office in the Cotroceni Palace, built by Carol I in neo-Brâncoveanu style so evocative of Greece. But there is an old part to this palace, built in the late seventeenth century, whose arched and narrow, cavernous hallways reminded me of the wondrous monastic complexes I had visited on Mount Athos decades earlier. The courtyard was graced by a new church that had replaced a seventeenth-century one built by the Cantacuzino family (a branch of the medieval Greek Phanariots), which Ceauşescu had ordered demolished.

An entire wall of Fota's office was covered with a map of the Marea Neagră (Black Sea) and Greater Middle East. This map, he explained, was an outgrowth of his concerns in the previous decade, when Romania had troops in Afghanistan and Iraq, with Romania's Black Sea coast used as a support base for U.S. forces in the Middle East. "Now I need another map—still of the Black Sea, but showing Ukraine and the rest of Central and Eastern Europe. And now after helping you Americans fight in Afghanistan and Iraq for years, Romania requires your assistance with troops and air and sea defense."

In a small ceremonial hall blessed by stained glass windows showing the various Cantacuzino rulers of Wallachia, Romanian president Traian Băsescu spent an hour with me poring over three maps he had brought along with him: of Central and Eastern Europe, Ukraine, and Moldova/Transdniestria. In his tenth and last year as president, Băsescu, tilting his bald head as he talked, was consumed by I-told-you-so frustration. His entire small, frail body had the tension of a fist. "We are a somewhat energy-rich island surrounded by a Gazprom empire," he told me, tracing with his finger how Romania's neighbors such as Bulgaria and Hungary were almost completely dependent on Russian natural gas. Romania—because of its own hydrocarbon reserves—still had a significant measure of independence. "In the twenty-first century, Gazprom is more dangerous than the Russian army," and thus was another weapon of unconventional, subversive war. Băsescu's frustration boiled over when he talked about how Nabucco, a planned pipeline network to bring Azerbaijani natural gas across Anatolia to the Balkans and Central Europe, had been killed by a combination of "economic interests"—Russian bribery and sabotage—and the failure of the West to see Nabucco for what it truly was: a geopolitical necessity, not a phenomenon of economics. Instead, South Stream, a pipeline project that would transport Russian natural gas to the Balkans, was going forward at least for the moment.

Băsescu then traced for me a line from the Ukrainian city of Odessa westward along the Black Sea to Romania's Danube Delta, indicating Russia's territorial acquisition plans for the coming years and decades. I argued that Odessa was an immense city with stores of cosmopolitanism and Ukrainian nationalism. He and others I met that day countered that the Russians needed only more time, to buy up media and other assets in Odessa, in order to undermine municipal politicians and public opinion. The area from Odessa westward to Romania's own Black Sea coast—in the former Turkish Budjak, south of Moldova— was populated with ethnic Russians. Odessa was the hinge for the whole crisis, I was told. As for Ukraine, the squabbling politicians in Kiev had no common philosophy of governance, in the Romanian view. Unlike Romania, Ukraine never had an Iliescu to give it coherence. Ukraine is all oligarchy and bankruptcy, one Romanian official said, waving his hand in dismissal.

These men in high positions of power in Bucharest labored under the knowledge that the average Romanian would never again accept a border with Russia—but if Ukraine were ever overrun, that would be Romania's fate. Underscoring the crisis was also the knowledge that Romania's greatest vulnerability, albeit to a lesser extent than Ukraine, was its own weak governing institutions; the reason why the Orthodox Church, the army, and the post-Ceauşescu-era security services were the most trusted organizations in the country, according to recent polls.

Whereas the Romanian president occupies palatial surroundings, the office of the Romanian prime minister, Victor Ponta, was in a Communist-era, architecturally desolate building oppressed by concrete. In the waiting room there was a wall of photos of Ponta's predecessors going back to the late nineteenth century. I gazed at the faces of Iuliu Maniu, Octavian Goga, Nicolae Iorga, and Marshal Ion Antonescu—a humanist hero, two anti-Semites, and a mass murderer. Ponta, a generation younger than Băsescu, wore fashionable jeans and went without a necktie. His office was crammed with sports memorabilia. While Băsescu, a former Communist-era merchant mariner, was all sturdy internal tension, Ponta, a former student leader, was all breezy surface charm. The two men despised each other, as everyone knew. Ponta's message was similar, though. It was all about Russian subversion.

Ponta said that Romania's most capable regional allies in the com-

ing struggle had to be Poland and Turkey (ironically, the former Ottoman enemy). Members of the Romanian elite looked up to Poland as
a much better governed and more powerful version of themselves,
even if Poland felt, in a certain sense, quite distant: you had to cross
the winding Carpathians not once but twice to get to Warsaw from
Bucharest. Polish foreign minister Radosław Sikorski, along with Swed-
ish foreign minister Carl Bildt, were at the time pushing the European
Union toward a tougher stance in defense of Ukraine. Turkey, meanwhile, was just *there*: the great geographical fact dominating the Black
Sea's southern seaboard, which constituted both a potential and necessary ally against Russia, though Turkey itself was also heavily dependent on Russian natural gas, arriving via the Blue Stream pipeline
from across the Black Sea.

Precisely because Romania was historically a victim of geography,
nobody here dismissed geopolitics. And geopolitics, in a variation of
Polish statesman Józef Piłsudski's 1920s concept of an Intermarium
("between the seas"), demanded the re-creation of a belt of independent states between the Baltic and Black seas, to guard against Russian
expansion westward. On this visit to Bucharest, I constantly had maps
and pipeline routes thrust at me.

AFTER A FEW DAYS IN BUCHAREST, I repeated my journey from the
previous autumn to Jassy. From there I would cross the Prut River
eastward into Moldova: historic Bessarabia. In Jassy I was met by the
county council president, Cristian Mihai Adomniței, who immediately reflected on how a relatively small group of Bolshevik conspira-
tors had taken the great cities of Moscow and St. Petersburg in
November 1917. "Putin is heir to this tradition," Adomniței said. "In
his heart, he is a Bolshevik. He knows that you can conquer vast territories without big armies. If Odessa ever falls, the Moldovans next door
fear that they are doomed." Adomniței took me inside Jassy's National
Theater. Whereas the Athenaeum in Bucharest is an exuberant statement of an age (the Belle Époque prior to World War I), Jassy's Na-

tional Theater, built in 1840 and renovated in the mid-1890s, is a precious, intimate little jewel, dripping in gold leaf, in celebration of the rococo and baroque styles. Verdi's *Traviata* was to be performed here in only a few days. Alone with me in the empty theater, Adomniţei declared, "Here is Europe, here is its history and its culture, its artistic values, and maybe soon its political values. Here is the borderland of the Habsburg Empire. We need your help to defend us."

THE SOMNOLENT PRUT, little more than a creek almost, was smothered in vegetation. I spotted acacias and walnut trees as I crossed the Prut from Romania east to Moldova. Immediately the quality of the road deteriorated and the houses became more poverty-stricken: marked by rust, scrap iron, and undressed concrete, just like the Romania I had known from a generation before, though with a sprinkle of new signage and gas stations. I knew that the houses along the road were all connected to a natural gas pipeline network coming from western Siberia—the quality of life here was dependent upon Russia. Men and women in dusty fedoras and kerchiefs rolled by in horse-drawn *leiterwagens*. In the first town through which I passed, Ungheni, the park and sidewalks were all devoured by weeds. Mint-and-white Russian neoclassical architecture, with the dimensions of the columns and capitals exaggerated, dominated the square. A massive Moldovan flag hung from a building, differentiated from the Romanian flag only by a slightly altered coat of arms: with the eagle—a symbol of Latinity—still there.

The lack of development meant an undefiled landscape between the little towns, with immense plains and sprawling, monumental hills pleated with corn and wheat fields, and the sides of the road thick with chestnuts, poplars, oaks, young birch, and those beech trees that the Russians so loved to plant, as though a conscious symbol of empire. I spotted a rail line. Russian imperial control of Moldova was most effectively witnessed in the width of the railway gauges: the wider Russian gauge of five feet on all the tracks in Moldova compared with the

European gauge of four feet eight and a half inches throughout Romania proper.[7] The difference in the gauges helped protect Russia from an invasion from the west.

I stopped for coffee by a willow-shaded lake filmy with pine needles and poplar feathers, and lined with potted petunias, the kind of scene that rewarded solitude.

It was time to think.

I WAS NOW IN historic Bessarabia, so named after the fourteenth-century family of Wallachian *voivodes* known as the Basarabs, who extended their rule northeastward from the Danube Delta in order to take advantage of the Black Sea trade. They may have been, at least in part, of Cuman (Turkic) origin, and this—at least one historian suggests—might have assisted them with the other Tatars in the region.[8] Bessarabia, with a few minor territorial adjustments, has gone by the name of Moldova in recent decades: it encompasses the part of Moldavia inside the former Soviet Union, as opposed to the part which forms eastern Romania.

Moldova was in the second half of the twentieth century a small Soviet republic in the southwestern corner of the empire, more or less squeezed between the Prut River—on the other bank of which lay Romania to the west—and the Dniester River—on the other bank of which lay Ukraine to the east. Whereas Ukraine had always been a Soviet republic, Moldova had been part of Romania between 1918 and 1940. In 1989, when the Berlin Wall fell, over 70 percent of the population was ethnic Romanian, with the remainder including ethnic Russians and ethnic Ukrainians. But these ethnic Romanians have their own distinct identity owing to the fact that they were not part of Romania during the nineteenth century, when Romania's modern national consciousness was being formed and when the Latin script had replaced the Cyrillic one. Mikhail Gorbachev's political liberalization of the Soviet Union in the second half of the 1980s encouraged Romanian nationalism in Moldova, and at the end of the decade Moldova made Romanian the state language and adopted the Latin script, along with the Romanian flag with some variations, and—until 1994—the Romanian national anthem. This drew ferocious protests from Moldova's Russian and Ukrainian minorities, whose demographic stronghold was in a sliver of Moldova east of the Dniester (and west of the Southern Bug) in the heavily industrialized region of Transdniestria ("beyond the Dniester," the site of Antonescu's Holocaust of the Jews).[9]

Whereas Moldova is agricultural, Transdniestria is a production center for metals, chemicals, and energy derivatives. And while Bessarabia had changed hands between Romania and Russia several times over the past two hundred years, Transdniestria has always remained within the Russian orbit. It was in Transdniestria that the Soviets had placed one of the largest ammunition dumps in Europe, at Colbasa in the north of the territory, for it was from here that the Soviets designed a staging post for the invasion of the Balkans and Greece.[10]

Moldova is dominated by ethnic Romanians, but only a third of Transdniestria's population of 400,000 is of Romanian descent (though reliable demographic data was unavailable at the time of this writing). At the beginning of the 1990s, Moldova declared its independence from the Soviet Union, even as Transdniestria, with encouragement from the Kremlin, seceded from Moldova in a political drama that included a war which left over a thousand dead and 130,000 internally displaced. As Georgetown professor Charles King has written, while the conflict was not about ancient hatreds, "history did play an important role."[11]

Transdniestria, in sum, was not part of historic Greater Romania: it was only Stalin's arbitrary decision that made Transdniestria part of Moldova. Stalin had a habit of creating republics deliberately composed of rival ethnic groups so as to make their secession from Moscow impossible without bloodshed. (Stalin and his successors in the Kremlin had always spoken the rhetoric of interethnic comradeship, yet they trusted only ethnic Russians in the key security posts in Moldova.) "Transdniestria is not a country or even a territory, it is a Stalin-invented logistics and intelligence base for any Russian strike south," explained

Sergiu Celac, a former Romanian foreign minister and interpreter for both Ceaușescu and Gheorghiu-Dej. And it wasn't only Transdniestria that was controlled by the Russians, but adjacent parts of Moldova proper itself. For example, there was Tighina (Bender in Turkish), just on the western bank of the Dniester in Moldova proper, which was now in the hands of pro-Russian separatists.

Yet Moldova—even following Transdniestria's and Tighina's secession from it—remains an ethnic stew beyond its Russian and Ukrainian minorities. For example, in southern Moldova live 160,000 Gagauz, a Turkic people who migrated from Bulgaria and the Dobrudja and converted to Orthodox Christianity. Their existence as Christian Turks is testimony to the influence of the former Ottoman Empire this far north, as well as to the complexity of cultural identity that can undermine stereotypes.[12] In fact, cultural identity is so complex that Professor King, among the leading experts in the field, calls nationality here a "decidedly negotiable proposition."[13]

Moldova (or geographic Bessarabia) is now crucial in the world of geopolitics, far out of proportion to its small size and meager population of 3.56 million. And this would not be the first time in modern history it was so. The transfer of southern Bessarabia to Romania was considered by Russian czar Alexander II as the last surviving "humiliation" of the Crimean War. Russia's determination to get back Bessarabia in the middle and latter parts of the nineteenth century, in order to keep it out of a Turkish sphere of influence, formed a central part of the so-called Eastern Question of the era: that is, *How should the great powers respond to the slow-motion demise of the Ottoman Empire?*[14]

Located between the Black Sea and the Carpathians, Moldova is central to Ukraine's security to the same extent that Ukraine's security is central to Russia's. Were Moldova to fall into hostile hands, Ukraine would be threatened, for Moldova combined with Transdniestria occupies what I like to term the Pontic Breach, the hinterland of the Black Sea that offers an invasion route to (or from) the Balkans and the Mediterranean.[15] Just as the North European Plain—Poland, Belarus, and the Baltic States—comprises the northern invasion route between

Europe and Russia, the Pontic Breach comprises the southern invasion route.

As for Ukraine, it is the pivot state that in and of itself transforms
Russia. Ukraine was the heartland of ninth-century Kievan Rus, and
thus is historically and emotionally fundamental to Russia's identity.
Ukraine's very independence both geographically and demographi-
cally keeps Russia to a significant degree out of Europe, even as Russia
must struggle to maintain some strategic control over Ukraine despite
the latter's claim to sovereignty. This is a reason why Russia maintains
thousands of troops and military assets in Transdniestria.[16] It is why
Putin is able to manipulate Russian public opinion on the issue.

So, having considered in the last chapter the humanitarian cost of
Antonescu's 1941 invasion and occupation of Bessarabia and Transdniestria, we should now consider the strategic one. For not only was
the great Soviet-Ukrainian metropolis of Kiev at least theoretically
threatened by Antonescu's forces: by occupying the port city of
Odessa—the farthest point of advance of Antonescu's army in
Transdniestria—the Nazi-allied Romanians during Operation Barbarossa cut off Stalin's major outlet to the Black and Mediterranean
seas. No wonder Stalin moved his troops so decisively into Romania in
1944 when he had the chance! No wonder he insisted on a show trial
and the execution of Antonescu, and after that proceeded to hammer
the Romanian population down into abject submission in the late
1940s and early 1950s. The Warsaw Pact was created not only out of
Stalin's evil intent, but out of Soviet strategic necessity immediately
after the Kremlin had experienced a strategic nightmare. And what
Russia now fears, nearly three-quarters of a century later, is the same
nightmare recurring with NATO forces in the place of Antonescu's
pro-Nazi ones: forces that are equally anti-Russian, whatever the vast
differences in moral or ideological orientation. As George Friedman,
founder of the private intelligence firm Stratfor, writes: "Moldova is
valuable real estate. It is a region that in the hands of NATO . . . could
provide leverage against Russian power, and perhaps strengthen
Ukraine's desire to resist Russia. Putting NATO troops close to Odessa,

a Ukrainian port Russians depend on, would cause the Russians to be cautious."[17] That's putting it mildly. NATO troops close to Odessa might in and of itself signal strategic defeat for the Russians, especially given the ongoing East-West crisis in the region since early 2014. Therefore, any attempt of Moldova (historic Bessarabia) to reunite with Romania, a member of NATO, would have to be strongly resisted by the Kremlin.

Moldova, if not a pro-Russian state, must, from Moscow's point of view at least, remain fundamentally separated from both Romania and NATO. Thus Moldova's perennial entreaties to the European Union for a closer relationship, combined with the stirrings for unification with Romania that are never really off the table, force Russia to continually attempt to undermine Moldova from its perch in Transdniestria.

THREE HOURS AFTER LEAVING Jassy, I entered the Moldovan capital of Chişinău (Kishinev in Russian). Soviet-era apartment blocks sprouted like yellowing teeth. "Giant tombstones . . . termite towers," the Polish traveler Andrzej Stasiuk had called them.[18] I had memories of the grim outskirts of Sofia, Tiflis, Tskhinvali, and Tashkent in the 1980s and 1990s. I noticed some Russian neoclassical buildings, new German-financed Plexiglas ones, and a glitzy mall. There were streets leafy with linden trees that gave an aura of Old World stateliness and brought Pushkin to mind. The great Russian poet had lived in Chişinău unhappily in internal exile in the early 1820s, banished to what in his mind were the seedy provinces by the czarist regime for his reformist views. While the women I saw were dressed with prideful elegance, the men looked like slobs. For away from the grand boulevard, Chişinău, with a population of 670,000, was actually little more than a big village. On the buses, recently purchased from Belarus, I saw many stickers of the European Union flag, even though Moldova was not a member. The aspiration was undeniable, though. There was a church in a clearing in the Maramureş style with a Gothic spire, another poignant symbol of the West. And, as though a rebuke to the adjacent blockhouse griminess of the Soviet-era parliament building, there was the fin de siècle Italian Gothic of the city hall, with a tower that reminded me of Florence.

This was the poorest country in Europe, behind Albania even. The drive from Jassy recalled to me the descriptions of the English traveler Henry Baerlein. From a prominent Jewish family in Manchester, Baerlein published *Bessarabia and Beyond* in 1935. "Whenever we were on the road, sunk in the black and viscous mud, we were like miserable flies endeavoring to walk along a ribbon of fly-paper." Yet this very underdevelopment also meant scenes of stark and searing beauty, as revealed in the black-and-white photographs of the book's first edition. It was a time, barely a few years before the Holocaust in Bessarabia and Transdniestria, when the cobblestoned Jewish quarter of Tighina had eighteen synagogues and Chişinău itself boasted some sixty-five places of Jewish worship. Premonitions of trouble in the form of group-against-group loathing creep into Baerlein's 1935 manuscript. As one person tells the author, "Boil a Jew . . . and you get two Greeks, boil an Armenian and you get three Jews."[19]

THE SICKENING PAST HERE, for which there was simply no adequate description, and for which Baerlein's experience was but a minor foreboding, did not determine the present or the future, I had to tell myself. To wit, the first person I met the following morning was Vitalie Marinuța, Moldova's defense minister from 2009 to 2014, who in his own biography personified the robust involvement of the West and the United States in this part of the world. A graduate of a military academy in the Soviet Union at the time of its collapse, Marinuța went on to study at Lackland Air Force Base in San Antonio, at Fort Leavenworth, and at the Naval Postgraduate School in Monterey, before being assigned to U.S. Central Command in Tampa. "I lived with a local family in Leavenworth, Kansas. That was my first experience with the culture and values of democracy," he told me.

In his early forties with close-cropped black-and-gray hair, Marinuța said that his time in government was spent at "deep military restructuring" along the Western model, for which there was uncertain political support. "I wanted new uniforms, a new form of marching. You might think this is unimportant but symbols do matter, because they can change a mindset. It is all about military professionalization."

But the Moldovan army numbered only 5,000 soldiers, plus border police and interior ministry troops. The air force, except for a few helicopters, existed only on paper. Russian forces next door in Transdniestria were clearly superior. "But the Russians would more likely back an insurgency here like in eastern Ukraine," Marinuța explained. "They would use local proxies" such as the Gagauz and ethnic Russians. It would be a matter of training individual companies (of roughly 150 men each) to take back buildings and engage in small-scale, close-quarters combat. "We have twenty-eight thousand veterans of the 1992 Transdniestrian war in Moldova," so it isn't only the army that knows how to fight.

He then told me with soldierly reserve: "The state bank was taken over by Russians. The airport is a Russian concession. The gas supply is Gazprom. Russia supplies ninety-seven percent of the energy to Moldova. If Transdniestria is formally annexed by Russia, then Moldova should unite with Romania. We should have done it in the 1990s when Russia was weak. Now Russia is strong and only sixteen percent of the Moldovan population support Romanian unification."

What began as an optimistic briefing descended steeply into a very negative one. Marinuța confidently assured me that Russia "will never be liberal." In fact, almost every person I met in Chişinău, without any prompting, would tell me the same thing. I recalled one of Dosto-evsky's characters in *The Idiot* saying that "liberalism" is an "attack . . . on Russia itself": on its culture and values.[20] And yet Russia, I knew, could never really prosper, or productively decentralize its vast territory, without liberalism.

Russian illiberalism was present in the most mundane and obscure ways in Moldova, a territory ruled by Russia for much of its history, and for most of the second half of the twentieth century. For example, I was heading north from Chişinău to the monasteries of Saharna and Tipova on the banks of the Dniester (Nistru in Romanian) River, Moldova's border with Transdniestria. As had happened the day before, when driving with someone else from Jassy, my driver this time was stopped for speeding. The local police had noticed the Romanian plates and decided on a shakedown. A bribe was probably paid. In Romania, one can no longer negotiate with, or bribe, the traffic police. Membership in the European Union has changed that, by bringing the rule of law to the country. In Moldova, the police still have little dignity and are underpaid, and so they ask for bribes. This is just how it is in so many other ways throughout the former Soviet Union.

It was a better road than the one from Jassy, built to handle the traffic going to the metallurgical complex in Râbniţa, just across the Dniester. But with Transdniestria closed off and having become a hostile Russian satellite, especially since the Ukraine crisis, the road was practically empty—even as some metallurgical products still managed to be smuggled into Moldova by trucks from across the river.

The smoke from the metallurgical complex appeared, and in the distance I spied the clay ridges on the other side of the Dniester—Transdniestria. Soon I was driving along the still and shallow river itself. It was much wider than the Prut. The Dniester, which gave off a breeze, felt like a frontier in a way that the Prut did not. Here Latinity finally comes to an end on the road east, I thought. On the other side there was a monument in honor of Transdniestria's liberation by the Soviets from Antonescu's marauding and murderous Romanian army of the era.

The Saharna monastery had been rebuilt in the Russian style in the late nineteenth century, complete with onion domes and light blue shades. "For almost a century down to the First World War, the church in Bessarabia was subject to relentless centralization and Russification [emanating from St. Petersburg]," writes the historian Keith Hitchins.[21] It was mainly through the institution of the Orthodox Church that Russia's imperial control made itself felt, especially by the Church's implementation of the czarist legal framework. The Russian Orthodox Church has always sought to emulate across an immense tract of Eurasian territory the pivotal role of the Greek Orthodox Church in medieval Byzantium. Whereas the Romanian Orthodox Church was historically an agent for the preservation of ethnic consciousness during Muslim Turkish rule, the Russian Orthodox Church was all about empire. Both were national churches, but the political circumstances for each were different. As recently as 2013, Russian patriarch Kirill, in a bow to Kremlin imperialism, suggested publicly that Moldova was traditionally part of Russia. Except for the interbellum period, the Moldovan church has been subordinate to Moscow, even as the hymns and liturgy have been allowed to be sung in Romanian. It was a complex relationship, as the Romanian Orthodox Church claimed equal canonical rights here, even if Russian religious domination was often the reality on the ground. To this day, the Orthodox Church here is anti-European, Virgil Pâslariuc, a Byzantine historian in Chişinău, had told me.

The icons and iconostasis of Saharna told the story of a more brutal form of Russian imperialism than that of the czars. After 1944, when Stalin regained Bessarabia from Antonescu, the Soviets burned and erased much of the art here and converted Saharna into a psychiatric hospital.[22] Local ethnic Romanian villagers were able to save some of the icons, which were later brought back to the monastery in 1990–91 when an independent Moldova emerged from a collapsing Soviet Union. But overall the art here now was new, unimpressive, and hastily arranged, and more touching for it. The new and immense iconostasis faced only a small area for worship—again, in the Russian style—making for an especial, otherworldly intimacy. The bones of monks deceased through the ages had only been rediscovered in the wake of the long Soviet occupation, and were finally back on display. Ferocity had bred ferocity, in other words: first Antonescu in Transdniestria, then the Soviets in Bessarabia. It was as though the centuries of Bessarabia existing as a fought-over borderland had culminated in the most inhuman intensity during World War II and the Cold War.

As Igor Cașu, another historian in Chișinău, had told me, pro-Russian elements in both Moldova and Transdniestria to this day use the war crimes committed by Antonescu against the Jews and others as proof of the evil of Romania and—by extension—of the West.

More rescued icons were displayed in the nearby cathedral, amid the masses of censers and an iconostasis from Bukovina that was about fifteen feet high, though it might as well have been ten stories given its majestic effect on me. Listening in the incense-filled darkness to the hymns sung in Romanian, the cultic primitiveness that was early Christianity provided as close a re-creation of heaven as one is likely to find on earth.

An hour away through the interminable, undefiled breadbasket that are the rolling hills of northeastern Moldova, I came to Tipova, a smaller monastery perched on an upland overlooking the Dniester, where some men and women were cutting and piling the grass with hand tools, and horses and goats frolicked in the fields. It might have been a scene from a previous century. The small church was empty. The sound of the sparrows outside seemed to intensify the silence inside. I walked down the steep and seemingly endless switchback trail to the bottom of the riverbank, where there were a series of caves. Here the skeletons of twenty-two monks had been reburied after the Soviet occupation. In one of these caves, according to legend, Stephen the Great—whose life story as told in Greater Romania can sometimes be as vague and monumental as that of Christ himself—is reputed to have been married to Maria din Mangop in 1472. Or was it to Maria Voichița in 1478? I never could get a firm answer, and no work of history that I found could provide it for me.

The Dniester was a shallow band of leaden ocher in the receding sun. I was extremely fatigued and dusty, and in a grumpy mood. For an instant I was rude to my guide, a local woman who had the appearance of having been beaten down by the years, and I could tell that she was hurt. I felt miserable about it for days afterward. For I knew that as an outsider my behavior was being constantly scrutinized. The more fragile and embattled the country, the more sensitive the people are to what a stranger thinks. I gazed at the opposite bank of the Dniester. The river's beauty only increased my remorse. I recalled momentarily the events of 1941–42 in Transdniestria, and, overwhelmed, choked slightly, with nothing useful to say, or think even.

A final thought on Transdniestria: not mine, but a poet's. Paul Celan was born to a Jewish family in northern Bukovina in 1920. In World War II his parents were deported to Transdniestria, where his father died of typhus and his mother was killed by a shot in the neck. Celan commited suicide in Paris in 1970. Claudio Magris, the lyrical historian and encyclopedist of Central Europe, calls Celan "the last Orphic poet," whose work "leans out over the brink of silence" and evinces a "blinding, primeval purity," thereby casting a spell. Here is Celan in 1952 remembering his mother:

> *Aspen tree, your leaves glance white into the dark.*
> *My mother's hair was never white.*
>
> *Dandelion, so green is the Ukraine.*
> *My yellow-haired mother did not come home.*
>
> *Rain cloud, above the well do you hover?*
> *My quiet mother weeps for everyone.*
>
> *Round star, you wind the golden loop.*
> *My mother's heart was ripped by lead.*
>
> *Oaken door, who lifted you off your hinges?*
> *My gentle mother cannot return.*[23]

BEFORE THE STATE AND THE KINGDOM there was the monastery. I was again north of Chişinău, at Old Orhei, amid another set of caves overlooking an immense valley sectioned with farm fields far below. In one cave there was a deep recess with man-made walls for the cells of individual monks who had lived here in the fifteenth century, during the lifetime of Stephen the Great. Though sunlight poured in, the shadows were cool and wondrous. A short passage led to an even larger cave crammed with icons and lit candles and an iconostasis. This had been a place of Orthodox worship through the ages, until Stalin's reconquest of Bessarabia in 1944. "But God is not lazy, he rebuilds," a monk told me.

In this cave there was no Russian Orthodoxy or Romanian Orthodoxy, there was only Eastern Orthodoxy, that is, Christianity in its original Byzantine form emerging out of the darkness of paganism. Thus, perhaps, the crowds came to this cave to make some sense out of who and what they were as a nation; to seek what defined each of them beyond their far more tangible individuality. Democracy, as corrupt and imperfect as it was in Moldova, encouraged people to be individuals. But the Church promoted life as a community, explained George Grigoriță, a counselor to the Romanian Patriarchate whom I had met in Bucharest. "It is an anchor against loneliness in the modern world."

IURIE LEANCĂ, MOLDOVA'S PRIME MINISTER at the time, greeted me in his office, a more elegant version of Prime Minister Victor Ponta's in Bucharest. Leancă, fifty, represented a pro-European party that was facing elections the coming fall. He ripped off his jacket and tie before sitting down. It had been a long day, he said. With an angular face and a full mane of white hair, he looked taller than he actually was. There was something both miniature and deeply cerebral about him. He exuded tension and was clearly preoccupied. In parliamentary systems, the monarch or president gets all the glory and the prime minister does all the work.[24] And because Moldova was an East-West war zone, politics here were particularly nasty. His was a coalition built on corruption and the dividing up of economic sectors by party barons. Yet it was probably the best government Moldova could manage, at least at the moment. Thus did the legacy of the Soviet Union live on a quarter century after Communism had collapsed.

We talked for almost an hour.

Leancă kept using the words "nervous" and "uncertainty" to describe the political atmosphere that had gripped the country since January 2014, when the Ukraine crisis had begun. His eyes half-closed in both fatigue and thought, he said: "The European security architecture that had existed since 1989 has vanished before our eyes." He paraphrased Zbigniew Brzezinski as saying that Russia without Ukraine cannot be an empire, and it was Putin's desire to convert Russia "from a regional power to a world power." Just as Romanian president Băsescu had done, he drew a line westward along the Black Sea beyond Odessa, through the former Bessarabian Budjak, to the Danube Delta, in order to indicate Russian imperial aims. "Moldova is an easy target. What could we do? Resist for a few hours?" he said in a bitter tone. As one foreign diplomat had told me, "Moldova is simple for the Russians compared to Ukraine."

This wasn't just a military matter. For Moldova's very identity was "still an issue in motion," Leancă explained, with strong Russian, Ukrainian, and Turkic elements coexisting in the country, and a Romanian majority that until the end of the Cold War had used the Cyrillic alphabet to read and write. And with corruption the overwhelming fact of political life that dare not speak its name, nationality questions received more public prominence than they deserved.

The prime minister did not have to tell me that Moldova, which had never really been independent in its history, was a psychological battlefield between East and West. Moldova had not fought for its independence, but like the Central Asian republics of the former Soviet Union, had independence thrust upon it. And because, since 1991, Moldova has decided on neutrality, with little possibility of joining the European Union, Russian influence remained formidable: Moldovans could afford to travel to Russia, while they could not afford to go to Europe. Meanwhile, Leancă went on, Russian influence through the media and the banks in the country was "hugely negative." I thought of my hotel, the Leogrand, filled with burly Russian-speaking men. Whenever I was conducting an interview in the upstairs lobby, they hovered barely a few feet away from me with satchels large enough to conceal an old-fashioned recording device. They were quite brazen about it, as if they owned the country. As one high-ranking Moldovan government official responded when I told him that his conversation with me could be off the record: "it doesn't matter, in this hotel nothing is secret."

The meeting with the prime minister ended, like so many other meetings here, with a discussion of natural gas pipeline routes. Moldova, Leancă said, could reduce its dependence on Russian energy by a pipeline from Romania that was to be activated in the near future. His voice and whole manner only appeared hopeful as we were saying goodbye, when he spoke of potential gas discoveries in Romania and off its Black Sea coast.

I WAS NOW HEADING NORTHWEST. The sensuous, undulating landscape, with its black bars of cultivation, must have been a bounty to the invading Russians from the early nineteenth century onward, arriving as they did from across the flat and blistering immensity of European Russia and the Ukraine. I spotted vineyards that I knew from visits to Moldovan wineries, as well as from experiences at the dinner table here, were evidence of some of the finest unrenowned wines in the world, with dessert variations equal to some of the most expensive French Sauternes. (But Moldova wasn't wholly a wine country: kvass, a fermented rye beverage, was also drunk here as in Ukraine and Russia, if not in Romania.) Bălți, Moldova's second city, appeared at first as a disease growth of Soviet-era apartment buildings and a smattering of new shops: so ugly all I could think of was rotten teeth. But then came the rows of stately trees which helped redeem the view. How awful the city must look in winter, without leaves on them, I thought. A statue of Stephen the Great dominated the square, where a statue of

Lenin had been toppled after the Soviet Union collapsed. The frescoes inside the cathedral in Bălți, along with its solemn and formidable icons, comprised an oasis of beauty amid the bleakness outside.

It was the festival of St. Nikolai, and crowds filled the main promenade in their Sunday best: women in blocky high heels and men in cheap suits wearing heavy cologne, though the young wore T-shirts as they do everywhere. Balloons and children were ubiquitous. However, there was the familiar hollowness in the ambience common to cities and towns throughout Eastern Europe where the Jews had either been killed or had emigrated. A Soviet tank stood on a plinth, in memory of the 1944 liberation from Antonescu's retreating army. It was a scene out of late Communism in Budapest in the 1980s and early post-Communism in Bucharest and Sofia in the 1990s. When I mentioned this to someone in a café, he said: "You should see Tiraspol [the capital of Transdniestria] now, it looks even further behind, like the old Soviet Union."

Such crowds made me realize that progress occurs when history becomes less that of the state or nation and more that of the individuals within it, so that one grand narrative fragments into millions of parts, each with its own full-bodied story. Because Communism constricted the life of individuals through both political and economic repression, these millions of stories were less defined, and the look of a crowd showed it. The difference between the crowd in Bălți and those in provincial cities in Romania, which had joined the European Union seven years before, was vast. This crowd was more black-and-white, more monolithic; the ones in Romania were already in Technicolor.

In the gloomy shade of an empty office building in Bălți, I met Cecilia Graur, a heavyset woman with auburn hair and a pale complexion. Her stolid look made her appear the very stereotype of a Russian Communist official: she was actually the vice president of a local pro-European political party, who had only bad memories of growing up in the Soviet Union, where her parents had been looked down upon as teachers on a nearby *kolkhoz*, or collective farm.

"Everyone is afraid," she told me. "The situation in eastern Ukraine could happen here. We all know this because of our own divisions," political, ethnic, and linguistic. "People talk about it all the time." (To be sure, Bălţi, with its pro-Russian sentiment, could become a Moldovan Donetsk, a Western diplomat had warned me.) I remarked that observing the holiday crowd it seemed to me that all the young mothers and fathers cared about was a better life for their children—so that they could become individuals in a way that their parents couldn't. "Yes, that's it exactly," she exclaimed. "But what can we do?"

"The crisis has deepened nostalgia for the stability of the old Soviet Union, when there was an armaments factory here that had employed thousands of people," she said. Bălţi is 20 percent ethnic Russian, and even the ethnic Romanians here are resigned to the fact that Russia must be engaged. "Putin's appeal is widespread because his nationalist propaganda is like the old Communist propaganda." Thus was Adam Michnik's insight played back to me.

Alexander Nesterovskii was the vice president of a pro-Russia political group. He dressed in cheap polyesters and smiled always as he talked. He spoke in Russian, whereas Cecilia Graur had spoken in Romanian. But he had the same message as she did. "We must avoid turbulence now. We must avoid more polarization. Nobody wants trouble like in Donetsk or Slavyansk. But Ukraine is the first topic of conversation." He said that 60 to 70 percent of Bălţi's population supported Putin, meaning that 30 to 40 percent did not. "Odessa is the pivot. If Putin can ever dominate Odessa, Russian influence will explode throughout Gagauzia and Moldova." He said that local support for Putin represented a rational choice. People could never afford to have Russia slow down natural gas deliveries or cease buying the region's agricultural products. Because aid from the European Union had been relatively meager over the years, there was little harm the West could do here. While the Europeans were present regarding this project and that, the Russians were everywhere apparent at the grass roots. Communism no longer meant Communism per se, but an advantageous economic relationship with Russia. "My mother," he happened to mention, "is Moldovan, that is, ethnic Romanian. My father is Ukrainian. I think of myself as Russian." In better economic and political circumstances, such eclectic forms of identity could make for a vibrant cosmopolitanism. Here it made for debate and confusion.

HEADING SOUTH NOW. AGAIN, the landscape was a caressing blanket, rippling up and down in all directions in stern green shades. Ninety minutes after leaving Chișinău I spotted the flag of Gagauzia with three stars and blue, white, and red stripes waving alongside the Moldovan one. Gagauzia was legally part of Moldova, but many of its inhabitants felt alienated from the government in Chișinău.

I entered Comrat, the Gagauz capital. The signs were all in Cyrillic amid weedy streets, undressed cement, and corrugated iron. It was the same old story: the countryside was magnificent; the outskirts of the towns miserable.

The dining room of the main hotel in Comrat was designed in a hideous tubular plastic and cheap metal, with black-and-white paisley wallpaper more suited for a cramped bathroom. For me the hotel represented all the ugliness of the old Soviet Union. My memories of bad hotels in the Caucasus and Central Asia welled up. Vitaliy Kyurkchu was, according to his business card, the "chief of the general department of economic development, trade and services of Gagauzia." He had a stocky build inside his business casual attire, and acted very much like the quiet boss of the town. He told me how Czar Alexander I in the early nineteenth century had encouraged the Gagauz to move northeast from Bulgaria and the Dobrudja into the Budjak and southern Bessarabia, close to the Black Sea, by offering them privileges such as low taxes and exemption from military service. Now these Orthodox Christian Turks, numbering some 160,000, comprised almost 5 percent of the Moldovan population living on more than 5 percent of the territory. "We are deeply engaged in the Turkic and Russian worlds, but we have no emotional links whatsoever to Romania and Moldova. Russia is a more natural market for us. Our experience with Romania under its occupation between 1918 and 1940, and especially under the Antonescu regime between 1941 and 1944, was extremely negative. Such a bad memory lasts."

He went on: "We still celebrate our [short-lived] declaration of an independent Gagauzian republic on August 19, 1990, when the Soviet Union was breaking up. In 1994, Moldova gave us special autonomous status. But in reality, Chişinău does not recognize our autonomy. We Gagauz are hardworking. We produce wine, cosmetics, textiles. . . . But the budget and social services we get from Chişinău are unsatisfactory."

A lunch was brought of lamb, stuffed vine leaves, goat cheese, and other mainstays of Turkish imperial cuisine. "Forty-thousand Gagauz are stranded just on the other side of the border in the Odessa region of Ukraine. Stalin made divisions here just like he did with Transdniestria." If Ukraine and Moldova were ever to dissolve, he told me, the Gagauz will be prepared. "We have had ongoing kitchen discussions—discussions mainly among ourselves, I mean—about the creation of a Greater Gagauzia" uniting the Christian Turks on both sides of the Moldovan-Ukrainian border into a single state. "We have created forty-seven maps of the Gagauzian people and their migrations throughout history."

I walked down the street to the parliament building, marked by a large statue of Lenin striding forward with a book under his arm, presumably Marx's *Kapital.* Inside I met three local historians: Stepan Bulgar, Svetlana Romanova, and Sergei Zachariya. They plied me with books and maps. "We have a strong ethnic and national consciousness, but with few written documents and many hypotheses," Bulgar said. There then ensued a friendly argument among them about whether the Gagauz had originally come from the Dobrudja, the Caspian, or the Altai region of Central Asia; and whether their stock was not only Turkic, but also included Bulgarian and Greek forebears. "In any case, we in Gagauzia believe in our ethnic identity," one of them announced.

Here was a place where you didn't have to ask questions. People just poured out their feelings, accompanied by maps. To an extent, it brought me back to my experiences in Yugoslavia in the 1980s. But here in the spring of 2014 the gratuitous, vulgar assaults against rival ethnic groups were missing from the conversations. Hate was muted here, even regarding the Romanians, and the word "compromise" punctuated the end of many a monologue. But the Russians were reported to be buying off local leaders in Gagauzia, in an attempt to stir up ethnic animosities and further weaken Moldova as a state.

And yet Russia was seen as the ultimate protector, a country with which the Gagauz required a "strategic partnership." Russia "is a fact here and throughout Greater Ukraine. We cannot change our geography," all three historians said, almost in unison, adding that Europe has often been seen in Gagauzia through the prism of Romanian influence, which in Gagauzia has distinctly negative connotations.

"Russia gives us gas, it is to Russia where our students and migrants go. Russia was always friendly to the Orthodox peoples of the Balkans. We speak Russian," one of them declaimed matter-of-factly. Then Zachariya countered: "I know, the West has the rule of law. In Russia there is no rule of law. Europe, though, is something barely known to us. We don't know what it is."

I was taken ten miles southeast beyond Comrat, in the direction of Ukraine. Had I traveled farther, I would have encountered Moldovan villages of pro-Russian ethnic Ukrainians and pro-Russian ethnic Bulgarians. But we stopped at the town of Ferapontievca, still in Gagauzia. Here Kyurkchu showed me a brick-lined enclosure where the grass had been neatly cut, with fifty black granite slabs, each with a long list of Gagauz names in Cyrillic. These were the local dead of every conflict in the twentieth century. In most of them, the Gagauz had fought on the Russian or Soviet side. People gathered in ones and twos from the street to judge my reaction. Everyone stared. As small as Moldova was, in Gagauzia it felt vast and full of unsolvable contradictions. For Gagauzia, like the breakaway city of Tighina, like the ethnic Russian community in Bălți, and the ethnic Ukrainian and ethnic Bul-

garian communities just down the road, was the borderland of a borderland.

GIVEN, THEN: MOLDOVA CONSTITUTED a bleak political environment. Whether it was interethnic relations, the stability of its institutions, the vulnerability of its economy, the utter corruption of its
political class, the manifest Russian subversion everywhere apparent,
or the very fact of this place being a frontier region with a confused
identity, there was demonstrably much to be pessimistic about. "Since
1812, Russia has always, in the end, been able to consolidate its position here," a top-ranking Moldovan official told me. "The czars and
the Soviets destroyed our intellectual class in previous eras, now our
[Western-oriented] intellectuals are leaving for Europe."

It occurred to me that the Russians loved weak, *murky* systems,
whether autocratic or democratic—it made little difference—where it
was easy for them to bribe parliamentarians even as a handful of oligarchs controlled the economy, always hedging their bets based on
which faction and imperial system called the shots.[25] The Russians
simply hated strong governments, even authoritarian ones in some
instances. After all, the Titos of the world had little trouble keeping
the Soviets out. (So did Ceaușescu, up to a point at least.) But give the
Russians a weak and chaotic democracy like Moldova's, without the
rule of law, and the Russians were in their element. And because they
liked murkiness, whether legal, political, or otherwise, they preferred
the confused legal status of Transdniestria just as it was: if Putin officially annexed it, then Moldova would be rid of hundreds of thousands
of ethnic Russians and might then be in a position to one day reunify
with Romania. Transdniestria, a smugglers' paradise, had been the perfect Stalinist creation: one built on ethnic divisions rather than on
ethnic reconciliations.

So it wasn't a conventional land invasion of eastern Ukraine that
Putin desired so much as the creation of mini-Transdniestrias there—

a much more efficient way to weaken the Ukrainian state. *Nothing should be legally settled.* Putin had annexed Crimea only because he had to, in order to satisfy public opinion back home in Russia after the loss of the pro-Moscow Kiev regime. Crimea was *clean,* as little else would be in this new age of Russian imperial subversion, which bore striking resemblances to a nonlinear insurgency of sorts.

But while the ground-level analysis I am providing is, perforce, unsentimental and cold-blooded, the policy that emanates from it must be, if at all possible, moral and inspirational. For the future is open to all manner of possibilities, however miserable the present may seem. In the 1980s, when I reported from Ceaușescu's Romania, Moldova was about to undergo a revival under Mikhail Gorbachev's policy of perestroika, and thus would be comparatively better off. So who knows how things may look a decade hence under brave policy formulations from the West, deftly executed?

Indeed, I had been down this road before. I had described a dark human landscape in the Balkans, specifically in Yugoslavia, while reporting there in the 1980s, in advance of the violent breakup of that country in the 1990s. My writing apparently influenced a White House policy of inaction from 1993 to 1995. But, I repeat, it is only the darkest human and political landscapes where intervention is ever required in the first place. Therefore, you should never have to romanticize a landscape—or shade your analysis in any way—in order to take action on its behalf. And you should know the worst about a place before you craft even the boldest and most humanistic policy toward it. I am not in this book recommending any particular policy toward Moldova or the other Central and Eastern European states facing Russia. That is for others to do. But I am saying that there are incalculable human costs to Western inaction. And as others have said, there is a large space of opportunity between doing nothing and *putting boots on the ground.* I feared for Moldova, because I knew that what was I writing at the moment would soon be dated by events. I worried that Moldova had a future in the headlines.

CROSSING THE CARPATHIANS

WHEN I RETURNED TO ROMANIA FROM MOLDOVA IN THE SPRING of 2014, I wanted to kiss the ground. From the vantage point of Moldova, a former Soviet republic never a member of the European Union, Romania unambiguously signified the West, complete with NATO membership and institutions slowly becoming more transparent, thanks to the influence of the EU. Romania might be an Orientalized backwater when viewed from Western Europe or Poland even, but travel can be a matter of painstaking comparisons with the last place you visited. To wit, the differences between Romania and Moldova showed how *Europe* as a concept did not end at this border or that. Instead, it was a series of gradations, major and minor, gradually thinning out as one traveled east, until, at least in my own experience, it terminated finally on the Caspian Sea.

Since that visit to Romania the previous spring, much had happened by the early summer of 2014. At first, Russian president Vladimir Putin had gotten bogged down in eastern Ukraine, with pro-Russian separatists there unable to make dramatic headway in the early stages against a surprisingly effective and methodical Ukrainian military, even as those same masked separatists had notably failed to ignite a popular uprising. Tellingly, the Ukrainian Black Sea port of Odessa,

which, for a moment in the spring of 2014, looked like it might become destabilized by the Russians, showed no signs of unrest and was
completely absent from the news. But my relief didn't last long. In
August 2014, the dramatically deepening Russian military involvement in eastern Ukraine—in order to establish a land bridge to Crimea
from Russian territory—made me realize that Europe's struggle with
Russia might not occur only over the Baltics, but over the Black Sea
and involve Romania. Russia would not relent in splitting off eastern
Ukraine from the rest of the country, or in attempting to undermine
the Ukrainian government in Kiev through the various forms of subversion that the Romanian national security advisor had warned me
about months back.

Driving my fear was the sickening feeling that the governments of
Europe, sinking economically and addicted to Russian energy, simply
had too little of a bottom line; the same with the administration in
Washington. "If South Stream is ever built, Ukraine is finished," said a
Romanian friend who specialized in energy matters. He was referring
to the gas pipeline network that the Russians had hoped at one time to
construct, transiting the Black Sea through the Balkans to Central Europe, thereby bypassing Ukraine. Not needing Ukraine to transport
natural gas to Central Europe would allow Russia to cut off supplies to
Ukraine at will. Meanwhile, the other countries involved in South
Stream were all falling in line with Russia: Bulgaria, though a NATO
and EU member, was a political and institutional basket case; Serbia
was becoming a veritable satellite of Russia, in organized crime and
politics both; Hungary was adopting neo-authoritarianism; and Austria
had a certain reputation for double-dealing. The temporary halt to the
South Stream project, coupled with the collapse of energy prices
months later, would give Europe a certain respite. Meanwhile, the
fighting and Putin's creeping annexation of eastern Ukraine went on.

I anxiously hoped that Romania would not be drawn into the maelstrom. For purely selfish reasons, I wanted Romania to remain out of
the news. Like many a traveler and not a few journalists, I liked having
a place to myself. After all, Romania was a quiet yet intense laboratory

for contemplating, among other things, the problem of Russia. Though the Soviet Union had disintegrated in 1991, the pulverizing effect of Leninism and Stalinism left deep scars on Russia to this day. Just witness the authoritarian Politburo style of Putin's rule. Russia was outside Europe less because of the deterministic yet undeniable force of geography, and more because of the still-lingering effects of the Bolshevik Revolution—an event full of dynamic contingencies that did not necessarily have to turn out as it did.[1] And yet a revanchist Russia notwithstanding, Romania was in spite of its troubles, I told myself, living through a relatively benign moment in its history. Its economy was growing, though more slowly than it did before the European economic crisis. A looming catastrophe did not draw me to Romania. Rather, I was attracted simply by Romania's cultural and historical uniqueness, even as it was so richly revealing of Central and Eastern Europe.

NOW HEADING NORTH FROM Bucharest in October 2014, I was leaving the flatland of Muntenia, a word which confusingly means "land of the mountains," perhaps because of the "mountain" origin of the Basarab dynasty that came to dominate it.[2] After an hour or so of driving, the sub-Carpathians curtained the horizon just beyond the Ploieşti oil fields—the same ones that had served as a gas station for Hitler's invasion force. Soon I was enfolded by hills and the oppression of the once ruler-flat Muntenian landscape, with its hovels and cornfields, lifted amid loud pink banners strung over the road proclaiming the arrival of T-Mobile in Romania.

Looking out at the sloping terrain, I could not help but think of Donald Hall's *Romanian Furrow*, published in 1933. Hall had come out from England, shortly before Patrick Leigh Fermor's own trek through the region, and intended to travel through the eastern Balkans and Turkey. But in the way of many a memorable journey, his plans went awry. He became besotted with the Romanian countryside, here near the southern slopes of the Carpathians, and he passed week upon week working in the fields alongside the peasants. *Romanian Furrow,* an account of those days of blissful labor, is the ultimate travel book: a song of the earth more than a rendering of cultures and ethnicities. He writes of rough peasant women who "wore blouses covered with exquisite embroidery in clear blues, reds, and yellows.... And at noon when the world slept they would free the cord at the side of their blouses' necks to suckle the babies that had lain in the shade while they worked." Their headdresses carried an air of "distinction" and "nobility" about them, he says. "On Trajan's column there are carved such women." While Romanian right-wing intellectuals of the 1930s were conflating Eastern Orthodoxy with the peasant life, as a means to delegitimize the Jews in the cities, Hall observes: "The Orthodox Church filled with pageantry and colour, icons and gorgeous vestments, though temporarily impressive was beyond their [the peasants'] understanding. They were too simple for it to penetrate to their lives bound close to the earth. For them," he goes on, "there was more glory in the sun than in lighted candles, more goodness in the smell of earth after rain than in swinging incense-burners." Romanian peasants were not irreligious, Hall explains: rather, they harked back to an earlier paganism, rooted in the seasonal cycle of the crops, which was more elemental and thus more powerful than any formalized Christian ritual.[3] Hall's book is an obscure and instructive treasure, of the kind that rewards one and in which the study of Romania abounds. The book was ranked below two million among books sold on Amazon the last time I checked. Albert Camus, quoting Herman Melville, said that if you want to perpetuate a name, carve it on a stone that sinks to the bottom of the sea, because "depths last longer than heights": the perfect and purest form of immortality, in other words, the kind I associate with Hall's book.[4]

Soon the landscape changed to thick forests of dark spruce, fir, birch, and beech, as well as the periodic fruit orchard. The sense of an impending frontier, more real than any official border, beckoned. The houses took on a noble character as wood began to compete with the undressed cement of Muntenia. Finally the Carpathians broke verti-

cally above the tree line, like glinting swords hoisted in the air. Peleş
Castle in the mountain town of Sinaia, built by Carol I at the turn of
the twentieth century, was like a backdrop for a fairy tale amid a dense
forest shattering sunlight all around. The castle was all Carol, I
thought, with a dark and mysterious Germanic quality despite the neo-
Renaissance architecture, owing to the wooden balconies and frames.
The very size and architectural ambition bespoke the new monarch's
need to impose himself on the country. Looking down into the forest
from the cool mountain air of the castle balcony I felt exhilarated.
Travel was about movement through stages of landscape, mirroring
one's journey through life. The more landscapes seen and deeply experienced, the longer and richer life seems.

The road switched back and forth until I found myself just beyond
the northern slopes of the Carpathians and into Transylvania proper. A
steep and towering line of granite peaks, flecked with snow and otherwise the color of blue smoke, seemed to dance across the plain. Technically I had entered Central Europe, but my first sight was of a
Romanian Gypsy village, the cars and satellite dishes indicating some
semblance of a middle-class existence. Over the coming weeks I would
see Gypsies in other settings, poor and not so poor, particularly the
Hungarian ones in broad-brimmed black hats and loud dresses. The
Roma, or Gypsies, are Europe's biggest minority with 11 million people, who left India during late antiquity or the early Middle Ages and
have adopted various religions and languages, although there is a Ro-
mani language with different dialects. The European Union is working to overturn centuries of discrimination against the Roma, which
culminated in World War II when Hitler tried to exterminate them.
According to the European Union's Fundamental Rights Agency, as
reported in *The Wall Street Journal*, "one-third of Roma are unemployed, 20 percent have no health insurance and 80 percent live below
the poverty line." Europe's resurgent far-right parties have appealed to
local prejudices by attacking the Roma in the way the Jews were ver-
bally attacked in the 1930s. Eight percent of the Romanian population
is Roma.[5] They are fundamental to the Romanian landscape.

Bran Castle stood on a spiky precipice with its turret and huddled, crenellated walls. An illustration of Bran Castle, built by the Hungarian king Louis the Great in the late fourteenth century, served to inspire the Irish writer Bram Stoker to set his vampire legend of Dracula here. Thinking back thirty-three years to 1981, I recalled Bran as dark and eerie, encased in wildness, with lonely staircases that creaked as I walked up and down. Now it was meticulously landscaped and surrounded by restaurants and a tacky tourist bazaar. Inside there were fresh potted plants, piped-in waltz music, well-lit exhibits, and hordes of tourists taking selfies. Yet I relished that earlier memory: the Communist-inspired underdevelopment, which had made the population miserable, had enhanced the experience of a young Western traveler. In November 1981, I had found the town's lone inn near the castle, and in that freezing autumn night I treated myself to a hearty meal with a bottle of red wine before taking a bus back to Bucharest. Because prices were relatively cheap compared to Israel, where I had been living, I suddenly discovered I could eat well. In Romania of the 1980s I first learned the joys of dining alone while writing in my notebook and savoring the experience, something I have associated with travel ever since.

Queen Marie was now more of a presence at Bran Castle than Count Dracula. She was the wife of King Ferdinand, Carol's nephew who had succeeded him, and known as a free-spirited Englishwoman who lifted Romania's morale during the grim travails of World War I. Marie maintained an apartment in Bran during the 1930s in a sort of exile from her son, the newly reigning King Carol II. With her oversize crown and beads hanging from her head, the black-and-white photos of Marie at Bran give her a theatrical, Bohemian look.[6] In 1981, Bran had been for me just another part of the creepy backdrop of Ceaușescu's Communism; in 1990, when I had traveled through Transylvania soon after Ceaușescu's fall, and in order to recover a sense of the past, I was intently focused on the Romanian royal family that had preceded the Communists. Now, on this latest trip in 2014, I was obsessed with large, more abstract questions such as the meaning of fate and determinism in Romanian and European history. Three visits, three Romanias—all in different political circumstances—and three phases of personal and intellectual life. I had seen different countries in a way as different persons.

THE NEXT MORNING I found myself in the center of Braşov, and the ambience of Central Europe descended on me like a benediction of autumn leaves. Settled by the Teutonic knights in the early thirteenth century at the invitation of the king of Hungary, Braşov immediately appeared as a monument to well-socketed urbanity, compared to the more wild-and-woolly Bucharest, which only came into its own in the seventeenth century in the marchland of the Turkish Empire. There were the cheerful pastel shades of the Gothic, baroque, and neoclassical exteriors, chipped and weary and down-on-heel in places, but elegantly decked with pots of flowering geraniums outside stately windows. The streets were studded with bookshops and smelled of coffee and pastry, smells made sharper by the mist and suggestion of rain. The pastries reminded me that, here in Transylvania, the inhabitants had inherited the cult of the dessert from the Austrians and Germans. And the bookshops! In 2014, Romania still had a vibrant bookstore culture, with online purchases rare rather than the norm, thus bestowing a coziness and intimacy to intellectual life, and intensifying the addiction to buying books simply because they are beautiful.

Braşov's fourteenth-century "Black Church" (the Church of St. Mary) dominated the townscape with its piercing steeple and vast, steep roof, which emitted a jaw-dropping red darkness: that of a dead leaf in November. It is named thus because its Gothic façade (with Romanesque brickwork) had once caught fire and still bore the dark traces of that inferno. Both inside and outside, centuries of dampness had produced every shade of brown and gray on the rising stones. Here was the elemental meaning of Gothic architecture: a sculptural rendering of human determination and struggle against *vast impersonal forces*—fire, earthquakes, and invasions, in this case. My heart reeled at the turned-down gazes of the disfigured saints scarred by the long-ago fire. It had originally been a Roman Catholic church, but in the early sixteenth century came the Protestant Reformation, of which Brașov became a center, owing to the influence of the local scholar and protean humanist Johannes Honterus. Ever since then, the Black Church had been Lutheran, with services conducted in German to this today. Claudio Magris speaks of the "keen, tenacious virtues" that made the Germans "the Romans of Mitteleuropa," creating "a single civilization out of a melting-pot of diverse races."[7]

Eyeing the massive organ, I could not imagine a better place to listen to Bach, with whom it all really begins in terms of sound as an expression of beauty. Bach was the ultimate Lutheran, in the sense that his music, in the words of the conductor John Eliot Gardiner, "carries a universal message of hope," a perfect accompaniment to these soaring Gothic contours.[8] Though Bach never traveled farther than Dresden in the east and Carlsbad in the southeast, I could imagine him performing here in this Lutheran outpost of Transylvania. The severe Germanic design was lightened by the Turkish carpets on the walls with their rich magentas, the gift of merchants and pilgrims.

Brașov's toy-store architecture revealed its origins as the Kronstadt of the Saxon Germans. It was likewise with Sibiu (Hermannstadt) and Sighișoara (Schassburg), whereas Cluj-Napoca (Kolozsvár) and Târgu Mureș (Marosvásárhely) had been mainly Hungarian towns, though they also carried German appellations from their past: Clausenburg and Neumarkt am Mieresch respectively. All these names spoke of a world where the aristocracy had been Hungarian, the bourgeoisie mainly Lutheran Germans from northwestern Germany, and the peasants Romanian. Almost 85 percent of Romanians in Hungarian-controlled areas of the late Habsburg Empire were rural dwellers; this was at a time when only a quarter or less of the population of Transylvanian cities was Romanian. Because a Romanian urban middle class barely existed, a class-based antagonism directed against fellow Romanians did not develop; Romanian resentment became focused rather on the wealthier Hungarians, as well as on the wealthier and more urbane Jews and ethnic Germans.[9]

The ethnic Germans were not limited to Transylvania. Several hundred thousand of them lived in the Banat region of southwestern Romania, for example. In the eighteenth century, they had been encouraged by the Habsburg emperors to settle that marchland of the Austrian Empire. Perhaps because they had embarked on the journey to the Banat from the south German city of Ulm on the Danube in Swabia, the ethnic Germans who settled the Banat were called Swabians. The Ceauşescu regime, as it merged ultranationalism with Communism, severely repressed these Swabian Germans along with the other ethnic minorities, and so the Swabians deserted Romania in large numbers during the last phase of the Cold War. For each émigré that was permitted to leave, the Ceauşescus demanded a bounty from the West German government. The same situation obtained for the other departing ethnic Germans, as well as for the departing Romanian Jews (whose bounty was paid by the American and Israeli governments).

I now bring up the Swabians because of the powerful effect that the prose of Herta Müller has had on me. In 2009 she won the Nobel Prize for her memoirs and novels of life as a Swabian girl growing up in the Banat during the Ceauşescu era. Oppression is everywhere in her work, yet she rarely writes about it directly. Instead, the reader is pierced with stark images of silence, cruelty, and emptiness: here is a material world that, while rural and traditional, is bereft of beauty or any uplifting aesthetic. Whereas mud and tools and earthen objects can become almost sensuous joys in the poetry of the late Northern Ireland–born Nobel laureate Seamus Heaney, the same images offer no respite in Müller's work. "Snow fell on stray dogs. . . . The cold eats away at the gables of the houses with its salt. In many places the inscriptions are crumbling off. . . . The muffled-up men who leave the pub with their moth-eaten fur hats walk by thoughtlessly talking to themselves. . . . [W]ater [here] is yellow and hard, and in the laundry it feels gritty, not foamy, and the clothes turn gray and rough from it. . . . Father comes home drunk every day. . . . Mother was leaning her whole body against the tiled stove and crying in shrieks. . . . There is neither dusk nor dawn. The twilight is in people's faces."[10]

Repression is not only about prisons and firing squads. It can also be about a more mundane and punishing tedium, a feeling that Müller faithfully reconstructs.

The Germans were an essential part of the Transylvanian aesthetic. The architecture could be, for example, Burgundian early Gothic, as at the fortress church at nearby Prejmer. The church, with its towering stone walls covered in smudged white plaster, dizzying clay roof tiles, mazelike wooden walkways, heavy and battered furniture with floral designs, and assemblages of blackened brass pots and tight weavings, had the aura of a complete and lost world of the high Middle Ages: the stern Lutheran equivalent of the Orthodox monasteries at Mount Athos in Greece (even though Prejmer was originally Roman Catholic). Then, too, there was Viscri, a rickety Saxon religious fortification dating to the late twelfth century. Its tower was the traditional, steep pyramidal hat, suddenly flattening out over a wooden platform, as is common in Transylvania, the clay tiles so discolored that they looked like ancient coins. Through the lacework of poplars and fruit trees was a rippling sculptural landscape, dotted with purple crocuses, which here and there took on the layered depth of an oil painting.

Wolfgang Wittstock, the head of the German Democratic Forum in Brașov, told me that while the ethnic German population in Transylvania had stopped declining, it was mainly an urban culture now. The Saxon village civilization, whose architecture I had so marveled at, had almost completely died out. The monuments were now supported by a historical trust whose benefactors included Prince Charles of Great Britain, who owned land in Transylvania and was an enthusiast of the region.

When Ceaușescu had come to power, there were some 400,000 ethnic Germans in Romania. About a third or more of those who remained after Ceaușescu's execution fled in 1990 and 1991, when the borders were finally opened. Since then the numbers had dwindled further to 45,000, with mostly old people left. The latest twist, Wittstock explained, was that with the German economy in the doldrums, young Saxons were returning to Romania to launch start-up firms. The fact that ethnic Germans were newly welcomed in post-Communist Romania was evinced by the person of Klaus Iohannis, the respected ethnic German mayor of Sibiu, who ran for president in the 2014 Romanian national elections and won in a startling upset, promising institutional reforms, a fight against corruption, and closer alignment with the West against Putin.

THE VERY *IDEA* THAT I was in former Habsburg Central Europe while still in the middle of Romania, even as other parts of the country might arguably be labeled the Near East, ignited my thoughts in disparate directions. Just as the Byzantine, Russian, and Turkish marchlands of Wallachia and Moldavia made me consider their geographical and imperial traditions, the fact of my being in Transylvania made me consider other geographical, imperial, strategic, and even philosophical prospects.[11]

Let me begin.

IT MIGHT BE HENRY KISSINGER, not the controversial statesman of the late 1960s and 1970s, but the young Harvard graduate student of the 1950s, who most succinctly defined the Austrian Habsburg Empire, which after the *Ausgleich*, or "Compromise," of 1867 became the dual monarchy of Austria-Hungary. Habsburg Austria, particularly in the eighteenth and nineteenth centuries, with its "polyglot composition" of Germans, Magyars, Ruthenians, Czechs, Slovaks, Slovenes, Italians, and Romanians, was the "seismograph of Europe," Kissinger writes in his first book, *A World Restored: Metternich, Castlereagh and the Problems of Peace 1812–1822.* The young Kissinger then unpacks his thesis:

It [Habsburg Austria] was certain to be the first victim of any
major upheaval because war could only increase the centrifugal
elements of a state whose sole bond of union was the common
crown. And because Austria's need for stability was so great and
because law is the expression of the status quo, Austria stood for
the sense of limit and the importance of the equilibrium, for the
necessity of law and the sanctity of treaties. . . .[12]

More to the point, Habsburg Austria was the last remnant of feudalism that had survived into the early modern and modern ages. Indeed,
according to one of the leading historians of the Habsburgs, the late
Robert A. Kann, the Austrian Empire was "more diversified . . . in regards to ethnic, linguistic, and historic traditions" than any other imperium in modern times.[13] "It was closer to the European Community
of the twenty-first century" than to other empires of the nineteenth,
writes the Welsh historian and travel writer Jan Morris.[14] The empire
sprawled "clean across Central Europe," observes the late Oxford
scholar C. A. Macartney, from the Vorarlberg Alps and Lake Con-
stance in the west to the edge of Moldavia in the east; and from the
Polish Carpathians in the north to the Adriatic Sea in the south, uniting Germans, Slavs, and Latins. And yet "in no single case," Macartney goes on, "was one of its political frontiers also an ethnic frontier."
Germans lay inside and outside the empire; so, too, did the Poles,
Ukrainians, Croats, Romanians, and so on.[15] Thus, as Kissinger states,
the Habsburg Empire "could never be part of a structure legitimized
by nationalism," for as nationalism in Europe had an ethnic and religious basis, this polyglot empire would have been torn apart by such a
force.[16] Making the Habsburg Empire doubly insecure and so dependent on the status quo was its easily *invadable* and *conquerable* geography, compared to that of Great Britain, Russia, and even France.[17]

Habsburg Austria, whose history spans the late thirteenth century
to the early twentieth, by simple necessity elevated conservative order
to the highest moral principle. Liberalism was held in deep suspicion
because freedom could mean not only the liberation of the individual,

but the liberation of ethnic groups, which could then come into conflict with one another. Thus toleration, rather than freedom, was encouraged. And because (especially following the Napoleonic Wars)
the status quo was sacrosanct in Vienna, so too was the balance of
power.

For decades and centuries even, Austria's sprawling imperium defined European geopolitics. Austria was the highly imperfect solution
to Turkish military advances into Central Europe in the sixteenth century and the perennial Panslav stirrings that emanated from Russia,
absorbing as Austria did the blows from both forces, even as the
Counter-Reformation helped bind the heavily Catholic Habsburg
lands together. Austria's role as a geopolitical balancer was further fortified by its fear of vast, Panslavic, and police-state Russia on the one
hand and the liberal, democratic, and revolutionary traditions of
France and the West on the other. Indeed, Austria's position as a great
power was threatened by Russian imperialism from the east, while, as
Kann puts it, "western liberalism threatened the durability of her domestic structure."[18] Talleyrand himself championed the "relative
power" of Austria as a buffer to keep Russia out of Germany and Central Europe. And yet Austria was so often weak, something inherent "in
the far-flung nature" of her monarchial possessions and her attendant
"extraordinarily cumbersome administrative and decision-making ar-
rangements," writes Cambridge history professor Brendan Simms.[19] It
was Romania's geographical and historical fate to be caught between
and among empires, with its position at the southeastern extremity of
Habsburg Austria, the southwestern extremity of Russia's imperialist
ambitions, and the northwestern extremity of those of Ottoman Turkey.

According to other interpretations, Austria itself might have constituted a bourgeoisie civilizing force from the West, altogether benevolent in its influence. For Habsburg culture was reassuring, *burgerlich*,
and sumptuous, at least compared to what those other, bleaker impe-
riums from the East had to offer—partially defined, as Austria and the
Catholic Church were, by the inspirational miracle of Gothic and ba-

roque art. But what Romanians too often received from Habsburg Austria was not inspiring aesthetics but simply the appalling hardship of
war, so that the northern Transylvanian Gothic style was to remain an
aspirational curiosity amid copious bloodshed as empires clashed.

AND YET TO MY MIND, no individual in modern European history has
more practically stood athwart the hot-blooded, intemperate tendencies of so many clashing and chilling utopias and ethnic nationalisms—
the ideologies of mass bloodshed—than that personification of Austrian
Habsburg values, the statesman and archconservative Prince Clemens
von Metternich. Metternich exemplified how an individual could
bend fate. Metternich, whose wisdom and cynicism were key to arranging the post-Napoleonic peace, vouchsafed to Europeans a nineteenth century—absent as it was in relative terms of large-scale
war—that made them ironically naïve about the prospects for violent
great-power conflict in the century that was to follow. Crossing the
Carpathians northward into Central Europe, I very much wanted to
think of the ultimate preemptive, practical, and philosophical alternative, in human form, to the historical monsters that I had to confront
south and east of the Carpathians. And so I thought of Metternich, the
Habsburg statesman who had the answer to safeguarding the imperfect status quo from the violent revolutionary chieftains who sought to
overturn it, because therein, ultimately, lay the protection of weak minorities.

Metternich, that farsighted reactionary, was a man of peace—
contra Napoleon, that endemic progressive, who was a man of war.
Metternich believed in legal states, not in ethnic nations. States are
sanctioned bureaucratic systems governed by the rule of law; ethnic
nations are ruled by blood-and-soil passion, the very enemy of modera-
tion and analysis. Metternich was not a larger-than-life hero like
Churchill. He was something far more mundane, at times more necessary, something the top bureaucrats who are now struggling to maintain the European Union should aspire to be: a tireless protector of the

existing, compromising, pancontinental order. Given Europe's present situation, with right-wing nationalist parties banging at the door of a fragile EU, Metternich's efforts at *conserving* the status quo are truly relevant.

The Romantic poet Lord Byron, in his 1823 poem "The Age of Bronze," denigrated Metternich as "power's foremost parasite." What Byron could not have known was that precisely by wielding power as he had, Metternich would, from a later historical vantage point, appear to have done more than any other single statesman to give the coming hundred years in Europe a comparative respite from the to-ings and fro-ings of armed men. Professor Kann, who taught at both Rutgers and the University of Vienna, calls Metternich's success "far-reaching and doubly impressive, considering that he began his operations in 1809 from the position of a defeated state." The youthful Kissinger writes: "It was thus that the Enlightenment retained deep into the nineteenth century its last champion, who judged actions by their 'truth,' not by their success, an advocate of reason in an age of philosophical materialism, who never surrendered his belief that morality could be known and that virtue was teachable."[20]

Metternich encapsulated the principle, later elaborated upon by the British geographer and strategist Halford Mackinder, that a world defined by a proper balance of power is a world most likely to be at peace. And in organizing a balance of power, Metternich believed in secrecy as diplomacy's greatest weapon. He understood that the difficult negotiations upon which peace and the consequent avoidance of tragedy depend required statesmen to conduct the frankest of dialogues without being subjected to public scrutiny—and public ridicule. Metternich supported "the primacy of confidential exchanges" over media grandstanding. In our day, there is the hue and cry from a self-interested media for openness, even as it is precisely such openness that reduces the space for diplomats to do their work.[21]

Metternich believed in order over romance. He believed emotion to be the enemy of analysis. Whereas romance can lead to chaos, order leads to predictability. (Hitler, remember, was once defined by Kissinger as a "romantic nihilist.") Predictability is what ordinary men and women require to go about their daily lives in peace. In our day, order has been somewhat maligned because of its association with fascism and Communism, whose shocking results are in historical terms still recent. But we must all bear in mind that order in its normal form, common to democracies and mild authoritarian systems, is much to be preferred over risky, populist experiments. Metternich saw close-up as a student the horrors of the French Revolution.[22] In order to prosper and become a normal state, Romania required the kind of continental order that Metternich had once provided.

Metternich was the ultimate European: a man of maneuver. He was prepared to associate Austria with other European states against Napoleon, but he had no intention, in biographer Alan Palmer's words, of becoming an "instrument" of Russian policy, or of Prussia's. Maneuver is not given to friendly press notices. It is not about standing up for "good" against "evil"; nor is it about achieving a demonstrable victory. Rather, it is about recognizing the geographic, economic, and demographic limitations of one's own state and, as a consequence, seeking a favorable outcome in a roundabout way. Maneuver is subtle because geopolitics is thus. A proper reading of the map does not reward black-and-white judgments, because the geographies of most states offer both advantages and disadvantages. Maneuver emphasizes equilibrium over domination.[23]

The location of Metternich's Austria encouraged subtle geopolitical thinking. It was at the dead, potentially unstable center of Europe: a hinge connecting the Balkans with Central Europe, and Central Europe with Western Europe. Yet even as Austria's Habsburg Empire, associated as it was with the Danube, was at the crossroads of the Continent, it was itself militarily vulnerable. And so Austria's self-interest lay with a pan-European *system* that preserved the continental peace. The system that Metternich helped arrange at the conclusion of the Napoleonic Wars, a concert of great powers at the Congress of Vienna, provided for such stability. Metternich knew that the very illiberal nature of the Congress system—dependent as it was on conservative monarchs—could not last indefinitely, and at times he "delighted in the hopelessness of his mission." Metternich, the late British historian A. J. P. Taylor once observed, was "gentle" compared to what was to follow.[24]

Dresden, Pressburg (Bratislava), Vienna: such were some of the datelines of Metternich's diplomatic encounters. Brașov (Kronstadt), Sibiu (Hermannstadt), and Cluj (Clausenburg) here in Transylvania made me think of those other cities and their historical associations, for on this side of the Carpathians I was inside Mitteleuropa, if only just.

CENTRAL EUROPE AND ITS geopolitics also had my mind rushing in the direction of the protean Polish revolutionary, statesman, and military leader Józef Piłsudski and his concept of the Intermarium, Latin for "between the seas," *Miedzymorze* in Polish. Piłsudski, too, was most relevant to Romania's current predicament.

Piłsudski dominated Polish affairs from the middle of World War I until his death in 1935. He was from a "staunchly Polonized" family of "disestablished nobility" that had held lands in present-day Lithuania, and originally owed its position to the Polish-Lithuanian Commonwealth, one of the great powers of sixteenth- and seventeenth-century Europe. The destruction of that colossal geopolitical force at the hands of invaders from both east and west provided the motivation behind Piłsudski's vision of a belt of small states, between the Baltic and Black seas, to hold in check both Germany in one direction and Russia in the other.[25]

Piłsudski's vision was a product not only of his family history, but of his own personal bloody experience. For it was he who had saved Poland from invading Soviet forces in 1920 in the midst of a number of border wars, and then went on to become the primary founder of the Second Polish Republic in 1926. Piłsudski's belief in a multicultural Poland to encompass his own Lithuanian background played well with his expansive vision of this anti-Russian belt of states. This Intermarium was, in turn, a spiritual and territorial descendant of that vast tract of territory that had constituted the late medieval and early modern Kingdom of Poland and the Grand Duchy of Lithuania, a territory that had stretched at its zenith from the shivering flatlands of northeastern Europe by the Baltic Sea to the confines of the Ottoman Empire.

Piłsudski's realization that the independence of both the Baltic States in the north and Ukraine in the south was central to Poland's own security lives on today in the country's post–Cold War foreign policy. To be sure, the European Union's expansion in the first decade of the twenty-first century to include Poland, the Baltic States, the Czech Republic, Slovakia, Slovenia, Hungary, Romania, and Bulgaria, together with their incorporation into NATO, has represented the partial institutionalization of Piłsudski's idea, even if Belarus, Ukraine, Moldova, and the countries of the Transcaucasus lie stranded in the neither-nor geopolitical landscape of the EU's Eastern Partnership, which has offered insufficient protection against the designs of Russia. But while danger lurks in the east, the west is less worrisome. For Germany, in the words of the late scholar Alexandros Petersen of the Woodrow Wilson Center, "has come into her maturity as a . . . benign giant critically driving the European economy and generally satisfied with her borders, as well as with those of her consolidated East European neighbors."[26]

Thus, while the European security environment since 1989 is not altogether clear, especially given the fact of Putin's revanchism, it may still, arguably, contain more possibilities than at any time since some of those comparatively dull nineteenth-century decades bequeathed by Metternich and his diplomatic allies. Of course, those same decades had lulled Europeans into the false sense of security common to people who have lost their sense of the tragic. And the sense of the tragic must always be cultivated in order to avoid tragedy.

Poland and Romania are two countries that need no lessons in cultivating the sense of the tragic: both have long been borderlands between stronger states and forces. Though they appear distinctly separated on the current map, with Poland in northeastern Europe and Romania in southeastern Europe (even as both can claim whole or partial membership in Mitteleuropa), the shadow of Poland has in the course of history crept well into the Romanian lands. For example, in the Moldavian town of Târgu Neamț, I had craned my neck up at the citadel that had been attacked by Polish forces under Jan III Sobieski in 1691. Lionized by Milton and praised by Clausewitz, Sobieski waged war against the Muslim Turks far away to the south from his native Poland and Ukraine, in epic campaigns that helped save the Habsburgs and thus the Christian West. His Moldavian expeditions of 1687 and 1691 were among his last.[27] Sobieski's distant forays toward the shadowlands of the Black Sea were certainly part of Piłsudski's mental map, a map that is still vital to Europe's future, as a belt of independent and democratic states anchored by Poland in the northeast and Romania in the southeast, struggling to maintain their equilibrium in the face of Russian aggression.

FROM WHEN I HAD first taken the train northwest to Sighișoara from Brașov thirty-three years earlier, my notebook records the countryside "bathed in autumnal gloom with pockets of mist rolling through the fir trees." There were "vine-webbed houses and thick carpets of rotting leaves." Sighișoara was where that hideously cruel scourge of the Turks, Vlad Țepeș "the Impaler," was born. In Bram Stoker's 1897 gothic vampire novel, *Dracula*, Count Dracula is a descendant of Vlad. In Chapter 3, the Count boasts, "Who was it but one of my own race who as *Voivode* crossed the Danube and beat the Turk on his own ground? This was a Dracula indeed!" Stoker never visited Romania. And rather than the howling wolves, midnight thunderstorms, and evil-looking peasants of his tale, Transylvania in fact conjures up the Renaissance, the baroque, the Gothic, and the Enlightenment, in all their architectural and spiritual beauty.[28] Nevertheless, the lowercase gothic character of Romania found resonance in the Ceaușescu era, when the economic and political desolation of the country reduced much of the population to the status of a peasantry. Darkness, literally, hovered over the landscape. Ceauşescu had brought the country so low that it constituted, in truth, a gothic horror story, with elements of fantasy.

THE ASSOCIATION, HOWEVER CRUDE and lazy, between Stoker's *Dracula* and Ceauşescu's Romania became just too irresistible for many writers, including myself at times. There was also, as a friend of mine in the upper reaches of the Manhattan publishing world noted, a certain undeniable gothic element to Romania that went beyond *Dracula*. After all, Romania was poor; relatively marginal, backward, and little known compared to other parts of Europe; and with a particularly chilling history, especially concerning the Holocaust. But the fact is, Romania has been moving out of that quarry for over a quarter century now, however slowly and unevenly. The word "Gothic," in upper case, is more appropriately used in regards to Romania, applying to the many examples of such medieval architecture that originated in France and spread throughout Central Europe, and which are evidence of Romania's Westernizing ambition.

Sighişoara, on a Saturday in early November 1981, had been a derelict masterpiece. I had left my backpack at the nearly vacant hotel in the lower town and explored on foot the cobblestone streets of the upper town, with their empty storefronts and absence of facilities. I remember there was no toilet, no place to wash my hands even, and only one place to eat—a sordid collection of benches where fatty grilled meat and watery beer were served. The man next to me had a terrible body odor, I remember: Communist underdevelopment denied people even their most basic forms of dignity. But there was that clock tower—a giant, thirteenth-century Gothic dream-fantasy, with no less than five onion domes and steeples on a sloping platform of multicolored enamel tiles (gold, green, orange), like an infinitely absorbing puzzle. Now that the tower had undergone cleaning and restoration it amazed even more. The streets in the autumn of 2014 were teeming with tourists and cluttered with cafés, souvenir stalls, and bunting. The façades had all been freshly painted, and like everywhere in Transylvania, decked with flowering geraniums. There were exquisite inns and antique shops, and lush pergolas in manicured courtyards. A band played. As evening fell and the streetlamps came on, I espied a sumptuous interior with fine furniture and shades through the window, and thought that few things scream money and elegance like soft yellow lighting.

In the spring of 1990, four months after the revolution, there had been nothing here. Even in 1998, the post-Communist boom still remained limited to the big cities. But looking all the way back to my first visit in 1981 from 2014 in Sighişoara, it was like comparing a lonely and empty house to one where a family had been firmly and noisily established, with all of their belongings and with the love that came with them.

EVEN IN 1990, SIBIU (HERMANNSTADT) had oozed efficiency and tidiness. Its vast yet intimate old town square was dominated by a squat, onion-steepled council tower and baroque, neo-Renaissance, and Art Nouveau buildings, further elaborated by medieval chimney battlements, dormer windows, and oval slits in the roofs that looked like so many droopy, half-opened eyes. Lurking nearby was the Gothic Evangelical church, its sharp triangular roofs and steeple appearing to accelerate into the sky. There was just an authority to the architecture of this particular medieval church that nearly made me hold my breath. In 1998, many of the façades in Sibiu blazed with fresh paint, and the effect was that of a pulsing stage set. Always further along in urbanity than the other towns and cities of Romania, now Sibiu was disappointingly globalized, with a bit of a tourist-trap feel. The squares were cluttered with high-end generic cafés bearing international signage and some of the interiors suffered sports events and stupid American movies blasting from wall-mounted monitors. Loud amusement park rides had taken over the square during one of the days I was there. Again, the locals were no doubt much happier, especially the children, but I treasured my original memory of twenty-four years ago.

But then I had a coffee away from the square and focused on the gargoyles and creamy white, recently renovated façade of the Împăratul Romanilor and recalled my experiences at the same hotel in 1990. Sibiu had always been far advanced because it was the most truly *burgerlich* of the Transylvanian towns: that is, its inhabitants seemed to combine a dynamic ambition with a counterintuitive sense of slowness and relaxation, which, in turn, rested on a sense of relative security. Here there was still, I noticed, the tradition of dressing up for a Sunday stroll.

Professor Paul Philippi was particularly stylishly dressed, with a light tan sport coat over a pale violet shirt and matching maroon silk tie. His English was impeccable and there was a knowing, sophisticated air about him: not arrogant, just civilized. Philippi's neat, whitewashed office with expensive, simple wood overlooking the town square was also well appointed. Philippi was ninety-one, and had learned his English from American GIs as a German prisoner of war in the mid-1940s. Early in World War II, the Nazis forced Saxon men in Romania to enlist in the Waffen SS, and so Philippi found himself in uniform, often fighting, all over Central and Eastern Europe. In Hungary near the end of the war, his unit fled west to the American side to escape the Russians. In Germany the Americans incarcerated him until late 1947. He stayed in Germany, since his Saxon homeland in Transylvania had fallen under Soviet and Romanian Communist control. In postwar Berlin, he met a Saxon evangelical bishop who influenced him to study theology and history. It was in this period that Philippi came to know in full the crimes of the Nazis, crimes he had suspected but the extent of which he claimed he had never imagined. He matured intellectually in an impossible situation. At home, in Romania, his parents' generation was sent to forced labor in Russia, had their land expropriated, and lost their political rights under Gheorghiu-Dej's national Communism; meanwhile, in Germany, there were tensions between those Saxons who had fled Romania during the war because of an ideological affinity with Hitler and those like himself who felt used by the Nazis.

Philippi went on to a successful academic career at the great university in Heidelberg, retiring later on as an emeritus professor, as well as serving as a guest professor at Cambridge. After 1989, he returned to Romania and soon afterward became a professor at the university in Sibiu, "Hermannstadt," as he called the town. He developed a passionate hatred for Romanian Communism, which, he explained, besides perpetrating an economic ideology "against human nature and resulting in political and psychological misery," was also built on "the original sin of blood-based nationalism." Much of Romania has always been composed of minorities, he noted. As for the Saxons, "it is a mistake to call us Germans: when we came here in the twelfth century there was no such thing as 'Germany.' We are like the Swiss, a microculture, which had its territory taken away by the Austrians." His larger point—his life lesson actually—as he admitted to me, was that identity is too fluid for the primitive nationalisms of the nineteenth and twentieth centuries. That is why he worries about Romania, where despite the sheen of globalization, schoolbooks still offer an unreconstructed ethnic nationalism, even as religion here is often more superstition than Christian virtue. A sustained economic and political crisis could always unleash old demons, he warned me.

I LEFT THE OLD TOWN on foot and walked under a mile to the late-eighteenth-century Church of Peter and Paul, also known as the church "between the evergreens," owing to the fir, spruce, and pines in the courtyard. It was the oldest Uniate church in Sibiu: the land had been bequeathed by Habsburg Empress Maria Theresa in the eighteenth century. While inside it looked like any Orthodox church, teeming with icons and a formidable iconostasis amid frankincense, the outside was baroque with a Catholic-style cross alongside an Orthodox one, thus announcing its difference in religions.

The Uniates were Greek Catholics, that is, members of the original Greek or Eastern Orthodox Church which had in 1699 submitted to a union with the Catholic pope in Rome. All Romanian Christians had been originally Eastern Orthodox. But in the sixteenth and seventeenth centuries, with Hungarian princes controlling Transylvania and the Ottoman Turks looming on the other side of the Carpathians, the Hungarians were fired by, in Patrick Leigh Fermor's phrase, "Protestant vernacular zeal," and were eager to separate the Romanians north of the mountains from their coreligionists to the south. So they replaced the Slavonic mass in Transylvania with a contemporary Romanian translation. Later on, when Transylvania came under direct Catholic Habsburg rule and Turkish power waned, this vernacular Orthodoxy came under pressure to take the next step and join Rome. But while the congregation worshipped in Romanian and were officially Catholic, the icons, the priests—both bearded and married—and everything else remained as in any Orthodox church. But rather than undermine Romanian nationalism as the Hungarians and Habsburg Austrians had intended, the Uniate Church achieved the opposite by sparking a greater interest in the Romanian language. As Fermor recounts in his typical delicious prose, "after the Union [with the pope], gifted Transylvanian sons of the Uniat manse were sent to study in Rome, where the spiral carvings of Trajan's Column—Roman soldiers at grips with Dacian warriors dressed very like modern Rumanian mountaineers—filled them with exciting convictions of joint Roman and Dacian descent." Fermor goes on: "these gave body to traditions which, in more nebulous form, had long been in the air."[29]

The Uniates, in a word, represented the West because of their link to Catholicism. This both the Communists and the Orthodox Church could not abide, and thus the Uniate Church was abolished by Gheorghiu-Dej in 1948—only to resurface immediately after the collapse of Communism. The Church of Peter and Paul was filled with worshippers at the time of my visit, listening to a bearded priest deliver a Sunday school lesson to children seated around him. More people were streaming in as I left.

———

IN SIGHIȘOARA I HAD gone to bed in an airy loft of a room with a stirring view of the clock tower, surrounded by graceful antique furniture,
thankful for the ethereal silence of my surroundings. The next night I
was in a musty room in Sibiu and until past midnight the blasting
noise of the amusement park rides made sleep impossible. Travel was
a compressed, more vivid version of life: the highs and lows came
quickly upon each other; everything could change in the space of a
day, or in a few hours even. A city you had visited only a few days before might seem like a distant recollection now, though you could remember every detail of it. And yet at the end of your travels the entire
journey became richly embedded in memory—as though an epic—
even as years of workaday existence at home fade into a blur. We travel
in order to defeat oblivion.

MY NEXT DESTINATION WAS northward in Transylvania, from the land
of the Saxon-Germans to that of the ethnic Hungarians: from Sibiu
(Hermannstadt) to Târgu Mureș (Marosvásárhely), that is, "the market
on the Mureș River." When I had last visited Târgu Mureș in the
spring of 1990, only two months after violent clashes between Romanians and ethnic Hungarians here, and nearly four months after
Ceaușescu had fallen, the city had been eerie and tense. Because capitalism still lay in the future, there was a beautiful emptiness to the
place, and I was able to focus that much more on the handsome baroque architecture. Now it was hectic and noisy with late-model cars
cluttering the squares and double parking on sidewalks. Ugly new
buildings marred the urban landscape, making the place forgettable
and at the same time dynamic. My hotel room had a loud cherry carpet, a chair with a zebra-skin design, and a picture of a woman blowing
smoke in a man's face. The lobby was lit by red globes with piped-in
blues music. Of course, people in the lobby as well as the pedestrians
outside were preoccupied with their smartphones. I escaped the tu-

mult when a group of professors from the local university, Romanians and ethnic Hungarians both, took me to one of those long and leisurely lunches with ample wine at an outdoor garden restaurant, the kind of lunch that does not end till nearly 5 P.M.

The talk was not initially about ethnic divides between Romanians and Hungarians. It was about constructivism versus realism, about the distinction between early modern and modern history, about the banality and hollowness of existence in a twenty-first-century capitalistic society: "people are narrow, primitive, still of the village, despite their gadgets and new cars," one of my companions said. The local inhabitants were ripe for manipulation, in other words. And that led to the latent fear of ethnic nationalism resurfacing through Russian subversion: for Putin could potentially weaken Romania by encouraging ethnic Hungarian nationalism in Transylvania, through his support of the chauvinistic, increasingly neo-authoritarian regime of Viktor Orbán in neighboring Hungary. Yet my companions agreed that there was at the moment little basis for such a policy succeeding. Ethnic relations utterly lacked the tension of post-Ceaușescu Romania in the 1990s. Economic development and the communications revolution had led to incipient cosmopolitan identities, despite the surviving narrowmindedness mentioned earlier. Only a severe and sustained economic downturn, which Romania had so far escaped, could present Putin with possibilities. At the same time, though, one had to remember that Hungarians here still sent their children to Hungarian-language schools, while Romanian children studied in their own language. Because language is one of the most basic components of identity, people were not really united, even as they lived side by side. In sum, the situation was defined by extreme ambiguity.

Nationalism in its vulgar form eschews ambiguity. It "craves for uniformity," writes the late Hungarian-British academic László Péter. And yet the story of the Hungarians in these parts was not at all monolithic. In the sixteenth century, to take one example, Greater Hungary was divided among the Habsburgs in the north and west and the Ottomans in the south, while Transylvania and the Partium (northern and western Transylvania) were autonomous under Ottoman suzerainty. Then, in the late sixteenth and early seventeenth centuries, Hungarians sided with Romanians against the Turks but on other occasions with the Turks against the Habsburgs.[30]

"Today, the ethnic Hungarians in Romania are themselves politically divided," said Cornel Sigmirean, a European history professor at the University of Petru Maior in Târgu Mureș. I had walked up the hill from downtown, passing the monumental, wafer-brick walls of the medieval citadel, to the leafy Old World surroundings of the campus: another refuge of quietude, where I had coffee with the professor. He was worried that the local Székely community (a subgroup of the Hungarians) contained elements of aggressive nationalism, and were sympathetic to Jobbik, the radical Hungarian rightest party that is avowedly pro-Christian and pro–racially Hungarian, while being anti-Semitic and anti–European integration. But he also explained that most ethnic Hungarians in Transylvania were far more apolitical. "People need to discover their ethnic roots as an anchor in the face of a more cosmopolitan world. So history goes on. But tensions will continue to play out through democracy," he said, adding that "Russia will always look for opportunities to weaken and divide communities in this part of Europe." Romania, he concluded, was still in the process of recovering from the forces set in motion by World War I, which had begun a hundred years before my visit, in August 1914. Bolshevism, the Weimar Republic, and later Nazism all came originally out of the tumult of World War I, and have provided a story line in Romania ever since, in his view.

I LEFT TÂRGU MUREȘ in the rainy, predawn blackness. I wandered around a vacant lot near the railway tracks searching for the makeshift ticket office. The station building, undergoing renovation, was a confusing construction site. A tough Gypsy kid spotted me and began demanding money. I had to fend him off repeatedly, until I saw someone with bags walking in a determined manner. I followed along and found the ticket office. The three-hour ride westward to Cluj-Napoca took me past a succession of rotting villages by the tracks where rowdy, greasy men kept getting on and off. Once again, the trains were a reminder of the underside of Romanian life. Yet as the dawn lifted, along with the rain and fog, the landscape revealed a deeper, more beautiful mystery swathed in dark oily greens and burgundy shadows. The autumn here had begun. The rivers were still and silent under a remaining layer of fog, like mirrors thickly coated with dust. A grimy taxi took me through the leafy, worn-down streets of Cluj to my boutique hotel, where I had a restorative breakfast in the late morning.

The first time I saw Cluj was in the summer of 1973, while backpacking through Eastern Europe. How ignorant I was! Coming from Hungary, Romania appeared wild and unkempt in comparison. I wandered into a bar near the main square where a group of Gypsies were playing music while others drunkenly caroused, and I stupidly thought to myself, Now I am in the East. I knew nothing of Cluj as the Kolozsvár of the Hungarians and as the Clausenburg of the Saxon-Germans. I did not know then that Central Europe both as a concept and as a culture had extended deep into Romania, unto the Carpathians south of Brașov, and in more subtle ways even farther beyond. Because Gheorghiu-Dej's and Ceaușescu's Communism had obliterated the bourgeoisie and turned once-proud cities into big, scruffy villages, downtown Cluj for me in 1973 appeared several steps more primitive than the most rural parts of eastern Hungary. In early 1990, when I returned to Cluj to research *Balkan Ghosts*, I was by now at least conscious of its rich past. But it was only when I read Miklós Bánffy's *The Transylvanian Trilogy* that I was able to actually imagine what Cluj, or more properly, Kolozsvár, had once constituted.

Bánffy's three masterly novels, *They Were Counted, They Were Found Wanting*, and *They Were Divided*, were initially published in their native Hungarian between 1934 and 1940. But they were obscured during World War II and the Cold War, and it wasn't until 1999 that the first English translation appeared. Though they do not reach the level of Stendhal, Tolstoy, Proust, or Joseph Roth, as the publisher's publicity and some reviewer notices indicate, the three novels do draw open the curtains on a period obviously much known about but not adequately imagined by those of us on the other side of a gulf created by widespread industrial warfare, mass murder, and suffocating decades of Communism. Here, against a dark and mountainous landscape where the forest greenery glistens as though enamel, there had once been a densely packed world of high culture and aristocracy, even as it was decadent and profligate, during the last phases of the Habsburg Empire. Transylvania had not simply been part of Austria-Hungary, or even just an extension of Hungarian ethnic demography emanating from Budapest. Transylvania, according to Bánffy, himself a Hungarian nobleman and politician, exhibited "a living form of national consciousness" different from Hungary proper. Here, after a fashion, was a distinct microcivilization that did not support the Habsburgs during the Thirty Years' War and seemed to have backed the Turks during the 1683 siege of Vienna. Bánffy restores the memory of this world, at once precious and wasteful, not merely in sentences but in vivid pictures where wineglasses clink and card games go on until dawn, inside castles built before the Tartar invasions and surrounded by brooding oak and beech forests. It is a world going about its petty intrigues even as the Europe around it builds toward cataclysm.[31]

The backdrop to Bánffy's saga is the outskirts of Kolozsvár, with its baronial estates built in some cases on the sites of former Roman and medieval forts, graced by "stone pilasters with elaborate capitals," in addition to the "fantastic intricacies of rococo taste" and Empire-style interiors that had become the rage of Europe in the time of Napoleon. Here lived a Hungarian aristocracy that had its origins far back in a once-dynamic people at the western edge of the great Eurasian steppe, a people that had to check other Asian nomads from making a similar migration. There were smoking rooms crowded with hunting trophies, and vast and dim libraries with thousands of "beautifully bound books" between cherrywood columns on carved shelves, as overwhelming in size as they were underused by the owners. A visitor would find the

portico steps lined with waiting servants and be offered an elaborate
tea service with plum cake, cold ham, and sugared biscuits. A "rhythmic carillon" of bells would announce dinner. There were shooting
parties, ballroom dances, glittering meals at immense candlelit tables
that went on until dawn, as well as violinists playing the music of the
young Richard Strauss in drawing rooms warmed by burning logs.[32]

The political discussions that went on at these fin de siècle feasts
were consistently bitter and intense, centered as they were on the
mounting frustrations of these Hungarians, who saw themselves as
mere tools of Austrian hegemony inside the Dual Monarchy. The atmosphere was one of continual crisis: parties, factions, coalitions all in
perpetual motion. The Magyar lands were in and of themselves held
up as a moral principle. Whereas the Austrians saw the Dual Monarchy, established in 1867, as the end of a process and a final compromise
toward awarding equal status to the Hungarian kingdom, the Hungarians saw the Ausgleich as merely a stage in an ongoing negotiation to
secure their rights.[33] Bánffy's heroic protagonist, Balint Abady, offers a
romantic late-nineteenth-century-style defense of ethnic nationalism:

> How much would be destroyed if men were to be treated as
> robots! What of the myriad individual characteristics, passions,
> aspirations, triumphs and disappointments that together made
> one people different from another? How could anyone ignore
> all the different threads of experience that, over the centuries,
> had formed and deepened the differences that distinguish each
> nation?[34]

The target here was the homogenizing tendency of the Habsburg
system, which, to a degree, was ahead of its time in seeking a universal
consciousness that rose above the bonds of ethnicity. And yet Abady's
nationalism allows him an enlightened attitude toward the Romanian
peasants on his estate, whose difficult lot he unswervingly tries to al-
leviate.[35] For though the events of the story take place at the turn of the
twentieth century, this is still a nineteenth-century nationalism more

connected to a groping liberalism than to the vicious zero-sum ethnic and racial politics of the 1930s.[36] *The Transylvanian Trilogy* deals with a world that was about to go up in smoke in the desolation of World War I, ushering in a century when ethnic consciousness would lose all of its idealistic glamour, as this aristocratic microcivilization of Kolozsvár simply, utterly vanished — surfacing only as an observed reality here and there in the pages of a vintage book such as Patrick Leigh Fermor's *Between the Woods and the Water.*

CLUJ, DESPITE THE VICISSITUDES of world war and decades of Communism, despite the loss of this entire world of aristocracy so long ago, merely because of its location at one of the trade intersections of Central Europe was still a city of high culture and learning, evinced by both its Gothic masterpiece of a church on the main square and the great Babes-Bolyai University. Vasile Puşcaş, the Jean Monnet professor of diplomacy at Babes-Bolyai, was an example of how Cluj represented a cosmopolitan milieu every bit the equal of Bucharest, Romania's capital city. It was Professor Puşcaş, more than any other Romanian, who was responsible for negotiating the country's ascension to the European Union in the previous decade.

We were in the tony lobby of a boutique hotel for businesspeople. Because the hotel was relatively new, I could not associate it with any of my previous visits to Cluj, and thus those earlier visits now seemed more distant and disconnected in memory. I simply let Puşcaş talk in his calm, albeit frustrated, urbane manner, since his understanding of Romania's security predicament was so pellucid:

"Ultimately, it is strong institutions that will protect us from aggressors. But the ascension to the European Union was only a partial success. Our various governments over the years never internalized the process of reform. They thought we had an alliance with the EU. We didn't. We had become part of the EU and had to measure up. They thought EU development funds were for financial assistance, not for institutional reform. The EU money was supposed to be for investing, not for spending. Because all parties and factions were at fault, one has to say that the problem was with our general political culture, which isn't quite Western, which is now no better than in the interbellum period, of course without the external horrors of that time.

"As for the European Union itself," he went on, "it has no foreign policy vision to speak of, since it is paralyzed by the need to defend its own domestic order—preventing the separation of Scotland, Catalonia, and so on. This inward focus occurs while the challenges of the early twenty-first century are much greater than in the 1990s. You cannot, for instance, drag [Vladimir] Putin to the International Criminal Court at The Hague the way you could drag [Slobodan] Milošević. Milošević represented a negligible power: Milošević's Yugoslavia was not Putin's Russia.

"Unlike the European Union, which lacks a foreign policy, Putin operates in a neo-czarist imperial fashion. Putin uses his secret services the way the last czars used the Okhrana, as a major tool of aggression. Putin knows that NATO's northern flank around the Baltic Sea is much stronger than its southern flank around the Black Sea. He also knows that a Russian move in the Baltic States or Poland would trigger a NATO response much more quickly than a Russian move in Moldova and Ukraine. So he concentrates Russian hard power on the Black Sea region, starting with Crimea and eastern Ukraine. Thus, Romania becomes the southeastern flank of the Western alliance: a position not unusual for Romania given its long history."

THE RAIN CONTINUED INTO the next day, only enhancing the city's beauty: Cluj's corroded Gothic and baroque majesty was badly in need of a facelift, even as its blackened and scabrous exteriors lent the place a certain depth and authenticity. There was character to this city. Cluj was grand and beautiful without being pretty. Its steeples and bell towers seemed to levitate above the Habsburg understories.

Valentin Naumescu, another Babes-Bolyai professor, had a panoramic view of the city skyline from the terrace in his office. He, too, was at once clear-cut and deeply concerned about how the situation in Ukraine had crystalized Romania's historical predicament.

"Romania cannot have a normal relationship with Russia," he said. "We want cheaper gas from them. But they don't want to give it. They want closer political and military ties with us, but we are not interested. In Romania now, unlike in many other countries of Central and Eastern Europe, there is no political force or faction that desires better relations with Russia." Romania, because of its Latinity and because of the difficult history with Bessarabia, was arguably the most pro-American and anti-Russian country in the Balkans and southeastern Europe. "Ceauşescu's mistake," Naumescu went on, "was to think he could play East off against West. He couldn't, because Romania was insufficiently crucial to either side. Ceauşescu merely succeeded in impoverishing us. We will never make that mistake again. We have to be part of a bloc. And the only choice for the good of the people is to be part of the West."

Naumescu openly called the new struggle "the second Cold War," which at least in late 2014 seemed to be settling into a kind of stasis. He explained that the West did not want Ukraine to join Russia, but neither did the West really want Ukraine as a member of its own alliance system. The European Union bureaucracy in Brussels wasn't enthusiastic about dealing with a poor and unstable country of 45 million. And neither Washington nor Brussels truly wanted Ukraine as a member of NATO, for that would make relations with Russia permanently impossible. Russia, for its part, did not want to fully incorporate Ukraine, but neither did it want Ukraine to join the West. So the further institutionalizing of both Ukraine and Moldova as buffer states was likely, since it served the purpose of the two camps. There was no conspiracy here, it was just a certain overlapping of interests. Naumescu said to me: "The West may integrate Ukraine and Moldova into some of their institutions, but will not admit them as full-fledged members. Meanwhile, if the West ever went too far, Putin can activate the separatism of the Gagauz in southern Moldova and further inflame the crisis in Ukraine."

Then there was the issue of the 1.6 million ethnic Hungarians in-side Romania, mostly in Transylvania, a factor that Russia's intelli-gence services could try to turn to their advantage as a gift to a populist and neo-authoritarian Hungarian prime minister. "[Viktor] Orbán and his circle might support some form of radicalization in regards to the ethnic Hungarians," István Horváth, the president of the Roma-nian Institute for Research on National Minorities, told me. Horváth was a member of the Székely community, which comprised roughly half of the ethnic Hungarians in Transylvania. The Székelys, he ex-plained, were "a border people," that is, Hungarians who had an intense experience living in proximity to Romanians and ethnic Saxon-Germans. They had a tradition of defending the southeastern frontier of the old Hungarian kingdoms, and by some accounts had Turkic origins, even though they had been Magyarized. "The Székelys have sometimes felt themselves losers in both a Hungarian and a Ro-manian context," Horváth said. Here was another possible, albeit vague, opportunity for chauvinism and separatism, in the event of a severe economic downturn or manipulation from outside. Horváth told me, somewhat sadly, that the only time that both ethnic Hungar-ians and Romanians felt themselves to be proud and equal members of a united Romanian political community was during the December 1989 revolution that toppled Ceauşescu, since both communities shared a part in it. This made me think of something that Naumescu had said:

"A right-wing ethnic populism combined with an anti-EU senti-ment barely exists in the Romanian political sphere today. But that is mainly because the present generation in power in Bucharest has a living memory of the horrors of Ceauşescu's national Communism. Yet that generation will pass, and if Romania does not more fully inte-grate into Europe, the crises to come could lead to a right-wing, popu-list backlash."

Professor Gabriel Bădescu, who holds the political science depart-ment chair at Babes-Bolyai, agreed that the generation with a living memory of Ceauşescu moors the country's moral values. But he was less worried about the future because the present was suitably encouraging in his view. An expert in quantitative analysis who closely follows opinion polls, Bădescu told me that most of the passions he finds in Romanian society are economically related, and tied to the rigors of capitalism and globalization. Ethnic, populist nationalism is just not much of an issue today in Romania, he said. Ironically, Gheorghiu-Dej's and Ceaușescu's national Communism had turned Romania into a "unitary" state, without any divisive regional issues regarding public opinion. Because the Hungarian population in Transylvania had declined over the course of the decades due to discrimination (today's Babes-Bolyai was originally a Hungarian university in the late nineteenth century), the increasing uni-ethnic character of Romania was, sad to say, a force for stability. There had been a brief spark of nasty populism in the 1990s and at the turn of the century in Cluj, when the anti-Hungarian firebrand Gheorghe Funar was mayor. But it had passed. And as the others had told me, Romanians were united about wanting to be in the European Union and NATO. Finally, in a future economic crisis, Romanians would still have the benefit of an escape valve through the ability to migrate elsewhere in Europe and the West in search of work.

Listening to Bădescu rattle off statistics in his terse, meditative voice, it occurred to me that having seen Romania at its worst in 1990, following a half century of world war and fascist-style Stalinism, I was now seeing the country at its best, with a population freely united on the main issues and as free of hatreds as it would ever likely be, even as its rulers, with a vivid memory of a dark and brutal past, remained relatively sober. Ukraine had made the Romanian governing class that much more serious, without (at least as yet) constituting a demonstrable threat. History surely had not ended here, but it had for the moment become more benign.

Chapter VIII

FISHERMAN'S BASTION

FROM CLUJ I DROVE NORTH INTO MARAMUREŞ, WHICH HAD THE CALM purity and femininity of a New Testament landscape, reminding me of the way that Nikos Kazantzakis described the Galilee in his travels in the 1920s.[1] Each tree, as he would say, was a hieroglyph, speaking so much with just a few lines, and with wine and gold on its breath as the autumn advanced. How distinct the colors were! We think of the past in black-and-white because of the state of photography at the time. But the past before the age of smokestack economies was even richer in primary colors than the world of today. And in Maramureş, mountainous isolation had meant a degree of safety from the environmental ravages of Communism. In the glistening swards, the hayricks took on a remote, prehistoric quality. Fruit orchards and flower beds abounded. Nothing in this landscape was unnecessary. I thought not of painting but of music: Saint-Saëns, Debussy, with their spare and haunting notes, touching you for moments after. There was such abundance yet concision everywhere.

In 1918, Maramureş was a province of Austria-Hungary. Following the Paris Peace Conference, in 1920 the area south of the Tisza River became attached to the Kingdom of Romania. In 1940, Hitler oversaw an arrangement called the Second Vienna Award, which returned

Maramureş to Hungary. But in 1945 it became part of Romania again. Maramureş typified a phenomenon in Romania that I had observed in my travels in early 1990, whereby the people of the mountains, as I had intimated, were protected against the worst ravages of collectivization, as though they had been partially forgotten by the Communist authorities.[2] Indeed, so forgotten were they that their language constituted a "brogue" that other Romanians found difficult to understand. No foreign writer captured the virtues of peasant life here better than the Englishman William Blacker in *Along the Enchanted Way*. Blacker actually lived for years among these last surviving peasants, and among the Gypsies in particular, in the first decade of this new century. Because of his love for the peasants and their material life, his book is a song of the earth much like Donald Hall's *Romanian Furrow*, and so the crimes the Communists did commit against these people achieve an especial horror in his lapidary voice. Something he wrote about the horses of peasants sticks in my memory. In the 1950s and 1960s, he explains, the years of Gheorghiu-Dej and the rise of Ceauşescu, the regime killed hundreds of thousands of horses—among the peasants' most prized possessions—merely because the animals were a sign of backwardness, as well as a sign of the owners' wealth. Thus did the regime's brutality cut at the very heart of peasant life.[3]

I myself had come to Maramureş to enjoy a particular Romanian aesthetic: wooden churches, both Orthodox and Uniate (Greek Catholic). Until the fifteenth century, notes the British expert on Romania John Villiers, "virtually all the churches in Maramureş, as elsewhere in the Romanian world, were built of wood." The conclusion of the peace of Satu Mare in 1711, which reestablished Habsburg rule in these parts following a rebellion of the local nobility, gave further encouragement to this kind of church-building. These blessed monuments are made of the pine, spruce, and oak trees that grow in the region. Ancient folk traditions are as much in evidence as the Byzantine and Gothic influences, though virtually all the churches draw their basic design from the early Byzantine basilica, with the tapering

Gothic spires their most arresting architectural detail. The walls are adorned with tempera paintings of pure vegetable and mineral dyes, such as malachite for green, cobalt for blue, and iron oxide for yellow.[4] The vividness of the colors makes the decades and centuries contract.

But it was the needlelike spires that particularly gripped me. They had reduced the Gothic principle—born of what the nineteenth-century British art critic John Ruskin identified as an icy northern fortitude[5]—down to its purest and most abstract form, giving it the power of a mathematical theorem. And that theorem was an affirmation of faith: by pointing so dynamically toward the heavens, these spires signaled the higher moral law that men and women must live under, and conquer fate by so doing. The ultimate purpose of human existence is to appreciate beauty, and beauty requires a spiritual element—an intimation of another world.

In the village of Plopiş I drove down a warren of narrow, cratered roads past silent tin-roofed houses. It was a feathery landscape, where the olive leaves were as dark and shiny as tar in the shadows. The church was a uniform silvery brown, with thousands of layered, puzzle-piece roof tiles creating the impression of a single smooth surface. Four small steeples guarded a massive one, all resting atop a square tower that, in turn, was adorned by winglike protrusions near the bottom. The power was all in the steepness of the design. I wasn't interested in measurements. As I stood next to the church, the steeple seemed to reach to the heavens. There was a particular purity to the construction, as the wooden blocks of the main frame were fitted together without mortar, and rested on ashlars. Romanian Orthodoxy has an especial intimacy with wood. I noted the semantron (*toacă*) used for banging the notes that announce vespers. On this fine October day I felt that I was back in an earlier Romania, without a sign of virtually anyone or even a person to open the church for me.

In Şurdeşti the wooden church was Greek Catholic. I had someone call the local priest, who said that he would come over with the key, after his wife finished cooking a stew for him. It was worth the wait. The flagstones complemented the half-eroded frescoes on the walls, with their thick traces of beet red and inky blue against an ashen background that evoked mist and candle smoke. The Byzantine icons seemed of a piece with a photo of Pope Francis. It is said that the architect of this church, Ion Macarie, designed it in 1721 as penance for some transgression or other: a creation of beauty to atone for a sin.

Still heading north, I crossed a mountain range and found a pruned, Italianate landscape exploding in every shade of ocher. The town of Sighetu-Marmației (Sighet) was hard up against the Ukrainian border and in the shadow zone of the Hungarian and Slovak ones. Here was Central Europe's back of beyond. The beauty came with a price, though.

SIGHET AT FIRST SIGHT was a scrap heap of a town, as if everything that had gone before, and all of history for that matter, had been erased, bulldozed over, and replaced by some of the cheapest prefabricated apartment blocks I have ever seen save for those from the Communist 1950s and 1960s. Grizzled peasants rattled by in horse-drawn *leiterwagens* beside economy cars and groups of Gypsies. People came out on balconies of these hideous buildings to hang clothes. Despite all the people I felt an emptiness.

In the center there was a mix of old- and new-style architecture, almost none of it distinguished, with the occasional rusted baroque dome or two and a café with bad American pop videos playing on a wall monitor. The difference in the generations seemed profound, as young people in stylish dress strode past hobbling old people in headscarves and fedoras. The sight of people smoking was more noticeable than that of people using smartphones. I was deep in the provinces.

Markus Hari greeted me at the entrance to the handsome, Sephardic-style synagogue built in the mid-nineteenth century, located on a side street. I had called in advance for someone to let me inside. The yellow interior was majestic with its mass of benches surrounding the *bima* and the lofty balcony spaces for women. I could imagine the Sabbath here with the close and intimate scents of wor-

shippers crowded together. Our voices echoed sharply in the emptiness and silence of the large space. "Seventy percent of Sighet's
population was Jewish before the Shoah [Holocaust]," Hari explained.
"There were tens of thousands of Jews throughout the Maramureş
then, along with ethnic Hungarians and ethnic Ukrainians. This was
one of eight synagogues in Sighet and one of three hundred in the region. This synagogue was once a lovely, crowded, and joyous place."
Pointing through a door, he said, "Elie Wiesel went to *heder* [Jewish
religious school] in that room." Hari, an old Jewish man with a no-
nonsense, matter-of-fact demeanor, added, "Sighet now has a hundred
and fifty Jews left, including twenty-eight children. The synagogue still
functions."

Elie Wiesel, the author, Auschwitz and Buchenwald survivor, and
1986 Nobel Peace Prize winner, grew up in a house down the street
which is now a small museum of the Holocaust in northern Transylvania. Again, I had to call in advance to gain entrance. The exhibits inside told the story of how the Nazis and Hungarian authorities had
methodically confiscated Jewish property here, had Jewish children
removed from local schools, had Jewish adults fired from their jobs,
forced all Jews here to wear yellow stars, herded all the Jews of Sighet
into a ghetto, and, between May 16 and May 22, 1944—after the Easter holidays that year—had four sealed "death trains" take 12,849 Jews
of Sighet to the Auschwitz-Birkenau concentration camp in Polish
Silesia. Of them, there would be 2,308 survivors after the war.

The museum contains an eyewitness account of the last days of the
large Jewish community of Sighet, written by Father Grigore Dăncuş,
a local Greek Catholic priest. The priest's account is moving in its
stark recitation of the facts. But it is the horror of the black-and-white
photos of local adults and children being herded into one of the
death trains outside Sighet that increases one's sense of utter
incomprehension—precisely because you are aware that this actually
happened, not far from where you are standing, and happened in the
intense, chromatic springtime of Maramureş.

My next stop was Romania's most comprehensive museum of the decades of Communist rule, located inside the country's most notorious Cold War prison, which had happened to be here in the center of Sighet. For in this building adjoining a restored pedestrian promenade, prisoners were tortured while naked, fed miserably, and kept in damp cell rooms with only a bucket. Here in cell number "nine," arguably the greatest Romanian politician of the twentieth century, Iuliu Maniu—who publicly opposed both the Nazis and the Communists—died in 1953.

Whereas the Jewish sites in Sighet are somewhat forlorn and opened only on request (at least when I was there), the prison museum functions as a lively, much-visited center of continuing education about the crimes of Romanian Communism. The walls are covered with the faces of individual victims, and each of the prisoners' cells functions as an exhibit of a separate facet of Communist tyranny. Every subject is unflinchingly dealt with: the literally spine-breaking torture techniques of the Securitate, the deportations to the Bărăgan Steppe, the Danube Canal prison labor system, the repression of ethnic and religious minorities, the decimation of the intellectuals. The prison memorial came into being in the post-Ceauşescu years largely because of the passion and energy of the poet and civic activist Ana Blandiana and her husband, the historian Romulus Rusan. Blandiana has famously said that "memory alone can be a form of justice." The prison is vast. Sighet is a concentration of horror amid beauty all around.

Almost within walking distance at the northern edge of town, past streets with new and prosperous dwellings, is the Tisza River, crawling silently between beech and poplar trees, and alongside farm fields and fruit orchards. Here, too, each tree had an iconic quality. On the other side of the Tisza is Ukraine, literally a few feet away from where I was standing. The fact that this was a border seemed unreal, given the narrow and somnolent quality of the river. But states have to end somewhere, I thought. Beyond the river I spotted a few houses in the middle distance. There the language and many of the concerns of the inhabitants would likely be different. The struggle with Russia would have an immediacy it did not have on this side of the Tisza. This border, like so many others, had real meaning.

This was no longer an imperial world of looser frontiers. Empires were cruel in their way but also allowed a mechanism for intercommunal coexistence, where borders and identities built on race, language, and religion mattered less, since everyone obeyed the same sovereign. The horrors of the twentieth century in Europe had as their backdrop the collapse of empires and the rise of modern, uni-ethnic states, with fascist and Communist leaders replacing the power of traditional monarchs. We still lived in the aftershocks of that nightmare. No solution had as yet been found in the Middle East for the collapse of the Ottoman Turkish Empire. Could the European Union endure to permanently solve the riddle of the collapse of the Austrian Habsburg Empire?

MORE DAYS IN MARAMUREŞ. More early mornings when, as the fog lifted in the sunshine, a perfect velvety landscape revealed itself, as though just surfacing from a biblical flood: sunlight crashing on leaves; rivers as hard as slate; wooden roofs, almost vertical in their steepness, overwhelming one as man's most protective form of embrace. Rococo, baroque, and Byzantine frescoes floated out of the darkness of church interiors. The small church windows, rather than being filled with stained glass, opened up to something more beautiful: the forest outside, beyond rows of apple, cherry, and plum trees. At the church in Bârsana, Father Gheorghe Urda took an hour to explain to me the Old and New Testament themes on the frescoes. "Religion," he said, "is about 'to be,' not about the materialistic 'to have.'" Everything you need to know about how to act in today's world, he went on, "is revealed in these frescoes." In Soconzel, a village far off the main road in the region of Satu Mare, men and women coated with dust and earth labored in the fields among scampering water buffaloes. I had come to see the wooden church here, built in 1777, but it had burned down

only a few years before, they told me. I was disappointed, but grateful
for having made the journey.

I IMAGINED ONE OF HAYDN'S exquisite and stately string quartets playing in my ears as I gazed up at the buildings in the heart of Oradea,
near the Hungarian border. This was Mitteleuropa with all of its architectural flourishes. From Piața Unirii to Piața Ferdinand to Calea Re-
publicii is a pageant of Habsburg monumentality. Amid the wedding
cake swirls on the façades, I checked off baroque, Empire, Secession,
Art Nouveau, and neoclassical in various shades of yellow, pink, and
cream, with a touch of Gothic and—given that this was still Romania—
Brâncoveanu and neo-Byzantine as well. The generic global cafés and
broken, worn-down sidewalks, crowded with smart-looking young men
and women, combined urban dynamism with a run-down seediness,
made slightly chaotic by the building renovations under way. Thus I
stopped hearing Haydn with his embodiment of a complete and finished culture and heard something all at once discordant, energetic,
and universal that I could not quite identify. As I people-watched at an
outdoor café, yet again a national history seemed to be shattering into
innumerable individual ones. I sensed neither liberation nor apoca-
lypse (or else Stravinsky would have been appropriate). Maybe it was
just something with a pulsing, metallic beat that the students at the
café, mixing Romanian with other languages, could name.

After only a few hours in Oradea, I boarded an international train
westward to Budapest. At Biharkeresztes I was stamped into Hungary
and as passengers boarded the train, the vaguely sensuous, staccato
slush of Hungarian consonants replaced the more euphonic Latin syl-
lables of Romanian. My first impressions were just those: superficial,
albeit distinct. The train stations appeared better kempt, with new plat-
forms; the housing plots and agricultural fields more neatly divided;
the passengers more prosperous on this side of the border. The Hungarians, or Magyars, represent a nomadic horse people of the Central
Asian steppe who had migrated into the heart of Europe. Without a

trace of Latin, Slavic, or German blood, they were distantly related to the Finns and Turks, the latter of whom had also migrated westward from Asia's interior reaches. The Hungarians' adoption of Latin Christianity more than a millennium ago completed an extraordinary process of cultural transformation; yet another of history's surprises and virtuoso acts that could not have been foreseen.

The land was yawningly flat, like a dryland sea. I was now beginning my train journey across the Alföld: the Great Hungarian or Pannonian Plain, also known in places as the Puszta, bordered in the north and bisected toward the west by the wide, curving signature of the Tisza, which cuts through the middle of Hungary and also borders the north of Romania.[6] I thought of the Romanian phrase *De la Nistru pin' la Tisa* ("From the Dniester to the Tisza"), with its misty inoperable longing for a Greater Romania.[7] Did such feelings matter anymore? I doubted it. Yet I also knew that if the European Union continued to weaken, it was prudent to think of these things, if only to be forewarned and, therefore, to try to prevent the sort of irredentism we have already seen in Russia. With irredentism comes attendant passions—virulent forms of populism, anti-Semitism, and so on—that can be even more toxic. While we should never acquiesce to these passions, neither should we deny their existence, or deny their attraction in a world where the masses, unable to sufficiently benefit from globalization, reject globalization outright.

IN THE EVENING THE TRAIN arrived at the vast shed of Budapest's Keleti ("Eastern") Station. After checking into a hotel on Castle Hill, I took a walk, despite feeling clammy and grubby from six hours on a second-class train car. Crowds of international tourists were everywhere, mainly Asian, a sight that had been strikingly absent in Romania. I gazed up at the flying, late-Gothic towers of the heavily restored fourteenth-century Matthias Church, glassy and white in their floodlit, sand-castle magnificence, and recalled a certain history: a history central to my journey. The aged historian Neagu Djuvara, whom I had met in Bucharest, recounts the story better than most:

Toward the end of the fourteenth century, there was a Romanian *knez*, or prince, called Voicu—reputed to be a good soldier—who was enlisted by the king of Hungary, Sigismund of Luxembourg, and given the fief of Hunedoara in southwestern Transylvania, near the Banat. His son, Iancu de Hunedoara, better known in history by his Hungarian name, János Hunyadi, would become among the most storied fighters against the Turks. Iancu de Hunedoara, to call him by his Romanian name, rose to become *voivode* of Transylvania and governor of Catholic Hungary. Iancu ranged far and wide in his military exploits in the mid-fifteenth century, battling the Turks, albeit unsuccessfully, as far southeast as Varna on the Black Sea coast of Bulgaria and as far west as Kosovo in south Serbia, though he would free Belgrade in 1456 from the armies of Mehmet II, "the Conqueror," who had taken Constantinople only three years earlier. That victory would give Balkan Christendom a respite from the Turks for seven decades. In Hunedoara, Iancu had built a magnificent castle from where he dominated the *voivodedoms* of Muntenia and Moldavia. It was Iancu, known throughout Europe (and especially among Hungarians and Serbs) as the "White Knight," who may have ordered the killing of Vlad Dracul (the father of Vlad Ţepeş, "the Impaler"), fearing a reconciliation between Vlad and the Turks.[8]

Upon Iancu's death from the plague in 1456, two years of disorder followed in Greater Hungary. There appeared to be no choice but to elect his fifteen-year-old son, Matei, who had followed his father on his campaigns, as the new king. Born in Cluj (Kolozsvár), Matei would become the great ruler Matei Corvinul, after the *corb*, or raven, with a ring in its beak on his coat of arms.[9] That was his Romanian name; he would become more famous by the Hungarian appellation of Matyas Hunyadi (or Matthias Corvinus). Western Poland, Bohemia, the eastern half of Austria, and the Adriatic coast of Italy would number among his conquests and the locations of his battles. He became king of Bohemia and duke of Austria. Though he regained Otranto, in Italy's far southeastern corner, from the Turks, he may have spent too many resources against his western neighbors, instead of concentrating on the containment of the Ottoman Empire. Perhaps as a result, thirty-six years after his death, in 1526, the Kingdom of Hungary for which Matei was so ambitious fell to the Turks at Mohacs.[10]

Matei, or Matthias, may be better remembered for the style of his rule, which was that of a "splendid Renaissance prince," in Patrick Leigh Fermor's words: a monarch who "was profoundly learned, a polyglot, a passionate humanist," who brought scholars and artists from Italy to his palace.[11] (He erected a royal oratory and rebuilt the south bell tower of this church on Castle Hill, and helped establish the Black Church in Braşov.) He was also an example of a fifteenth-century absolute monarch who helped put an end to the autonomy of feudal domains, leading, in turn, to the creation of modern unified states. He introduced a new system of taxation. He limited the power of feudal masters over the serfs, and maintained the equivalent of a national army: the famous "Black Army," composed mainly of mercenaries.[12]

Again, now what was it: Matei Corvinul or Matthias Corvinus; Iancu de Hunedoara or János Hunyadi; a Romanian or Hungarian? Iancu was nominally a Romanian who may not have known more than a few Romanian words, Magyarized as he was, Professor Paul Philippi had told me back in Sibiu. In these late medieval kingdoms, identity was less rigidly established than it was to become in the age of modern ethnic nationalism. We cannot even be sure of the parentage of Iancu and Matei. For someone like Matthias, who in any case was educated in Italian, today's identity questions might have seemed incomprehensible or beside the point, just as they might on some future morrow, when what we call globalization is further advanced and allows for identities that are in part a throwback to a more flexible age. "It doesn't matter what precise national identity those heroes had!" Philippi had exclaimed to me. But for the moment, in too many places, we will have to endure divisions of blood and myth: divisions that are frankly undeniable because people believe them, even as they must be resisted.

TIME IS A MOVING SEA OF FOG, rent with holes that reveal intense, sacred moments of memory, even as all the rest is dim. I remember vividly the neo-Gothic and neo-Romanesque terrace known as Fisherman's Bastion, a few feet from the Matthias Church, coated with snow in early December 1981, dancing almost in its multilevel, spiraling conquest of the night. I was completing a journey through the Balkans and part of Central Europe that had changed my life, giving it a direction that would never really alter afterward. The friendships I had before that autumn would, for the most part, gradually fade away, while the new friendships I would acquire would hold steady over all the coming decades. From the vantage point of 1981, my previous nighttime visit to this terrace in 1973 had seemed like ages ago. For in those intervening years I had moved in a directionless pattern from being a young traveler in Eastern Europe, to being a newspaper reporter in New England, to traveling about the Mediterranean for many months, to living in Israel for a few years, only to return to Eastern Europe. The distance from 1973 to 1981 seemed vast only because I had gained so many different kinds of personal experiences in between, something normal in a young person uncertain of his bearings. "You do not describe the past by writing about old things, but by writing about the haze that exists between yourself and the past," observes the novelist Mircea Cărtărescu.[13] The haze obscuring 1973 from the vantage point of 1981 was thick indeed. But now in 2014, 1981 appeared so close—so immediate—I could almost touch it, though thirty-three years had passed! For I felt I was a similar person now to what I had been back then on that snowy terrace in 1981. Then I had started on a path that I was still on, even as marriage, a child, the anticipation of a grandchild, the intense pain of professional mistakes, and the process of aging had matured me further (at least I hoped it had).

But time told a different story for the politics of the region. While

1973 and 1981 encompassed an immense gulf in my personal life, Eastern Europe had barely changed in those eight years, governed as it was by the same Communist system and by the same dictators in 1973 as in 1981. Thus, only when I became utterly self-absorbed did I think that much had happened during those eight years; since for the peoples of the region, tragically, very little had happened. And yet while 1981 might have been like yesterday for me, the world in that intervening third of a century had collapsed and was reborn for those who actually lived here.

Throughout the 1980s, I repeatedly returned to Budapest and visited its dissidents in their disorderly apartments: young men and women who lived and dressed like sixties protestors but whose intellectual world was so much more mature and realistic. Whereas the youth rebellion in the United States had been about denouncing the imperfections of a democratic system, Hungary's dissidents were battling, in semi-secrecy and at great personal risk, a Moscow-based totalitarian system. Of course, Communist Hungary tolerated dissidents to a degree that Communist Romania did not. While Hungary's regime under János Kádár bore elements of Central European autocracy, Romania's under Nicolae Ceauşescu was sheer Oriental despotism.

But history is not only about the ground moving slowly under one's feet and observing subtle differences. History is also about convulsions that wipe away decades of previous patterns. So it was that in 1989 the Berlin Wall fell, and these and all the other regimes throughout Communist Eastern Europe suddenly collapsed. Various experiments in democracy and free market economics transformed Romania and Hungary irrevocably. Elected governments rose, succeeded or failed, and were replaced by others. The deadening silence of Communism had been replaced by the need to adapt to ruthless capitalism, which bred its own, less heroic anxieties at the personal level. Indeed, people will always have their heartrending problems, and so the job of a statesman is not to make people happy, but to substitute one set of problems for another.

The geopolitics of Europe had also completely altered. Between my Cold War visits of 1973 and 1981, two blocs had continued to reign, one free and one Communist; the former protected by a security umbrella provided by the United States and the latter by one provided by the Soviet Union. Piłsudski's idea—born of necessity—of an Intermarium had, back then, been all but forgotten; now it was newly relevant, as Russia had passed from post-Communist chaos to a more threatening neo-authoritarianism and Germany had emerged to become the regional economic hegemon. The United States, meanwhile, was somewhat less significant in Europe than it had been during the Cold War, partly distracted as it was by crises in the Greater Middle East and the Pacific Basin. The present situation was not so stark as during the Cold War, nor was it given to post-historical optimism like in the 1990s, when NATO and the European Union were expanding and Russia was conveniently helpless. And yet neither was it like the 1930s—utterly without hope, with Hitler and Stalin looming, and the West nowhere in sight. Carol II and Antonescu, even if they had been wise and good (which they obviously weren't), would still have had few palatable choices in those circumstances.

But geography remained now, as always, disturbingly relevant. To repeat: the Warsaw Pact might be dead, but Russia was still big, illiberal, and right next door. Ukraine was crucial to Russia's destiny, and Romania and Moldova combined had a longer border with Ukraine than had Poland, even as Romania also provided an invasion route between the Black Sea and the Mediterranean. Officials in Washington acted as if they had less at stake in these matters than officials in the Kremlin. And that was both Romania's challenge and tragedy. The fact that Hungary now had a prime minister, Viktor Orbán, who was moving steadily in an authoritarian direction, eroding the judiciary, individual rights, and a free press—as if he cared more about the opinion of Moscow than of Brussels—demonstrated that all was not well here in Central Europe, and that a Russia-backed Orbán regime had the theoretical possibility to stoke anti-Romanian unrest among Romania's ethnic Hungarian minority.

Hungary's turn toward a low-calorie form of Putinism also suggested how the past was not such a sure guide to the present and future, since throughout much of the Cold War and the first two decades afterward, Hungary compared to Romania had been the more Westernized country. Now, at least for the moment and at the macropolitical level, the situation was reversed. Who could have foreseen that? This is ultimately why all foreign correspondency and travel writing, however clairvoyant it may sometimes be, is merely the record of what was seen and heard at a particular moment in time. A place may change beyond recognition in just a few short years. Whether or not a journalist or travel writer is able to discern the middle-term future in a given location, capturing a perishable moment in time is perhaps even more important.

Looking out over the glittering Danube between the neo-Gothic towers, I broke my own advice, as I had done so often throughout this journey: I took refuge in a book rather than solely in the magnificent pageant of water and light before me. It was just that the memory of the subtle brown and yellow shades of the jacket cover and the wonderful maps inside appeared welcoming, and the author's voice had been wise. Indeed, the printed book was still for me the greatest expression of art. I had carried the tome with me during part of my travels, despite the weight of its nearly seven hundred pages, because, like the process of memory itself, Cambridge University professor Brendan Simms's *Europe: The Struggle for Supremacy, from 1453 to the Present* makes the past hum with immediacy. In the mid-eighteenth century, as Simms writes, Bourbon France and Habsburg Austria (and later Russia) combined against Prussia and Great Britain with the consequence being the Seven Years' War. In the mid-nineteenth century, France and a German federation used Austria to block Russia. In the early twentieth, it was France, Britain, and Russia against Germany and Austria. And so it continues in his narrative until the Götterdämmerung of World War II.

With Europe at this moment in so much economic disarray, with Germany rising, and with Russia back to its default autocratic and militaristic normal, it would be tempting to predict that Europe will simply rediscover its demons and revert to its disunited self, threatening competing coalitions and conflict once more, as in its long and bloody past. For as the Romanian expatriate and Bard College professor Norman Manea exquisitely writes: "The modern world faces its solitude and its responsibilities without the artifice of a protective dependency or a fictive utopian coherence."[14] And so we see the return of various kinds of exclusivist identities: national, ethnic, tribal, and sectarian.

Yet, I wasn't sure. So much is contingent on the decisions of individual men and women and especially of political leaders themselves. Just look at the Hungarian leader Orbán! Furthermore, one had to consider the unifying tendencies of new communications technologies that are creating an authentic global civilization, however uncertain and superficial that civilization may still be. Czesław Miłosz, writing from the vantage point of the end of the Cold War, says that "our bond of being born at the same time, thus being contemporaries, is already stronger than that of being born in the same country."[15] To be sure, feeling oneself part of an era can in many circumstances be less destructive than feeling oneself part of a racial or ethnic group, for the former identity leads to bonds across ethnicities, and the latter does not. Moreover, while the masses in individual countries might be restive and alienated from the elite vision of a united Europe proffered by the Eurocrats in Brussels, the nationalisms to which some of them now regress simply lack the thickened intensity of the nationalisms of the 1920s and 1930s, when contact with the outside world was so much less seamless than it is in a postmodern era. As the American intellectual Michael Walzer says, "When identities are multiplied, passions are divided," and, therefore, I would add, those passions also have the possibility of being less lethal.[16]

Europe will not simply reinhabit the demons of the past, in other words. The Continent will enact something new, or at least some variation of former ages. It will, with any luck, retain the basic liberalism, best epitomized perhaps by the Swiss-French philosopher Benjamin Constant, that has thus far broadly defined the West.

Rightly, Professor Simms eschews prophecy and makes only observations at the end of his text. And his most arresting observation is both geographical and historical: that Europe as a whole has always had its destiny shaped by what takes place inside the boundaries of the medieval Holy Roman Empire, an area that today encompasses a united Germany and stretches from the Netherlands eastward to Czech-Bohemia, and from Denmark southward to the Italian Piedmont. In short, the geography that matters most currently signifies Berlin and the major cities of the European Union: Brussels, The Hague, Strasbourg, and so forth. That means the region from Budapest to Bucharest to Chişinău, all more or less part of Piłsudski's Intermarium, will likely still have its fate significantly determined by an interplay of outside forces: in geographic terms, the same as in the past. Of course, Hungary, Romania, and Moldova can mitigate those outside forces by strengthening their own governing institutions so that vibrant civil societies take root, societies that are less susceptible to subversion. Nevertheless, as minor powers all, they must always be cognizant of shifts in the international and European strategic balance. If Germany and the powers within the European Union cannot stand up to a revanchist Russia, if the EU crumbles from within, Romania and its shadow zones will be in trouble, since the United States is not likely to provide quite the same level of support to its allies as it did during the Cold War. The West will be far away, Russia in whatever form will be close, and Ukraine will continue to be perhaps more central to the European drama than Spain or Portugal.

To forecast a return to belligerent and shifting alliances within the Continent is simply too deterministic; but so is the forecast of a united and pacifistic Europe stretching from Iberia to the Black Sea. The future may feature gradations and levels of complexity yet unseen in terms of geopolitics and group identity. The divisions between those states inside the European Union and outside, and between those states both within the Eurozone and the so-called borderless Schengen Area and those not, attest to this emerging complexity. Among much else, as I've said, a lot may hinge on how communications technology, as it continues to evolve, either empowers or undermines the forces of ethnic and religious nationalism—not to mention the forces of new ideologies as yet unimagined. Nationalism, after all, was modernism writ large. As men and women lost their literal belief in God and thus their belief in individual immortality, they sought refuge in a "collective immortality."[17] As the Romanian philosopher Andrei Pleşu patiently explains, it isn't that nationalism per se is bad: it is only nationalism that puts its values above all other values that is destructive.[18] Truly, nationalism will have to evolve, as Middle Eastern refugees flow into Europe, adding further complexity to its demography. Europe, throughout history, has had its destiny affected by migrations from the east—the various Gothic tribes, Slavs, Magyars, and others. So this latest wave is not as unprecedented as the media suggests. Furthermore, we must keep in mind that Europe's southern border was never really the Mediterranean but the Sahara Desert, and the Balkans have often been a zone of human passage. A classical geography has now reasserted itself in Europe, uniting it with Africa and Eurasia.

So what will postmodernism bring? At the very least, we can hope that the central horror of the twentieth century—that "baroque synthesis" of Communism and fascism, as epitomized by the Ceauşescu regime, in the words of scholar Vladimir Tismăneanu—will not be equaled or even approached.[19]

To guarantee a better century than the last one, a European Union in some form will be essential. The European Union, despite its economic woes that for years have been producing the most lugubrious headlines, was still a favored destiny in the lands of Europe's southeast through which I had traveled. And this came as no surprise to me. For the European Union, I repeat, represented more than a balance sheet: it represented states rather than ethnic nations, and impersonal laws over corrupt and arbitrary fiat; thus it defended the individual against prejudice and reaction. Group consciousness is all well and good as long as it defends the rights of the individual—regardless of origin or political tendency. Only with that in mind does nationalism have legitimacy. Though people from time to time still thought vaguely and wistfully, with their eyes half-closed, about Greater This or Greater That, their immediate concerns were for safety and predictability in their own lives. And those concerns were ultimately communicated through the clenched resolve, however roundabout and half-measured, that European Union officials continued to manifest at one summit after the other. *We will get through this crisis, and that one, because we have no other choice, given the past.* I hoped that I was not being naïve. I knew that the leaders of the European Union would have to do far, far better than they had, if only because half measures were themselves a form of self-deception. They would have to confront head-on the structural and financial issues that they had infinitely postponed. But I reasoned that they must ultimately do so because, again, there was no other choice. If the European Union crumbled, there was only un-bridled German power, exclusivist ethnic nationalism, and the de-mentia of ideologies. To wit, Russia was now a threat not because it was Russia essentially, but because Putin's neo-czarist oil and gas em-pire had reduced geopolitics to the zero-sum factor of ethnicity.

I now thought of the Romanian philosopher Constantin Noica and his disciples living in the Carpathian Mountains during the worst years of the Ceauşescu regime, holding intense discussions that went on deep into the night about Kierkegaard, Heidegger, Foucault, Hegel, and Goethe—keeping the flame of humanism alive, since it was the canon of Western philosophy and literature that constituted, in and of itself, a hopeful rebuke to the low culture of Communism all around them. I thought, too, of the massive stone busts of postwar Europe's founders in Herăstrau Park in Bucharest, in whom Romanians still put so much faith. And—as I looked out over the nighttime Danube and its many bridges strung with lights—I thought of an Orthodox priest I had met seven hundred miles downstream on this same river at Giur-giu, who had told me about the Gothic-inspired roof of his wooden church, and how it indicated Romania's yearning for the West.

ACKNOWLEDGMENTS

OANA-ANTONIA COLIBĂŞANU, AN ASSOCIATE PROFESSOR AT THE University of Bucharest, has been a guiding spirit in the research behind this book since I began serious work on it in 2012. Her shrewd perceptions about individuals and historical context immensely improved the manuscript, which she checked and commented upon. This is in addition to helping me on everything from arranging travel to inserting diacritical marks for Romanian words.

Dennis Deletant, visiting professor of Romanian studies at Georgetown University and emeritus professor at University College, London, read and corrected the manuscript, as did his erudite Georgetown colleague, Professor of International Affairs Charles King. Vladimir Tismăneanu of the University of Maryland, the author of several books on Communist and post-Communist Europe, also read and commented upon the manuscript, and in general plied me with advice on the subject matter, including books to read and people to interview. Dr. Ernest H. Latham Jr., a former American diplomat in Romania and an assiduous researcher in his own right, also made corrections on the manuscript, and opened up his vast library on Romanian subjects for me to explore. I am deeply grateful for all of this assistance, though,

I emphasize, all mistakes and other flaws herein are completely my own.

My wife, Maria Cabral, continues to put up with my absences and provide a loving and gracious home for me always to return to, which she has done for well over three decades now. She has truly been the silent hand behind whatever I have been able to achieve. My chief assistant, Elizabeth M. Lockyer, in addition to helping me on the maps, photographs, and bibliography, continues—with help from Dede Rathbun—to punctiliously organize my professional life, which has allowed me the luxury to devote so much attention to writing books.

Gail Hochman, Marianne Merola, and Henry Thayer at Brandt & Hochman Literary Agents worked prodigiously to provide me with the resources and much else to proceed with this project, among others. The late Carl D. Brandt, my agent for a quarter century, helped me in the early stages to think through what I wanted to convey to the reader. My long friendship with Carl continues to yield fruit, and I expect will do so into the future. My former editor at Random House, Jonathan Jao, now at HarperCollins, was a source of excellent and canny judgment in the early stages of the publishing process. He and Gail Hochman were fierce defenders of my idea for writing a book about Romania, Romanian Communism, and the threat from Russia long before the Ukraine crisis made its relevance more obvious. At Random House, Kate Medina and Anna Pitoniak took this book project under their wing with fastidiousness and loving care. Kate runs a crisp and classy editorial shop within Random House, and Anna's judgment on the manuscript and much else was indicative of this. For a number of my books already, Steve Messina at Random House has handled the copyediting and correction process with extraordinary calm and efficiency, for which I remain grateful.

Joy de Menil, who along with Jason Epstein was my editor at Random House in the 1990s, advised me early on to highlight my Cold War memories in the book. Lidia Bodea, the director general of Editura Humanitas in Bucharest—my Romanian publisher—encouraged me to keep the narrative deeply personal throughout. Simona Kessler, my literary agent in Bucharest, made me aware of various books on Romanian philosophy that I otherwise might have missed. Whatever merits this book has are due substantially to such guidance.

My preoccupation with Romania has, over the past three and a half decades, resulted in a number of enduring friendships and professional relationships, as well as kindnesses offered. In this vein, let me thank Cristian Mihai Adomniței, Adriano Bosoni, Sergiu Celac, Eugene Chausovsky, Corneliu Ciurea, Radu Dudău, Mircea Geoană, Lauren Goodrich, Andrei Hincu, Ioanna Ieronim, Major General (Ret.) Mihai Ionescu, Tudor Jijie, Ioana Leucea, Octavian Manea, Teodor Meleșcanu, Silviu Nate, Laurențiu Pachiu, Adam Reising, Alex Șerban, Kiki Skagen-Harris, Georgia Călin Ștefan, Professor Laurențiu Ștefan, Marius Stoian, and Berbeca Veaceslav.

There are, too, George and Meredith Friedman, who introduced me to their Stratfor colleague Antonia Colibasanu in the first place. George was born in post–World War II Hungary and did not speak English until he was seven. His knowledge of the region is profound, even as I have at times disagreed with him. My decision a half decade ago to write a book about Romania, along with a first encounter with George and Meredith in Jakarta, Indonesia, in 2011, was fortuitous. Stratfor, of which George is the founder, has pursued advisory services in a number of countries, including Romania. During the time I wrote a weekly column for Stratfor, from 2012 to 2014, I took no part in this activity. This book was generated by love of subject only.

I completed *In Europe's Shadow* as a senior fellow at the Center for a New American Security in Washington, which I rejoined in 2015 after four years there, from 2008 to 2012. I am grateful to its leadership— CEO Michele Flournoy, President Richard Fontaine, and Director of Studies Shawn Brimley—for integrating me back into a highly caffeinated and altogether meticulous organizational culture that both stimulated me intellectually and allowed me time alone to write.

SELECT BIBLIOGRAPHY

Appelfeld, Aharon. "Buried Homeland." Translated by Jeffrey M. Green. *New Yorker*, November 23, 1998.

Applebaum, Anne. *Iron Curtain: The Crushing of Eastern Europe 1944–1956*. New York: Doubleday, 2012.

———. "Nationalism Is Exactly What Ukraine Needs: Democracy Fails When Citizens Don't Believe Their Country Is Worth Fighting For." *New Republic*, May 13, 2014.

Arendt, Hannah. *The Origins of Totalitarianism*. 1951; reprint, New York: Benediction Classics, 2009.

Ascherson, Neal. *Black Sea*. New York: Hill & Wang, 1995.

Aspinall, D. "Romania: Queues and Personality Cults." *Soviet Analyst*, May 1984.

Baerlein, Henry. *Bessarabia and Beyond*. London: Methuen, 1935.

———. *Enciclopedia României*. Vol. 2, *Țara Românească*. Bucharest: Imprimeria Națională, 1938.

Bánffy, Miklós. *The Transylvanian Trilogy*. Vol. 1, *They Were Counted*. Vol. 2, *They Were Found Wanting*. Vol. 3, *They Were Divided*. Translated by Patrick Thursfield and Katalin Bánffy-Jelen, introduction by Hugh Thomas. New York: Knopf, 2013.

Baynes, N. H. *The Hellenistic Civilization and East Rome*. Oxford: Oxford University Press, 1946.

Bendavid, Naftali. "Europe Confronts Its Roma Problem." *Wall Street Journal*, April 23, 2014.

Berdyaev, Nicolas. *The Origin of Russian Communism*. Translated by R. M. French. 1937; reprint, Ann Arbor: University of Michigan Press, 1960.

Berlin, Isaiah. *Four Essays on Liberty*. New York: Oxford University Press, 1969.

Blacker, William. *Along the Enchanted Way: A Story of Love and Life in Romania*. London: John Murray, 2009.

Blake, Robert. *Disraeli*. New York: St. Martin's Press, 1967.

Bloch, Marc. *Apologie pour l'histoire ou Métier d'historien*. Paris: A. Colin, 1964.

Boia, Lucian. *Romania: Borderland of Europe*. Translated by James Christian Brown. London: Reaktion Books, 2001.

Bolovan, Ioan, et al. *A History of Romania*. Jassy, Romania: Center for Romanian Studies, 1996.

Boxer, Charles Ralph. *The Portuguese Seaborne Empire 1415–1825*. London: Hutchinson, 1977.

Brown, Peter. *The World of Late Antiquity: AD 150–750*. London: Thames & Hudson, 1971.

Byron, Robert. *The Byzantine Achievement: An Historical Perspective CE 330–1453*. 1929; reprints, London: Routledge, 2013, Mt. Jackson, VA: Axios Press, 2010.

Byron, Robert, and David Talbot Rice. *The Birth of Western Painting*. London: George Routledge, 1930.

Camus, Albert. *Lyrical and Critical Essays*. Translated by Ellen Conroy Kennedy. New York: Vintage, 1970.

———. *The Rebel*. New York: Vintage, 1991.

Canetti, Elias. *Crowds and Power*. Translated by Carol Stewart. New York: Penguin, 1981.

Cantacuzino, Sherban. "The Brâncoveanu Style: Art and Architecture in Romania in the Seventeenth Century." In John Villiers, ed., *Romania*. London: Pallas Athene, 2009.

——. "Bucharest and Its Architecture." In John Villiers, ed., *Romania*. London: Pallas Athene, 2009.

Caroe, Olaf. *The Pathans: 550 B.C.–A.D. 1957*. Karachi: Oxford University Press, 1958.

Cărtărescu, Mircea. *Blinding*. Translated by Sean Cotter. Brooklyn, NY: Archipelago Books, 2013.

Cavafy, C. P. *Collected Poems*. Translated by Edmund Keeley and Philip Sherrard, edited by George Savidis. Princeton, NJ: Princeton University Press, 1975.

Celan, Paul. *Poems of Paul Celan*. Translated and with an introduction by Michael Hamburger. New York: Persea Books, 1972.

Chausovsky, Eugene. "Transdniestria: The Geopolitics of the Ultimate Borderland." Austin, TX: Stratfor, July 2013.

Cioran, E. M. *Schimbarea la față a Românei (The Transfiguration of Romania)*. Bucharest: Editura Vremea, 1936.

Clark, Victoria. *Why Angels Fall: A Journey Through Orthodox Europe from Byzantium to Kosovo*. London: Macmillan; New York: William Morrow, 2000.

Codrescu, Andrei. *The Hole in the Flag: A Romanian Exile's Story of Return and Revolution*. New York: William Morrow, 1991.

Coles, Paul. *The Ottoman Impact on Europe*. London: Thames & Hudson, 1968.

Conrad, Joseph. *Lord Jim and Nostromo*. Introduction by Robert D. Kaplan. New York: Modern Library, 1999.

Davies, Norman. *God's Playground: A History of Poland*. Vol. 1, *The Origins to 1795*. New York: Columbia University Press, 2005.

Deletant, Dennis. *Hitler's Forgotten Ally: Ion Antonescu and His Regime, Romania 1940–1944*. New York: Palgrave Macmillan, 2006.

——. *Romania Under Communist Rule*. Jassy, Romania: Center for Romanian Studies, 1998.

Diță, Alexandru V. *Marele Mircea Voievod*. Bucharest: Editura Academiei, 1987.

Djuvara, Neagu. *A Concise History of Romanians*. Translated by Constantin Banica. Whitby, Ontario: Cross Meridian, 2012.

Dostoevsky, Fyodor. *The Idiot*. Translated by Richard Pevear and Larissa Volokhonsky. New York: Vintage, 2002.

Eksteins, Modris. *Rites of Spring: The Great War and the Birth of the Modern Age*. Boston: Houghton Mifflin, 1989.

Eliade, Mircea. *The Myth of the Eternal Return: or, Cosmos and History*. Translated by Willard R. Trask. Princeton, NJ: Princeton University Press, 1954.

———. *The Romanians: A Concise History*. Translated by Rodica Mihaela Scafes. Madrid: Stylos, 1943.

Eminescu, Mihai. *Poems*. Translated by Corneliu Popescu. Bucharest: Editura Cartea Românească, 1989.

Fall, Bernard. "The Theory and Practice of Insurgency and Counterinsurgency." *Naval War College Review*, April 1965.

Fermor, Patrick Leigh. *Between the Woods and the Water: On Foot to Constantinople from the Hook of Holland: The Middle Danube to the Iron Gates*. London: John Murray, 1986.

———. *The Broken Road: From the Iron Gates to Mount Athos*. Introduction by Colin Thubron and Artemis Cooper. London: John Murray, 2013.

Figes, Orlando. *A People's Tragedy: The Russian Revolution 1891–1924*. London: Jonathan Cape, 1996.

Fischer, Rudolf. "Romania or Rumania?" Impala Publishers blog, September 19, 2009.

Frederick the Great. *The History of My Own Times*, 1746.

Friedman, George. *Borderlands: A Geopolitical Journey in Eurasia*. Austin, TX: Stratfor, 2011.

Fussell, Paul. *Abroad: British Literary Traveling Between the Wars*. New York: Oxford University Press, 1980.

Gardiner, John Eliot. *Bach: Music in the Castle of Heaven*. New York: Knopf, 2014.

Georgescu, Vlad. *The Romanians: A History*. Translated by Alexandra Bley-Vroman. Columbus: Ohio State University Press, 1991.

Gibbon, Edward. *The Decline and Fall of the Roman Empire*. Vol. 1. New York: Knopf, 1993.

——. *The Decline and Fall of the Roman Empire*. Vol. 6. New York: Knopf, 1994.

Gide, André. *The Immoralist*. Translated by Richard Howard. New York: Knopf, 1970.

Hall, Donald. *Romanian Furrow*. London: Bene Factum, 2007.

Herodotus. *The Histories*. Translated by Tom Holland. New York: Penguin, 2015.

Hitchins, Keith. *Rumania 1866–1947*. New York: Oxford University Press, 1994.

Hobbes, Thomas. "On the Life and History of Thucydides." In Hobbes's translation of *The Peloponnesian War*. Ann Arbor: University of Michigan Press, 1959.

Ignatieff, Michael. *Isaiah Berlin: A Life*. New York: Henry Holt, 1998.

Illyes, Gyula. *Puszták népe (People of the Puszta)*. Budapest: Nyuget, 1936.

Inalcik, Halil. *The Ottoman Empire: The Classical Age 1300–1600*. London: Weidenfeld & Nicolson, 1973; London: Orion, 1994.

Ioanid, Radu. *The Holocaust in Romania: The Destruction of Jews and Gypsies Under the Antonescu Regime, 1940–1944*. Chicago: Ivan R. Dee, 2000.

Jelavich, Barbara. *Russia and the Formation of the Romanian National State 1821–1878*. New York: Cambridge University Press, 1984.

Judt, Tony. *Postwar: A History of Europe Since 1945*. New York: Penguin, 2005.

Kafka, Franz. *The Castle*. New York: Oxford University Press, 2009.

Kann, Robert A. *A History of the Habsburg Empire 1526–1918*. Berkeley: University of California Press, 1974.

Kaplan, Robert D. *Balkan Ghosts: A Journey Through History*. New York: St. Martin's Press, 1993.

——. "Balkans' Fault Line: Yugoslavia Starts to Feel the Tremors." *Wall Street Journal Europe*, November 30, 1989.

——. "Being There: Put Down Your Smartphone—the Art of Travel Demands the End of Multitasking." *Atlantic*, November 2012.

——. *Eastward to Tartary: Travels in the Balkans, the Middle East, and the Caucasus*. New York: Random House, 2000.

——. "Europe's New Map." *The American Interest*, April 12, 2013.

——. "Europe's Russia Factor." Austin, TX: Stratfor, May 23, 2012.

——. "Europe's Third World." *Atlantic Monthly*, July 1989.

——. "In the Balkans, No Wars Are 'Local.'" *New York Times*, April 7, 1999.

——. "Into the Bloody New World: A Moral Pragmatism for America in an Age of Mini-Holocausts." *Washington Post*, April 17, 1994.

——. "Joseph Conrad: God's Own Foreign Correspondent." Introduction to Joseph Conrad, *Lord Jim and Nostromo*. New York: Modern Library, 1999.

——. *The Revenge of Geography: What the Map Tells Us About Coming Conflicts and the Battle Against Fate*. New York: Random House, 2012.

——. "Rumanian Gymnastics: Ceauşescu Looks West but Acts East." *New Republic*, December 12, 1984.

——. "Why Yugoslavia Exploded." *Reader's Digest*, March 1993.

Kazantzakis, Nikos. *Journeying: Travels in Italy, Egypt, Sinai, Jerusalem and Cyprus*. Translated by Themi Vasils and Theodora Vasils. Boston: Little, Brown, 1975.

King, Charles. *The Moldovans: Romania, Russia, and the Politics of Culture*. Stanford, CA: Hoover Institution Press, 1999.

——. *Odessa: Genius and Death in a City of Dreams*. New York: Norton, 2011.

Kinross, Lord. *The Ottoman Centuries: The Rise and Fall of the Turkish Empire*. New York: William Morrow, 1977.

Kissinger, Henry. "Otto von Bismarck, Master Statesman." *New York Times*, March 31, 2011.

————. *A World Restored: Metternich, Castlereagh and the Problems of Peace 1812–1822*. Boston: Houghton Mifflin, 1957.

Kosary, Dominic G. *A History of Hungary*. Foreword by Julius Szekfu. New York: Benjamin Franklin Bibliophile Society, 1941.

Latham, Ernest H., Jr. *Timeless and Transitory: 20th Century Relations Between Romania and the English-Speaking World*. Bucharest: Editura Vremea, 2012.

Lewis, Bernard. *Istanbul and the Civilization of the Ottoman Empire*. Norman: University of Oklahoma Press, 1963.

Lieven, Dominic. *Empire: The Russian Empire and Its Rivals*. London: John Murray, 2000.

Liiceanu, Gabriel. *The Păltiniş Diary*. Bucharest: Cartea Românească, 1983; Budapest: Central European University Press, 2000.

Lubbock, Basil. *The Opium Clippers*. Boston: Charles E. Luriat, 1933.

Lucas, Edward. "How the West Lost Ukraine to Putin." *Wall Street Journal*, December 11, 2013.

Lukacs, John. "In Darkest Transylvania." *New Republic*, February 3, 1982.

Luttwak, Edward N. *The Grand Strategy of the Byzantine Empire*. Cambridge, MA: Harvard University Press, 2009.

Macartney, C. A. *The Habsburg Empire 1790–1918*. New York: Macmillan, 1969.

Machiavelli, Niccolò. *Discourses on Livy*, 1531, I:6.

Mackinder, Halford J. *Democratic Ideals and Reality: A Study in Politics of Reconstruction*. New York: Henry Holt, 1919.

Magris, Claudio. *Danube: A Journey Through the Landscape, History, and Culture of Central Europe*. Translated by Patrick Creagh. New York: Farrar, Straus & Giroux, 1989.

Manea, Norman. "Intellectuals and Social Change in Central and Eastern Europe." *Partisan Review*, Fall 1992.

————. *October, Eight O'Clock*. New York: Grove Press, 1992.

Mann, Thomas. *Buddenbrooks: The Decline of a Family*. Translated by H. T. Lowe-Porter. Middlesex, England: Penguin Books, 1957.

———. *The Magic Mountain.* Translated by H. T. Lowe-Porter. New York: Knopf, 1927.

———. "Tonio Kröger." In *Death in Venice and Seven Other Stories.* Translated by H. T. Lowe-Porter. New York: Vintage, 1963.

Martines, Lauro. *Furies: War in Europe, 1450–1700.* New York: Bloomsbury Press, 2013.

Matynia, Elzbieta. *An Uncanny Era: Conversations Between Václav Havel and Adam Michnik.* New Haven, CT: Yale University Press, 2014.

McGuinness, Patrick. *The Last Hundred Days.* New York: Bloomsbury, 2012.

Miłosz, Czesław. *Beginning with My Streets: Essays and Recollections.* Translated by Madeline G. Levine. New York: Farrar, Straus & Giroux, 1991.

———. *The Captive Mind.* Translated by Jane Zielonko. New York: Vintage, 1981.

Mitford, Nancy. *Frederick the Great.* New York: Vintage, 2011.

Moorehead, Alan. *The Blue Nile.* New York: Harper & Row, 1962.

———. *The White Nile.* New York: Penguin, 1983.

Morris, Ian. *War! What Is It Good For?* New York: Farrar, Straus & Giroux, 2014.

Morris, Jan. *Trieste and the Meaning of Nowhere.* New York: Da Capo Press, 2002.

Müller, Herta. *Nadirs.* Translated and with an afterword by Sieglinde Lug. Lincoln: University of Nebraska Press, 1999.

Musil, Robert. *The Man without Qualities.* Vols. 1 and 2. Translated by Sophie Wilkins and Burton Pike. New York: Vintage, 1996.

Nabokov, Vladimir. "Cloud, Castle, Lake." *Atlantic Monthly,* June 1941.

Niebuhr, Reinhold. *Moral Man and Immoral Society.* New York: Charles Scribner's Sons, 1932.

Norwich, John Julius. *Byzantium: The Early Centuries.* New York: Knopf, 1989.

Ogden, Alan. *Romania Revisited.* Bucharest: Center for Romanian Studies, 2000.

Ormsby, Eric. "Hidden Affinities." *New Criterion,* June 2012.

Ostrogorsky, George. *History of the Byzantine State.* Translated by Joan Hussey. Oxford: Basil Blackwell, 1956.

Palmer, Alan. *Metternich: A Biography.* New York: Harper & Row, 1972.

Pessoa, Fernando. *Fernando Pessoa & Co.: Selected Poems.* Translated by Richard Zenith. New York: Grove Press, 1998.

Péter, László. *Historians and the History of Transylvania.* New York: East European Monographs, 1992.

Petersen, Alexandros. *The World Island: Eurasian Geopolitics and the Fate of the West.* Oxford: Praeger, 2011.

Petreu, Marta. *An Infamous Past: E. M. Cioran and the Rise of Fascism in Romania.* Translated by Bogdan Aldea. Chicago: Ivan R. Dee, 2005.

Pleşu, Andrei. *On Angels: Exposition for a Post-Modern World.* Bucharest and Berlin: Humanitas and Berlin University Press, 2012.

Pop, Ioan-Aurel, and Ioan Bolovan, eds. *History of Romania: Compendium.* Cluj-Napoca, Romania: Romanian Cultural Institute, 2006. "Dacia Before the Romans," by Aurel Rustoiu. "The North-Danube Region from the Roman Province of Dacia to the Emergence of the Romanian Language," by Coriolan Horaţiu Opreanu.

Psellus, Michael. *Fourteen Byzantine Rulers: The Chronographia.* Translated by E. R. A. Sewter. New York: Penguin Books, 1966.

Rapport, Mike. *1848: Year of Revolution.* London: Little, Brown, 2008.

Reed, John. *The War in Eastern Europe.* New York: Charles Scribner's Sons, 1916.

Renan, Ernest. "What Is a Nation?" In A. Zimmern, ed., *Modern Political Doctrines.* Oxford: Oxford University Press, 1939.

Rezzori, Gregor von. *Memoirs of an Anti-Semite.* Introduction by Deborah Eisenberg. New York: New York Review Books, 2008.

———. *The Snows of Yesteryear.* Translated by H. F. Broch de Rothermann. New York: Knopf, 1989.

Rothschild, Joseph. *East-Central Europe Between the Two World Wars.* Seattle: University of Washington Press, 1974.

Ruskin, John. *The Stones of Venice*. New York: Da Capo, (1853) 1960.

Sadoveanu, Mihail. *Tales of War*. New York: Twayne Publishers, 1962.

St. John, Robert. *Foreign Correspondent*. London: Hutchinson, 1960.

Seton-Watson, Hugh. *The Russian Empire 1801–1917*. New York: Oxford University Press, 1967.

Seton-Watson, R. W. *A History of the Roumanians: From Roman Times to the Completion of Unity*. New York: Cambridge University Press, 1934.

Shore, Marci. *The Taste of Ashes: The Afterlife of Totalitarianism in Eastern Europe*. New York: Crown, 2013.

Simms, Brendan. *Europe: The Struggle for Supremacy, from 1453 to the Present*. New York: Basic Books, 2013.

Skilling, H. Gordon. *The Governments of Communist East Europe*. New York: Thomas Y. Crowell, 1971.

Snyder, Timothy. *The Reconstruction of Nations: Poland, Ukraine, Lithuania, Belarus, 1569–1999*. New Haven, CT: Yale University Press, 2003.

Solonari, Vladimir. *Purifying the Nation: Population Exchange and Ethnic Cleansing in Nazi-Allied Romania*. Washington and Baltimore: Woodrow Wilson Center Press and Johns Hopkins University Press, 2010.

Solzhenitsyn, Aleksandr. *November 1916: The Red Wheel: Knot II*. New York: Farrar, Straus & Giroux, 1999.

Stasiuk, Andrzej. *On the Road to Babadag: Travels in the Other Europe*. London: Harvill Secker, 2011.

Steiner, George. *Language and Silence: Essays on Language, Literature and the Inhuman*. New York: Atheneum, 1982.

Stephenson, P., M. Wagner, M. Badea, and F. Serbanescu. "The Public Health Consequences of Restricted Induced Abortion— Lesson from Romania." *American Journal of Public Health*, October 1992.

Storrs, Sir Ronald. *Orientations*. London: Ivor Nicholson & Watson, 1937.

Strauss, Leo. *On Tyranny: Including the Strauss-Kojeve Correspondence.* Edited by Victor Gourevitch and Michael S. Roth. Chicago: University of Chicago Press, 1961.

Taylor, A. J. P. *Bismarck: The Man and the Statesman.* New York: Knopf, 1955.

Thomas, Hugh. *Armed Truce: The Beginnings of the Cold War 1945–1946.* New York: Atheneum, 1987.

Tismăneanu, Vladimir. *The Devil in History: Communism, Fascism, and Some Lessons of the Twentieth Century.* Berkeley: University of California Press, 2012.

——. *Fantasies of Salvation: Democracy, Nationalism, and Myth in Post-Communist Europe.* Princeton, NJ: Princeton University Press, 1998.

——. *Stalinism for All Seasons: A Political History of Romanian Communism.* Berkeley: University of California Press, 2003.

——. "The Tragicomedy of Romanian Communism." *East European Politics and Societies,* Spring 1989.

Tocqueville, Alexis de. *Democracy in America.* Abridged ed. New York: Penguin Books, 1956.

Tolstoy, Leo. *Resurrection.* Translated by Rosemary Edmonds. London: Penguin Books, 1966.

Toynbee, Arnold J. *A Study of History.* London: Oxford University Press, 1946.

Turgenev, Ivan. *Fathers and Sons.* Translated by Rosemary Edmonds. Harmondsworth, Middlesex, England: Penguin Books, 1965.

Verdery, Katherine. *National Ideology Under Socialism: Identity and Cultural Politics in Ceauşescu's Romania.* Berkeley: University of California Press, 1991.

Villiers, John, ed. *Romania.* London: Pallas Athene, 2009.

Waldeck, R. G. *Athene Palace Bucharest: Hitler's "New Order" Comes to Rumania.* London: Constable, 1943.

Walzer, Michael. "The New Tribalism: Notes on a Difficult Problem." *Dissent,* Spring 1992.

Watts, Larry L. *Romanian Cassandra: Ion Antonescu and the Struggle for Reform, 1916–1941.* Boulder, CO: East European Monographs, 1993.

——. *With Friends Like These: The Soviet Bloc's Clandestine War Against Romania,* vol. 1. Bucharest: Editura Militară, 2010.

White, Theodore H. *In Search of History: A Personal Adventure.* New York: Harper & Row, 1978.

Winder, Simon. *Danubia: A Personal History of Habsburg Europe.* New York: Farrar, Straus & Giroux, 2013.

NOTES

PROLOGUE: NABOKOV'S ROOM

1. Sir Ronald Storrs, *Orientations* (London: Ivor Nicholson & Watson, 1937), p. 609.

2. Vladimir Nabokov, "Cloud, Castle, Lake," *Atlantic Monthly*, June 1941.

3. Marci Shore, *The Taste of Ashes: The Afterlife of Totalitarianism in Eastern Europe* (New York: Crown, 2013), p. 106.

4. H. Gordon Skilling, *The Governments of Communist East Europe* (New York: Thomas Y. Crowell, 1971), pp. 11 and 234.

CHAPTER 1: BUCHAREST 1981

1. Fernando Pessoa (1888–1935), "Ah, the First Minutes in Cafes of New Cities," *Fernando Pessoa & Co.: Selected Poems*, translated by Richard Zenith (New York: Grove Press, 1998), p. 145.

2. André Gide, *The Immoralist*, translated by Richard Howard (New York: Knopf, 1970), pp. 148 and 170.

3. Lucian Boia, *Romania: Borderland of Europe*, translated by James Christian Brown (London: Reaktion Books, 2001), pp. 55–58.

4. Dennis Deletant, *Romania Under Communist Rule* (Jassy, Romania: Center for Romanian Studies, 1998), p. 118.

5. Robert D. Kaplan, "Rumanian Gymnastics: Ceaușescu Looks West but Acts East," *New Republic*, December 12, 1984.

6. Sherban Cantacuzino, "Bucharest and Its Architecture," in *Romania*, edited by John Villiers (London: Pallas Athene, 2009).

7. Kaplan, "Rumanian Gymnastics."

8. Robert Musil, *The Man Without Qualities*, vols. 1 and 2, translated by Sophie Wilkins and Burton Pike (New York: Vintage, 1996), vol. 1, p. 325.

9. Ibid., vol. 1, pp. 426, 538, and 606; vol. 2, p. 1535.

10. Thomas Mann, "Tonio Kröger," quoted from the translation of H. T. Lowe-Porter, *Death in Venice and Seven Other Stories* (New York: Vintage, 1963), p. 98.

11. Robert D. Kaplan, "Joseph Conrad: God's Own Foreign Correspondent," introduction to *Lord Jim and Nostromo* (New York: Modern Library, 1999).

12. Thomas Hobbes, "On the Life and History of Thucydides," in Hobbes's translation of *The Peloponnesian War* (Ann Arbor: University of Michigan Press, 1959).

13. Thomas Mann, *The Magic Mountain*, translated by H. T. Lowe-Porter (New York: Knopf, 1927), p. 32.

14. Robert D. Kaplan, *Mediterranean Winter: The Pleasures of History and Landscape in Tunisia, Sicily, Dalmatia, and Greece* (New York: Random House, 2004), p. 198.

15. Theodore H. White, *In Search of History: A Personal Adventure* (New York: Harper & Row, 1978), pp. 144–53.

16. Kaplan, "Rumanian Gymnastics."

17. Vladimir Tismăneanu, *Stalinism for All Seasons: A Political History of Romanian Communism* (Berkeley: University of California Press, 2003).

18. Czesław Miłosz, *The Captive Mind*, translated by Jane Zielonko (New York: Vintage, 1981), p. 29.

19. Modris Eksteins, *Rites of Spring: The Great War and the Birth of the Modern Age* (Boston: Houghton Mifflin, 1989), pp. 281–82.

20. Robert D. Kaplan, *Eastward to Tartary: Travels in the Balkans, the Middle East, and the Caucasus* (New York: Random House, 2000), p. 41.

21. R. G. Waldeck, *Athene Palace Bucharest: Hitler's "New Order" Comes to Rumania* (London: Constable, 1943), pp. 85 and 277–78.

22. Robert D. Kaplan, "Being There: Put Down Your Smartphone—the Art of Travel Demands the End of Multitasking," *Atlantic*, November 2012.

23. Leo Tolstoy, *Resurrection*, translated by Rosemary Edmonds (London: Penguin Books, 1966), p. 244.

24. I still held out hope for peace. As the article concluded: "A Yugoslavia propelled forward by Slovene reformist values will help the chances of successful liberalization. . . . The Balkans would then exist purely in a geographical sense." Robert D. Kaplan, "Europe's Third World," *Atlantic Monthly*, July 1989; Robert D. Kaplan, "Balkans' Fault Line: Yugoslavia Starts to Feel the Tremors," *Wall Street Journal Europe*, November 30, 1989.

25. In the March 1993 issue of *Reader's Digest*, the same month *Balkan Ghosts* was published, I wrote: "Unless we can break the cycle of hatred and revenge—by standing forcefully for self-determination and minority rights—the gains from the end of the Cold War will be lost. All aid, all diplomatic efforts, all force if force is used, must be linked to the simple idea that all the people of Yugoslavia deserve freedom from violence." Soon afterward I appeared on television (CNN, C-SPAN) to publicly urge intervention in the Balkans. I also unambiguously urged military intervention in the Balkans on the front page of *The Washington Post* Outlook section on April 17, 1994, more than a year before we intervened ("Into the Bloody New World: A Moral Pragmatism for America in an Age of Mini-Holocausts"). During the

NATO air campaign in defense of Kosovo five years later, on the op-ed page of *The New York Times* on April 7, 1999, when the campaign seemed to be going badly and much of the media was calling it a failure, I vigorously supported it.

26. More specifically, the American invasion, by dismantling the machine of bureaucratic authority, made survival for ordinary Iraqis a self-help game, in which they fell back on sectarian solidarity groups.

27. The division, albeit, was rough. For example, the Habsburgs, whose empire generally designated Central Europe, nevertheless ruled in the Banat and Oltenia, beyond the Carpathians, after the 1718 Treaty of Passarowitz. And the Turks, whose rule often ended at the Danube, maintained Transylvania, to the north of the Carpathians, as an Ottoman vassal state in the fifteenth and sixteenth centuries.

CHAPTER 2: BUCHAREST 2013

1. Gregor von Rezzori, *Memoirs of an Anti-Semite*, introduction by Deborah Eisenberg (New York: New York Review Books, 2008), pp. 140–41.

2. Gregor von Rezzori, *The Snows of Yesteryear*, translated by H. F. Broch de Rothermann (New York: Knopf, 1989), p. 16.

3. Patrick Leigh Fermor, *The Broken Road: From the Iron Gates to Mount Athos*, introduction by Colin Thubron and Artemis Cooper (London: John Murray, 2013), pp. 161 and 163.

4. For an erudite opinion on the matter, see Rudolf Fischer, "Romania or Rumania?" Impala Publishers blog, September 19, 2009.

5. Robert D. Kaplan, *Balkan Ghosts: A Journey Through History* (New York: St. Martin's Press, 1993), p. 83.

6. Kaplan, *Eastward to Tartary*, pp. 31–32.

7. Barbara Jelavich, *Russia and the Formation of the Romanian National State 1821–1878* (New York: Cambridge University Press, 1984), pp. 47–48 and 198.

8. Anne Applebaum, *Iron Curtain: The Crushing of Eastern Europe 1944–1956* (New York: Doubleday, 2012), p. 383.

9. Rezzori, *Memoirs of an Anti-Semite*, pp. 73, 116, and 173.

10. Marc Bloch, *Apologie pour l'histoire ou Métier d'historien* (Paris: A. Colin, 1964), p. 15; Boia, *Romania*, p. 47.

11. Kaplan, *Eastward to Tartary*, p. 33. The journalist Victoria Clark makes a related point about how connections rather than any established bureaucratic process were necessary if she were to visit the monastery of Snagov north of Bucharest. "I was back, I surmised, in the Orthodox world proper where personal contacts are the *sine qua non* of getting anything done." Victoria Clark, *Why Angels Fall: A Journey Through Orthodox Europe from Byzantium to Kosovo* (London: Macmillan, 2000), p. 229.

12. That Austro-Hungarian army had a large German component, and included among its ranks the future World War II field marshal Erwin Rommel.

13. Lauro Martines, *Furies: War in Europe, 1450–1700* (New York: Bloomsbury Press, 2013), p. 209. The civilians' suffering was both mundane and extreme, if that is possible. In the wars of the mid-eighteenth century, merely as a matter of course, armies stole the produce of peasants, trampled their crops, and often burned down their houses to make bivouac fires. Nancy Mitford, *Frederick the Great* (New York: Vintage, 2011), p. 182. Ian Morris, *War! What Is It Good For?* (New York: Farrar, Straus & Giroux, 2014), p. 201.

14. Kaplan, *Balkan Ghosts*, pp. 82–83.

15. Waldeck, *Athene Palace Bucharest*, p. 85.

16. Maniu, along with the Liberal leader Constantin Brătianu, also advised against Antonescu taking his war machine beyond Bessarabia and into Transdniestria. Had Antonescu heeded their advice, a great many Jews would have been saved and Romania's fate after the war might have been less harsh. Maniu was not perfect. A native Transylvanian, he harbored resentment toward Transylvanian Jews, whom he viewed as pro-Hungarian. In 1937, his National Peasant Party made a tactical alliance with the fascist

Iron Guard. But in an era when the West seemed to be deserting Central and Eastern Europe, the only debate in Romania was whether to align with Hitler or with Stalin. Charles King, *The Moldovans: Romania, Russia, and the Politics of Culture* (Stanford, CA: Hoover Institution Press, 1999), p. 94; Radu Ioanid, *The Holocaust in Romania: The Destruction of Jews and Gypsies Under the Antonescu Regime, 1940–1944* (Chicago: Ivan R. Dee, 2000), p. 292; Dennis Deletant, *Hitler's Forgotten Ally: Ion Antonescu and His Regime, Romania 1940–1944* (New York: Palgrave Macmillan, 2006), pp. 32–33 and 75; Larry L. Watts, *Romanian Cassandra: Ion Antonescu and the Struggle for Reform, 1916–1941* (Boulder, CO: East European Monographs, 1993), p. 339; Keith Hitchins, *Rumania 1866–1947* (New York: Oxford University Press, 1994), p. 545.

17. R. W. Seton-Watson, *A History of the Roumanians: From Roman Times to the Completion of Unity* (New York: Cambridge University Press, 1934), pp. 1 and 5.

18. Niccolò Machiavelli, *Discourses on Livy*, 1531, I:6; Frederick the Great, *The History of My Own Times*, 1746. See Brendan Simms, *Europe: The Struggle for Supremacy, from 1453 to the Present* (New York: Basic Books, 2013), pp. 28 and 111.

CHAPTER 3: LATIN BYZANTIUM

1. Thomas Mann, *Buddenbrooks: The Decline of a Family*, translated by H. T. Lowe-Porter (Middlesex, England: Penguin Books, 1957), pp. 17, 24, and 213.

2. Mann, *The Magic Mountain*, pp. 250 and 295.

3. Isaiah Berlin, *Four Essays on Liberty* (New York: Oxford University Press, 1969), ch. 2.

4. Michael Ignatieff, *Isaiah Berlin: A Life* (New York: Henry Holt, 1998), p. 200.

5. Hannah Arendt, *The Origins of Totalitarianism* (New York: Benediction Classics, 2009), p. 157.

6. Berlin, *Four Essays on Liberty*, ch. 2.

7. Sherban Cantacuzino, "The Brâncoveanu Style: Art and Architecture in Romania in the Seventeenth Century," in *Romania*, edited by John Villiers (London: Pallas Athene, 2009), p. 118.

8. Fermor, *The Broken Road*, pp. 181 and 184; Boia, *Romania*, p. 174.

9. Elias Canetti, *Crowds and Power*, translated by Carol Stewart (New York: Penguin, 1981), pp. 197–209.

10. Kaplan, *Balkan Ghosts*, pp. 132–33.

11. Alexis de Tocqueville, *Democracy in America*, abridged ed. (New York: Penguin Books, 1956), p. 27.

12. Ernest Renan, "What Is a Nation?" in *Modern Political Doctrines*, edited by A. Zimmern (Oxford: Oxford University Press, 1939), pp. 187–205.

13. Reinhold Niebuhr, *Moral Man and Immoral Society* (New York: Charles Scribner's Sons, 1932), pp. 83–97 and 110–12.

14. Boia, *Romania*, p. 63.

15. Mihai Eminescu, *Poems*, translated by Corneliu Popescu (Bucharest: Editura Cartea Românească, 1989), p. 165.

16. Marta Petreu, *An Infamous Past: E. M. Cioran and the Rise of Fascism in Romania*, translated by Bogdan Aldea (Chicago: Ivan R. Dee, 2005), p. 63.

17. Boia, *Romania*, p. 109.

18. Gabriel Liiceanu, *Jurnalul de la Păltiniş* (Bucharest: Cartea Românească, 1983), pp. 232–33 and 236–37; also published in English as *The Păltiniş Diary* (Budapest: Central European University Press, 2000), pp. xiv and xxv–xxvi; Katherine Verdery, *National Ideology Under Socialism: Identity and Cultural Politics in Ceauşescu's Romania* (Berkeley: University of California Press, 1991), pp. 258, 278–79, and 301.

19. Edward Gibbon, *The Decline and Fall of the Roman Empire*, vol. 1 (New York: Knopf, 1993), pp. 8–9, 273, and 325.

20. Mircea Eliade, *The Romanians: A Concise History*, translated by Rodica Mihaela Scafes (Madrid: Stylos, 1943), p. 7; Herodotus,

The Histories. Translated by Tom Holland (New York: Penguin, 2015), IV, 93; Ioan Bolovan, et al., *A History of Romania* (Jassy, Romania: Center for Romanian Studies, 1996) (authors include: Ioan Bolovan, Florin Constantiniu, Paul E. Michaelson, Ioan-Aurel Pop, Christian Popa, Marcel Popa, Ioan Scurtu, and Marcela Vultur), pp. 12 and 18; Ioan-Aurel Pop and Ioan Bolovan, eds., *History of Romania: Compendium* (Cluj-Napoca, Romania: Romanian Cultural Institute, 2006), "Dacia Before the Romans" by Aurel Rustoiu, "The North-Danube Region from the Roman Province of Dacia to the Emergence of the Romanian Language" by Coriolan Horatiu Opreanu.

21. Tismăneanu is, in turn, paraphrasing the point of literary historian Adrian Marino, whom Tismăneanu calls "one of the few genuine liberal intellectuals in post-Ceaușescu Romania" in the late 1990s. Vladimir Tismăneanu, *Fantasies of Salvation: Democracy, Nationalism, and Myth in Post-Communist Europe* (Princeton, NJ: Princeton University Press, 1998), p. 11 and footnote on p. 170.

22. Eliade, *The Romanians*, pp. 12–13; Bolovan, *A History of Romania*, p. 23.

23. Vlad Georgescu, *The Romanians: A History*, translated by Alexandra Bley-Vroman (Columbus: Ohio State University Press, 1991), pp. 12–13.

24. Eliade, *The Romanians*, pp. 14–15.

25. Bolovan, *A History of Romania*, pp. 43 and 45; Eliade, *The Romanians*, pp. 16–17.

26. Eliade, *The Romanians*, pp. 20–21.

27. Ibid., pp. 23–24; Bolovan, *A History of Romania*, pp. 67–73.

28. Eliade, *The Romanians*, p. 25.

29. Mircea Eliade, *The Myth of the Eternal Return: or, Cosmos and History*, translated by Willard R. Trask (Princeton, NJ: Princeton University Press, 1954), pp. 153–54.

30. Eliade, *The Romanians*, p. 26.

31. Ibid., pp. 28–31; Alexandru V. Diță, *Marele Mircea Voievod* (Bucharest: Editura Academiei, 1987), pp. 254–77; Bolovan, *A History of Romania*, pp. 99–100; Georgescu, *The Romanians*, p. 53.

32. Iancu de Hunedoara more commonly goes under the Hungarian name of János Hunyadi: more on him later in the narrative.

33. Neagu Djuvara, *A Concise History of Romanians*, translated by Constantin Banica (Whitby, Ontario: Cross Meridian, 2012), pp. 102–3.

34. Eliade, *The Romanians*, pp. 32–33; Bolovan, *A History of Romania*, pp. 105–9 and 112–14; Pop, *History of Romania: Compendium*, "Romanians in the 14th–16th Centuries: From the 'Christian Republic' to the 'Restoration of Dacia,'" p. 211; Clark, *Why Angels Fall*, p. 213.

35. Martines, *Furies*, pp. 153 and 209.

36. Bolovan, *A History of Romania*, p. 115; Pop, *History of Romania*, p. 266; Eliade, *The Romanians*, p. 33.

37. Eliade, *The Romanians*, pp. 33, 35, and 37; Bolovan, *A History of Romania*, p. 151.

38. Eliade, *The Romanians*, p. 40.

39. Bolovan, *A History of Romania*, pp. 143–51; Pop, *History of Romania*, pp. 305–14; Georgescu, *The Romanians*, pp. 54–55.

40. Eliade, *The Romanians*, pp. 41–42. There will be more about Cuza, Moldavia (Moldova), Carol I, and so forth later in the narrative. Clark, *Why Angels Fall*, p. 215.

41. Eliade, *The Romanians*, p. 44.

42. Ibid., pp. 45, 47, 50–52, and 55.

43. Tismăneanu, *Fantasies of Salvation*, pp. 21 and 72.

44. Ibid., p. 105.

45. Ibid., pp. 82–83.

46. George Steiner, *Language and Silence: Essays on Language, Literature and the Inhuman* (New York: Atheneum, 1982), p. 152; Tismăneanu, *Fantasies of Salvation*, pp. 64 and 157.

47. Timothy Snyder, *The Reconstruction of Nations: Poland, Ukraine, Lithuania, Belarus, 1569–1999* (New Haven, CT: Yale University Press, 2003), pp. 16, 22, 29, 41, 70, 205, 207, 230, and 293.

48. Snyder, *The Reconstruction of Nations*, p. 42.

CHAPTER 4: THE BĂRĂGAN STEPPE

1. Locating the Battle of Rovine by the Argeș River near Craiova would explain the fog mentioned in the Ottoman and Serbian historical writings. Craiova was also the more important location, though the route the Turks likely took was through Bărăgan.

2. Djuvara, *A Concise History of Romanians*, p. 24.

3. Fermor, *The Broken Road*, p. 143.

4. Peter Brown, *The World of Late Antiquity: AD 150–750* (London: Thames & Hudson, 1971), p. 22.

5. John Julius Norwich, *Byzantium: The Early Centuries* (New York: Knopf, 1989), pp. 325 and 339.

6. Edward N. Luttwak, *The Grand Strategy of the Byzantine Empire* (Cambridge, MA: Harvard University Press, 2009), pp. 82 and 94.

7. George Ostrogorsky, *History of the Byzantine State,* translated by Joan Hussey (Oxford: Basil Blackwell, 1956), p. 27; N. H. Baynes, *The Hellenistic Civilization and East Rome* (Oxford: Oxford University Press, 1946), p. 1.

8. Robert Byron, *The Byzantine Achievement: An Historical Perspective CE 330–1453* (1929; reprints, London: Routledge, 2013, Mt. Jackson, VA: Axios Press, 2010), p. 48 of Axios Press edition.

9. Robert D. Kaplan, *Mediterranean Winter: The Pleasures of History and Landscape in Tunisia, Sicily, Dalmatia, and the Peloponnese* (New York: Random House, 2004), pp. 187–88 and 190–93; Paul Fussell, *Abroad: British Literary Traveling Between the Wars* (New York: Oxford University Press, 1980), pp. 79–112.

10. Fussell, *Abroad*, p. 85.

11. Norwich, *Byzantium*, p. 25.

12. Byron, *The Byzantine Achievement*, pp. xxxiii, 39–40, 50, 122; Norwich, *Byzantium*, p. 27.

13. Byron, *The Byzantine Achievement*, pp. 177 and 326; Ostrogorsky, *History of the Byzantine State*, p. 33.

14. Luttwak, *The Grand Strategy of the Byzantine Empire*, pp. 3–5, 236, and 410.

15. Hitchins, *Rumania 1866–1947*, pp. 1 and 10.

16. Ostrogorsky, *History of the Byzantine State*, p. 31.

17. Nicolas Berdyaev, *The Origin of Russian Communism*, translated by R. M. French (Ann Arbor: University of Michigan Press, 1960); Kaplan, *Eastward to Tartary*, pp. 79–80.

18. Michael Psellus, *Fourteen Byzantine Rulers: The Chronographia*, translated by E. R. A. Sewter (New York: Penguin Books, 1966), p. 177.

19. C. P. Cavafy, *Collected Poems*, translated by Edmund Keeley and Philip Sherrard, edited by George Savidis (Princeton, NJ: Princeton University Press, 1975), pp. 189 and 245.

20. Jelavich, *Russia and the Formation of the Romanian National State 1821–1878*, p. 229.

21. Lord Kinross, *The Ottoman Centuries: The Rise and Fall of the Turkish Empire* (New York: William Morrow, 1977), pp. 18–19 and 139; Halil İnalcik, *The Ottoman Empire: The Classical Age 1300–1600* (London: Weidenfeld & Nicolson, 1973; London: Orion, 1994), pp. 5–6 and 67, Orion edition; Paul Coles, *The Ottoman Impact on Europe* (London: Thames & Hudson, 1968), p. 16; Eric Ormsby, "Hidden Affinities," *New Criterion*, June 2012; Bernard Lewis, *Istanbul and the Civilization of the Ottoman Empire* (Norman: University of Oklahoma Press, 1963), pp. 36 and 39–40.

22. Lord Kinross, *The Ottoman Centuries*, pp. 111, 143, and 155; İnalcik, *The Ottoman Empire*, p. 7; Coles, *The Ottoman Impact on Europe*, p. 154; Arnold J. Toynbee, *A Study of History* (London: Oxford University Press, 1946), part 3, ch. 9, p. 2.

23. Lord Kinross, *The Ottoman Centuries*, pp. 41 and 47; İnalcik, *The Ottoman Empire*, pp. 11–12 and 15.

24. According to the Romanian historian Neagu Djuvara, Phanariot rule "was the least evil of the possible ones, because we had no chance of becoming independent at that time, when the Turks were afraid we could have taken the side of Austria or Russia. The choice was between becoming a *pashalik* and having Greek governors from Constantinople. The second alternative was preferable. . . ." Djuvara, *A Concise History of Romanians*, p. 170.

25. Lord Kinross, *The Ottoman Centuries*, pp. 60, 113, and 613–14.

26. Ibid., p. 192.

27. Gibbon, *The Decline and Fall of the Roman Empire*, vol. 6, ch. 64.

28. Lewis, *Istanbul*, p. 48; Lord Kinross, *The Ottoman Centuries*, pp. 49–52, 61, 68–69, 187–88, and 192.

29. Coles, *The Ottoman Impact on Europe*, p. 34.

30. Jelavich, *Russia and the Formation of the Romanian National State 1821–1878*, pp. 10–11.

31. Hitchins, *Rumania 1866–1947*, p. 2.

32. Hugh Thomas, *Armed Truce: The Beginnings of the Cold War 1945–1946* (New York: Atheneum, 1987), pp. 282–83 and 285, and footnotes pp. 613–14.

33. Tony Judt, *Postwar: A History of Europe Since 1945* (New York: Penguin, 2005), p. 192; Applebaum, *Iron Curtain*, p. 249.

34. Deletant, *Romania Under Communist Rule*, pp. 10 and 16–17.

35. Ibid., pp. 17–18.

36. Ibid., pp. 18–19 and 104.

37. Ibid., pp. 58–63, 74–76, and 98.

38. Ibid., p. 65; Vladimir Tismăneanu, "The Tragicomedy of Romanian Communism," *East European Politics and Societies*, Spring 1989.

39. Georgescu, *The Romanians*, p. 288.

40. Deletant, *Romania Under Communist Rule*, p. 114.

41. Ibid., pp. 145–46; D. Aspinall, "Romania: Queues and Personality Cults," *Soviet Analyst*, May 1984; P. Stephenson, M. Wagner,

M. Badea, and F. Serbanescu, "The Public Health Consequences of Restricted Induced Abortion—Lesson from Romania," *American Journal of Public Health*, October 1992.

42. Leo Strauss, *On Tyranny: Including the Strauss-Kojeve Correspondence*, edited by Victor Gourevitch and Michael S. Roth (Chicago: University of Chicago Press, 1961), p. 45. Strauss is referring to Xenophon's dialogue between Hiero, tyrant of Syracuse, and Simonides, a wise poet.

43. Larry L. Watts, *With Friends Like These: The Soviet Bloc's Clandestine War Against Romania*, vol. 1 (Bucharest: Editura Militară, 2010), pp. 1, 2, 4–5, and 9.

44. Aleksandr Solzhenitsyn, *November 1916: The Red Wheel: Knot II* (New York: Farrar, Straus & Giroux, 1999), p. 337.

45. In 1998, I interviewed Silviu Brucan, another member of the group that determined the Ceaușescus' fate, about the decision to execute them. Kaplan, *Eastward to Tartary*, ch. 5, "Balkan Realists."

46. For a very short, elegant description of Ovid in Tomi see Neal Ascherson's *Black Sea* (New York: Hill & Wang, 1995), pp. 66–67.

47. The southern Dobrudja now belongs to Bulgaria, though it was in Romanian hands between the Second Balkan War of 1913 and World War II, a time when Queen Marie built a dream palace at Balchik there.

48. Clark, *Why Angels Fall*, p. 234.

49. Fyodor Dostoevsky, *The Idiot*, translated by Richard Pevear and Larissa Volokhonsky (New York: Vintage, 2002), p. 429.

CHAPTER 5: THE GREAT CEMETERY OF THE JEWS

1. Deletant, *Hitler's Forgotten Ally*, pp. 71 and 302 (footnote).

2. Quoted in Hugh Seton-Watson, *The Russian Empire 1801–1917* (New York: Oxford University Press, 1967), p. 262.

3. Albert Camus, *The Rebel* (New York: Vintage, 1991), pp. 23, 25, and 70.

4. I use Greater Romania here in the informal geographic sense. The formal term, Romania Mare, is more precisely used to describe Romanian territory between the two world wars, when Romania constituted the largest polity in its history.

5. Dominic Lieven, *Empire: The Russian Empire and Its Rivals* (London: John Murray, 2000), p. 222.

6. Lieven, *Empire*, pp. 236–37; Hugh Seton-Watson, *The Russian Empire 1801–1917*, p. 31; Jelavich, *Russia and the Formation of the Romanian National State 1821–1878*, p. x.

7. Jelavich, *Russia and the Formation of the Romanian National State 1821–1878*, pp. 17 and 19. Istanbul did not become the official name until 1930 under Mustafa Kemal Atatürk.

8. After the compromise of 1867, in which the declining Austrian Habsburgs agreed to share sovereignty with the government of Hungary, the empire is properly known as Austria-Hungary.

9. Jelavich, *Russia and the Formation of the Romanian National State 1821–1878*, pp. 1, 4, 7, 20, and 30–32; Coles, *The Ottoman Impact on Europe*, pp. 132 and 174; Hugh Seton-Watson, *The Russian Empire 1801–1917*, pp. 45, 48, 94, 299, 301–2, 313, and 320–21.

10. Jelavich, *Russia and the Formation of the Romanian National State 1821–1878*, pp. 39–41; Boia, *Romania*, p. 82.

11. Jelavich, *Russia and the Formation of the Romanian National State 1821–1878*, pp. 101–2.

12. Mike Rapport, *1848: Year of Revolution* (London: Little, Brown, 2008), pp. 3–5, 79, 111, 113, 132, 134, 139, 142–43, 149, 377, and 407.

13. Hugh Seton-Watson, *The Russian Empire 1801–1917*, pp. 280–81 and 430–31.

14. Hitchins, *Rumania 1866–1947*, p. 11.

15. Djuvara, *A Concise History of Romanians*, p. 216.

16. Jelavich, *Russia and the Formation of the Romanian National State 1821–1878*, pp. 239–42.

17. Lord Kinross, *The Ottoman Centuries*, pp. 520–21; Jelavich, *Russia and the Formation of the Romanian National State 1821–1878*, pp. 268 and 290. For vivid battlefield descriptions of the 1877–78 war, see the short stories in Mihail Sadoveanu's *Tales of War* (New York: Twayne Publishers, 1962).

18. Kaplan, *Balkan Ghosts*, p. 121.

19. Ibid.

20. At the time of this writing, Cristian Mihai Adomniței, president of the Jassy County Council, planned to raise money for the renovation of the Jewish cemetery and the sites of the 1941 pogrom here, complete with historical markers. As an Orthodox Christian, he told me, it was the right thing to do.

21. Kaplan, *Balkan Ghosts*, pp. 96–98 and 126–29.

22. Deletant, *Hitler's Forgotten Ally*, pp. 2, 62, and 280 (footnote); Joseph Rothschild, *East-Central Europe Between the Two World Wars* (Seattle: University of Washington Press, 1974), p. 317.

23. Deletant, *Hitler's Forgotten Ally*, pp. 2 and 182.

24. Larry L. Watts, "Ion Antonescu and Romania in Western Historiography," 2013, p. 2: an update to his 1993 work, *Romanian Cassandra: Ion Antonescu and the Struggle for Reform, 1916–1941*.

25. Deletant, *Hitler's Forgotten Ally*, p. 127.

26. Vladimir Solonari, *Purifying the Nation: Population Exchange and Ethnic Cleansing in Nazi-Allied Romania* (Washington and Baltimore: Woodrow Wilson Center Press and Johns Hopkins University Press, 2010), pp. 171 and 187.

27. Aharon Appelfeld, "Buried Homeland," translated by Jeffrey M. Green, *New Yorker*, November 23, 1998.

28. Ioanid, *The Holocaust in Romania*, p. 272. This was only a few months after the infamous Bucharest Pogrom, which included the notorious butchery of Jews at the local slaughterhouse. I numbered the victims at about two hundred in *Balkan Ghosts*, relying as I did on the account of the late Robert St. John, an American journalist in Bucharest and the Balkans at the time. Robert St.

John, *Foreign Correspondent* (London: Hutchinson, 1960), p. 180. But Ioanid numbers the Jews killed at the slaughterhouse at actually thirteen, even as more than one hundred others died in nearly as cruel and hideous circumstances during those same hours. Ioanid, *The Holocaust in Romania*, pp. 57–59.

29. Petreu, *An Infamous Past*, p. 73.

30. Hitchins, *Rumania 1866–1947*, pp. 164–65.

31. Hugh Seton-Watson, *The Russian Empire 1801–1917*, pp. 493–94; Ioanid, *The Holocaust in Romania*, p. xx; R. W. Seton-Watson, *A History of the Roumanians*, pp. 347 and 349.

32. A. C. Cuza, a Romanian politician and theorist of the early and mid-twentieth century, should not be confused with Alexandru Ioan Cuza, the founder of the Romanian state in the mid-nineteenth century. Nae Ionescu should not be confused with the famous playwright Eugène Ionescu.

33. Petreu, *An Infamous Past*, p. 124.

34. Antonescu was not in Romania at the time of the pogrom, but with the Romanian army advancing into the Soviet Union.

35. Deletant, *Hitler's Forgotten Ally*, pp. 136–37 and 139; Ioanid, *The Holocaust in Romania*, pp. 41–43.

36. Deletant, *Hitler's Forgotten Ally*, p. 38.

37. Hitchins, *Rumania 1866–1947*, p. 474.

38. Solonari, *Purifying the Nation*, p. 123.

39. This, in fact, is a theme of Vladimir Solonari's aptly titled book, *Purifying the Nation: Population Exchange and Ethnic Cleansing in Nazi-Allied Romania*, pp. xv and 1–3.

40. Deletant, *Hitler's Forgotten Ally*, pp. 79, 118, 127, 142, and 196; William Blacker, *Along the Enchanted Way: A Story of Love and Life in Romania* (London: John Murray, 2009), pp. 86 and 162.

41. Deletant, *Hitler's Forgotten Ally*, pp. 212–13.

42. Ioanid, *The Holocaust in Romania*, p. 248.

43. Watts, "Ion Antonescu and Romania in Western Historiography," pp. 1 and 26.

44. Petreu, *An Infamous Past*, pp. xi, 31–32, and 48–49.

45. Ibid., pp. 8–9 and 12.

46. Ibid., pp. 22, 97, 98–99, 152–53, and 169–70.

47. Ibid., pp. 33, 123, 128, and 133.

48. Ibid., pp. 115–17, 138, and 234.

49. Ibid., pp. 151, 179, 237–38, and 243.

50. Franz Kafka, *The Castle* (New York: Oxford University Press, 2009), p. 54.

51. Solonari, *Purifying the Nation*, pp. 17–20.

CHAPTER 6: THE PONTIC BREACH

1. Robert D. Kaplan, "Europe's Russia Factor," Austin, TX: Stratfor, May 23, 2012; Robert D. Kaplan, "Europe's New Map," *The American Interest*, April 12, 2013.

2. Elzbieta Matynia, *An Uncanny Era: Conversations Between Václav Havel and Adam Michnik* (New Haven, CT: Yale University Press, 2014), p. 52.

3. Vladimir Tismăneanu, *The Devil in History: Communism, Fascism, and Some Lessons of the Twentieth Century* (Berkeley: University of California Press, 2012), p. 186; Anne Applebaum, "Nationalism Is Exactly What Ukraine Needs: Democracy Fails When Citizens Don't Believe Their Country Is Worth Fighting For," *New Republic*, May 13, 2014.

4. Coincidentally, the office of the foreign intelligence service in downtown Bucharest was a villa once owned in the 1930s and 1940s by Marshal Antonescu's most important minister, Mihai Antonescu (a distant relation), who had been executed along with the marshal in 1946 for war crimes. The ghosts of one of the darkest eras in modern Romanian history lived on in these buildings.

5. In the Romanian view, the highest-ranking enemy agent in Europe was former German chancellor and Gazprom board member Gerhard Schröder, bought and paid for by the Russians.

6. Bernard Fall, "The Theory and Practice of Insurgency and Counterinsurgency," *Naval War College Review*, April 1965.

7. Ernest H. Latham Jr., *Timeless and Transitory: 20th Century Relations Between Romania and the English-Speaking World* (Bucharest: Editura Vremea, 2012), p. 67.

8. Djuvara, *A Concise History of Romanians*, pp. 52–56 and 60–61.

9. The Romanian name is Transnistria.

10. Andrzej Stasiuk, *On the Road to Babadag: Travels in the Other Europe* (London: Harvill Secker, 2011), p. 123.

11. King, *The Moldovans*, pp. 178–79.

12. Lieven, *Empire*, pp. 388–89; Stasiuk, *On the Road to Babadag*, pp. 114 and 124–25; Eugene Chausovsky, "Transdniestria: The Geopolitics of the Ultimate Borderland," Austin, TX: Stratfor, July 2013.

13. King, *The Moldovans*, p. 5.

14. Robert Blake, *Disraeli* (New York: St. Martin's Press, 1967), pp. 575–76.

15. Pontos is the ancient Greek shorthand for the Black Sea.

16. George Friedman, *Borderlands: A Geopolitical Journey in Eurasia* (Austin, TX: Stratfor, 2011), pp. 39–40; Robert D. Kaplan, *The Revenge of Geography: What the Map Tells Us About Coming Conflicts and the Battle Against Fate* (New York: Random House, 2012), pp. 180–81; Chausovsky, "Transdniestria."

17. Friedman, *Borderlands*, pp. 40 and 48.

18. Stasiuk, *On the Road to Babadag*, p. 118.

19. Henry Baerlein, *Bessarabia and Beyond* (London: Methuen, 1935), pp. 46 and 48. *Enciclopedia României*, vol. 2, *Țara Românească* (Bucharest: Imprimeria Națională, 1938), pp. 600 and 686; Latham, *Timeless and Transitory*, pp. 107 and 110.

20. Dostoevsky, *The Idiot*, p. 335.

21. Hitchins, *Rumania 1866–1947*, p. 244.

22. During the Khrushchev era especially, in the 1950s and early 1960s, monasteries here were closed and converted into warehouses and psychiatric institutions. In one case, in the central Moldovan town of Calarsi, the closure of a monastery in 1962 led to a brief armed resistance.

23. Paul Celan, *Poems of Paul Celan*, translated and with an introduction by Michael Hamburger (New York: Persea Books, 1972), pp. 21–22 and 41; Claudio Magris, *Danube: A Journey Through the Landscape, History, and Culture of Central Europe*, translated by Patrick Creagh (New York: Farrar, Straus & Giroux, 1989), pp. 320–21.

24. While Moldova's was a traditional parliamentary system, Romania's was an odd mix, with both the president and prime minister enjoying real power, hence the hatred between Băsescu and Ponta at the time of my visits in 2013 and 2014.

25. To wit, a few weeks earlier, Gazprom had paid off parliamentarians in Bulgaria to protect South Stream—a Russian pipeline network—against European Union efforts to regulate it.

CHAPTER 7: CROSSING THE CARPATHIANS

1. I was particularly influenced in this regard by Orlando Figes's *A People's Tragedy: The Russian Revolution 1891–1924* (London: Jonathan Cape, 1996).

2. Djuvara, *A Concise History of Romanians*, p. 53.

3. Donald Hall, *Romanian Furrow* (London: Bene Factum, 2007), pp. 11, 21, 25–26, and 35.

4. Albert Camus, *Lyrical and Critical Essays*, translated by Ellen Conroy Kennedy (New York: Vintage, 1970), p. 294.

5. Naftali Bendavid, "Europe Confronts Its Roma Problem," *Wall Street Journal*, April 23, 2014.

6. I wrote more extensively about Queen Marie in *Balkan Ghosts*.

7. Magris, *Danube*, p. 312.

8. John Eliot Gardiner, *Bach: Music in the Castle of Heaven* (New York: Knopf, 2014), p. 15.

9. Boia, *Romania*, p. 24; Hitchins, *Rumania 1866–1947*, pp. 218–20.

10. Herta Müller, *Nadirs*, translated and with an afterword by Sieglinde Lug (Lincoln: University of Nebraska Press, 1999), pp. 22–23, 34, 106, and 122.

11. There was an exception to this, though: Habsburg Austria did occupy Oltenia between 1718 and 1739, and had an army of occupation here from 1854 to 1856.

12. Henry A. Kissinger, *A World Restored: Metternich, Castlereagh and the Problems of Peace 1812–1822* (Boston: Houghton Mifflin, 1957), p. 7.

13. Robert A. Kann, *A History of the Habsburg Empire 1526–1918* (Berkeley: University of California Press, 1974), p. 27.

14. Jan Morris, *Trieste and the Meaning of Nowhere* (New York: Da Capo Press, 2002), pp. 45–46.

15. C. A. Macartney, *The Habsburg Empire 1790–1918* (New York: Macmillan, 1969), pp. 12, 16–17, 100, and 826–27.

16. Kissinger, *A World Restored*, pp. 207–8 and 233.

17. Simon Winder, *Danubia: A Personal History of Habsburg Europe* (New York: Farrar, Straus & Giroux, 2013), pp. 292–93.

18. Kann, *A History of the Habsburg Empire 1526–1918*, pp. 25 and 266.

19. Simms, *Europe: The Struggle for Supremacy*, pp. 94 and 163.

20. Kann, *A History of the Habsburg Empire 1526–1918*, p. 235; Kissinger, *A World Restored*, p. 196.

21. Alan Palmer, *Metternich: A Biography* (New York: Harper & Row, 1972), pp. 2–3.

22. Henry Kissinger, "Otto von Bismarck, Master Statesman," *New York Times*, March 31, 2011; Palmer, *Metternich*, pp. 15 and 19.

23. Palmer, *Metternich*, p. 103.

24. Ibid., pp. 155 and 202; A. J. P. Taylor, *Bismarck: The Man and the Statesman* (New York: Knopf, 1955), pp. 32–33.

25. Alexandros Petersen, *The World Island: Eurasian Geopolitics and the Fate of the West* (Oxford: Praeger, 2011), pp. 60–62. A similar concept had been proposed a few years earlier by British geographer Halford Mackinder in *Democratic Ideals and Reality: A Study in Politics of Reconstruction* (New York: Henry Holt, 1919). See Kaplan, *The Revenge of Geography*, pp. 74–76.

26. Petersen, *The World Island*, pp. 78–79; Edward Lucas, "How the West Lost Ukraine to Putin," *Wall Street Journal*, December 11, 2013.

27. Norman Davies, *God's Playground: A History of Poland*, vol. 1, *The Origins to 1795* (New York: Columbia University Press, 2005), pp. 357–69.

28. John Lukacs, "In Darkest Transylvania," *New Republic*, February 3, 1982; Kaplan, *Balkan Ghosts*, p. 149.

29. Patrick Leigh Fermor, *Between the Woods and the Water: On Foot to Constantinople from the Hook of Holland: The Middle Danube to the Iron Gates* (London: John Murray, 1986), pp. 184–85.

30. László Péter, *Historians and the History of Transylvania* (New York: East European Monographs, 1992), pp. 1 and 9–11.

31. Miklós Bánffy, *The Transylvanian Trilogy*, translated by Patrick Thursfield and Katalin Bánffy-Jelen, introduction by Hugh Thomas (New York: Knopf, 2013), vol. 1, *They Were Counted*, pp. x, xxii, 5, and 22; vol. 2, *They Were Found Wanting*, p. 268.

32. Bánffy, *They Were Counted*, pp. 26–29, 41, 63, 102, and 399–401; Coles, *The Ottoman Impact on Europe*, pp. 79–80.

33. Macartney, *The Habsburg Empire 1790–1918*, pp. 572–73 and 687.

34. Bánffy, *They Were Counted*, pp. 37 and 135.

35. Bánffy, *They Were Found Wanting*, pp. 47–48.

36. Miklós Bánffy, *The Transylvanian Trilogy*, vol. 3, *They Were Divided*, p. 529 (translators' note).

CHAPTER 8: FISHERMAN'S BASTION

1. Nikos Kazantzakis, *Journeying: Travels in Italy, Egypt, Sinai, Jerusalem and Cyprus*, translated by Themi Vasils and Theodora Vasils (Boston: Little, Brown, 1975), p. 83.

2. Gabriel Liiceanu makes an oblique reference to this phenomenon when he observes that he and his intellectual mentor, Con-

stantin Noica, would take walks in the mountains near Sibiu in the 1970s and 1980s to escape "the toxins of Bucharest." Liiceanu, *The Păltiniș Diary*, p. 94.

3. Blacker, *Along the Enchanted Way*, pp. 34–35, 49, and 211.
4. Villiers, *Romania*, pp. 167 and 169–70.
5. John Ruskin, *The Stones of Venice* (New York: Da Capo, [1853] 1960), p. 166.
6. See Gyula Illyes's 1936 classic, *People of the Puszta* (Budapest: Nyuget, 1936).
7. The phrase comes from the first line of Mihai Eminescu's poem "Doina," forbidden in Communist Romania because of its strident nationalism, not to mention the reference to the Nistru (Dniester), at the time in the territory of the Soviet Union (specifically the Moldavian Soviet Socialist Republic).
8. Djuvara, *A Concise History of Romanians*, pp. 98–100; Lord Kinross, *The Ottoman Centuries*, pp. 85–86; Fermor, *Between the Woods and the Water*, pp. 116–17.
9. Donald Hall tells us that the coat of arms has as its origin the story of how Iancu de Hunedoara's mother had a ring stolen by a raven, but it was subsequently recovered when Iancu's father shot the bird. Hall, *Romanian Furrow*, p. 126.
10. Djuvara, *A Concise History of Romanians*, pp. 100 and 107–08; Fermor, *Between the Woods and the Water*, pp. 117–18 and 144.
11. Fermor, *Between the Woods and the Water*, p. 118; Djuvara, *A Concise History of Romanians*, p. 107.
12. Dominic G. Kosary, *A History of Hungary*, foreword by Julius Szekfu (New York: Benjamin Franklin Bibliophile Society, 1941), pp. 65 and 68–70.
13. Mircea Cărtărescu, *Blinding*, translated by Sean Cotter (Brooklyn, NY: Archipelago Books, 2013), p. 20.
14. Norman Manea, "Intellectuals and Social Change in Central and Eastern Europe," *Partisan Review*, Fall 1992; Tismăneanu, *The Devil in History*, pp. 187–88; Robert D. Kaplan, "The Return of Toxic Nationalism," *Wall Street Journal*, December 23, 2012.

15. Czesław Miłosz, *Beginning with My Streets: Essays and Recollections*, translated by Madeline G. Levine (New York: Farrar, Straus & Giroux, 1991), p. ix.

16. Michael Walzer, "The New Tribalism: Notes on a Difficult Problem," *Dissent*, Spring 1992.

17. Miłosz, *Beginning with My Streets*, p. 87.

18. Andrei Pleşu, *On Angels: Exposition for a Post-Modern World* (Bucharest and Berlin: Humanitas and Berlin University Press, 2012), p. 146.

19. Tismăneanu, *The Devil in History*, p. x.

ILLUSTRATION CREDITS

Ion Antonescu reviewing maps with Hitler: ullstein bild/Granger, NYC

Mircea Eliade: Jeff Lowenthal/Lebrecht Music & Arts

Iuliu Maniu: ullstein bild via Getty Images

Emil Cioran: Rue des Archives/Granger, NYC

Gheorghe Gheorghiu-Dej: Keystone-France/Gamma-Keystone
    via Getty Images

Nicolae and Elena Ceauşescu walking past honor guard on visit to China:
    Reuters/Edward Nachtrieb

Nicolae and Elena Ceauşescu shortly before execution: Associated Press

Ion Iliescu: Mircea Hudek/AGERPRES

INDEX

ROBERT D. KAPLAN is the bestselling author of sixteen books on foreign affairs and travel translated into many languages, including *Asia's Cauldron, The Revenge of Geography, Monsoon, The Coming Anarchy,* and *Balkan Ghosts.* He is a senior fellow at the Center for a New American Security and a contributing editor at *The Atlantic,* where his work has appeared for three decades. He was chief geopolitical analyst at Stratfor, a visiting professor at the United States Naval Academy, and a member of the Pentagon's Defense Policy Board. *Foreign Policy* magazine twice named him one of the world's "Top 100 Global Thinkers."

robertdkaplan.com

cnas.org